Japanland

Japanland

A Year in Search
of *Wa*

Karin Muller

RODALE®

Rodale books may be purchased for business or promotional use or for special sales. For information, please write to: Special Markets Department, Rodale, Inc., 733 Third Avenue, New York, NY 10017

Cover photo © Grant Faint / Getty Images

Printed in the United States of America
Rodale Inc. makes every effort to use acid-free ∞, recycled paper ♻.

Book design by Patricia Field

Library of Congress Cataloging-in-Publication Data

Muller, Karin.
    Japanland : a year in search of wa / Karin Muller.
        p.   cm.
    ISBN-13 978–1–59486–223–6 hardcover
    ISBN-10 1–59486–223–0 hardcover
    ISBN-13 978–1–59486–523–7 paperback
    ISBN-10 1–59486–523–X paperback
    1. Japan—Social life and customs—1945–   I. Title.
DS822.5.M8   2005
306'.0952—dc22   2005014286

Distributed to the trade by Holtzbrinck Publishers

2 4 6 8 10 9 7 5 3 1 hardcover
    4 6 8 10 9 7 5 3 paperback

RODALE
LIVE YOUR WHOLE LIFE™

We inspire and enable people to improve their lives and the world around them

For more of our products visit **rodalestore.com** or call 800-848-4735

To the people of Japan

I remember turning twenty-one in a squatter's village on a remote island in the Philippines. I was celebrating a rather forlorn birthday in my tiny palm-leaf hut when a card arrived from my brother. The picture on the front showed a young woman laboring up a mountain to reach an unshaven guru sitting at its top. My brother had inked out the caption and scrawled "Still looking for the meaning of life?" in its place. It was an annoyingly perceptive comment from a guy who had already earned two degrees from MIT and had his eye on a Harvard MBA. My career, by comparison, was already starting to look like the scurrying tracks of a plover being chased by the waves.

After serving in the Peace Corps, I donned a gray suit and joined a consulting firm, then eventually started my own company. I got engaged. We bought a puppy and a hang glider. I filled our apartment with African violets and coffee-table books of exotic places that I would now almost certainly never get to see. We broke up. I sold my company. I put on a backpack, mothballed the suits, and got on a plane. For the next eight years I traveled the world with a video camera, looking for the meaning of life—in a Quechua hut on Lake Titicaca, among the Vietnamese Sea Gypsies anchored in forgotten caves on Halong Bay, and in the intricate Hindu battle scenes of Angkor Wat in Cambodia.

One day I woke up to find myself living in a hotel-like warren of twelve hundred identical apartments in Washington, D.C., and casually dating a divorce lawyer who was casually dating at least two other women. I had made it to that proverbial mountaintop—I was working at National Geographic, post-producing a documentary series I'd shot in South America for their global channel. And yet that birthday card still haunted me. *The meaning of life.* Was it just a childish quest, or had I given up too soon? I certainly wasn't going to find it here, in the tiny cubicles bathed in fluorescent light and the eight-year wait for a coveted underground parking spot.

But—as my parents kept reminding me—I was thirty-four, and I wasn't getting any younger. I'd already blown through half a dozen careers, learned six languages and forgotten three, and tried my hand at everything from flower arranging to flying ultralights. I approached relationships the same way I did a midwinter swim in an icy fjord: great expectations, wholehearted plunge, determined misery—and exit screaming. I had the uneasy feeling that the problem wasn't the system. It was me.

There was only one place where all of my worries would disappear, at least temporarily. Three times a week I'd strap my gym bag to my bicycle and ride through downtown traffic to a judo academy. I'd twist and throw and tumble on the mats for hours, then weave home drenched in sweat and utterly exhausted. On those nights I would sleep untroubled by either unsettling dreams or endless early-morning doubts.

I'd taken up judo soon after the Peace Corps and studied it doggedly for eleven years. It had lasted longer than any boyfriend, longer than all of my New Year's resolutions combined. It wasn't the rare moments of success that kept me coming back. It wasn't even the strength and coordination that I gradually acquired, or the confidence that I could defend myself under most circumstances. It was something . . . else. Most of my instructors were Japanese, and they approached judo with a sense of utter dedication to perfecting a profoundly difficult art. They seemed to glow with an almost ethereal calm and inner strength. They made it clear that you would never truly master the sport until you understood the philosophy behind it. And for that, they told me, you have to understand Japan. The spiritual peace the Japanese seem to find in simple objects and the contemplation of nature; their willingness to sacrifice their own needs for the common good. It was utterly alien to me, and I was fascinated. What could induce a monk to stare at a wall for seven hours a day? Or a geisha to spend a lifetime learning the elegance of a single gesture serving tea?

Focus. Harmony. *Wa*. I wasn't even sure exactly what *wa* was, but I wanted some.

But there was a catch. This wasn't something you could learn by cracking open the right fortune cookie. You had to dedicate yourself heart and soul to the effort. You had to go to Japan, immerse yourself in its culture and beliefs. You had to *become Japanese*. It would take at least a year, maybe more, and it wouldn't come cheap. I had spent most of the past decade working my way to the top; could I afford to throw it all away on another fool's errand in search of peace and happiness? A part of me wanted to settle down and maybe even start a family. My body no longer bounced off the mats the way it had when I was twenty-five. After a hard workout, I'd wake up stiff and shuffling, and injuries weren't healing like they used to. And Japan wasn't known for its soft mats or easygoing instructors.

Examined in the light of day, the idea seemed, well, absurd. So I ran it by a few people in an offhand way, ready to distance myself from it at the first sign of scoffing.

A lifelong friend—a man who had lived in Japan for twenty-eight years, married a Japanese woman, and raised three children—didn't mince words. "The only way you'll ever become a part of Japanese society," he told me, "is if you were born in a Japanese village to Japanese parents."

My old Asian-studies professor was somewhat more optimistic. "No problem," he said. "Just study Japanese etiquette for the next thirty years, speak through a ventriloquist, and wear a paper bag over your head."

"You?" scoffed an old hang-gliding buddy who had known me for years. "Ha!"

I finally had coffee with an art collector who had spent three decades studying antique woodblock cuttings and building his dream house on a remote island in the Japanese Inland Sea. He heard me out, then sat in silence for a few minutes. "What does everyone else say?" he asked.

Not optimistic, I conceded.

"But you're going to do it anyway?"

Of course.

"Then," he said slowly, "you are not Japanese."

Making up my mind to go turned out to be the easy part. Although Japan welcomes tourists, it almost never allows them more than a superficial glimpse of its culture and traditions. My plan to bring along a video camera and try to capture what I learned would make things even harder.

For six months I searched in vain for someone who could help me find a way into Japanese society. And then one day, when I was on the verge of giving up, he walked into my life.

Murata-san had been coming to judo workouts punctually every Monday night. He was sixty-nine, as strong as an oak tree, and as fast as a striking cobra. One day he overheard me talking of my plans to go to Japan and make a documentary and quietly offered to find me a host family in Tokyo. Within a few days he had contacted his old judo alumni network at a top Japanese university. An announcement was made at their quarterly meeting, and Genji Tanaka, a sixth-degree black belt, immediately raised his hand. He not only agreed to become my sensei, he also offered to rent me his empty granny suite for a pittance and to introduce me to life in Japan.

Japanland

CHAPTER 1

My new home in Fujisawa is the essence of wealth—
meaning it is a five-minute walk from the beach, fifteen minutes from the train station, and just under an hour's commute
to Tokyo. It is a house, not an apartment, and has a thin layer
of garden wrapped around it like a coat of varnish. The whole
thing is protected from the prying eyes of neighbors and foreign thieves by a high cement wall. Inside lies the sole domain
of my host mother, Yukiko.

There are two kinds of older women. There are those who
let their hair go gray and their figures fill out around their hips
and thighs. Their hands relax into their laps, and their faces
gradually sag into laugh lines and molded smiles. They no
longer bother with umbrellas and rarely vacuum under the bed.

Then there is Yukiko. Her hairdresser is one of her closest
friends. She wears tight pants that emphasize her long, slender
legs and exudes an air both regal and stylish, like a Victorian

lady in stiffly ironed jeans. I am jealous because I have never looked that elegant, though I am half her age. I am afraid of her because I cannot tell the difference between her smile and her grimace.

Yukiko met Genji when she was twenty-one. She'd worked briefly as a nurse's helper in a hospital and then spent two years at home, learning to cook and clean. When Genji proposed, she achieved her life's most important goal. Two children quickly followed. Now, at fifty-eight, she has a full-time maid, carefully dyed black hair, seamless skin, and a domain that includes everything from the mailbox to the back fence. In Japan, the man may command a company of several thousand employees, but the woman rules the home—and everyone in it.

This seemingly insignificant fact would have enormous consequences for us all. Because when Genji raised his hand in a moment of spontaneous generosity, he invited me not only into his home but also his wife's—without asking her if she wanted me there.

Our differences are obvious from the very first day. Yukiko is very traditional. I am not. She is quite sure, for example, that all these newfangled cooking devices, like microwaves, break down food. I've done nothing to disabuse her of this notion because there is only one microwave in the house, and it is now conveniently located on my kitchen counter. Nobody in my host family can figure out how I managed to decipher all the buttons in a matter of minutes without being able to read a word of Japanese. I haven't told them that when my oven broke down in my last apartment, it took me almost a year to get it fixed. I use the microwave more often than the telephone.

Yukiko also doesn't believe in using the clothes dryer.

Unfortunately, she doesn't believe in *my* using the dryer either, so I usually have to sneak upstairs with an armful of wet laundry when she's out shopping. Lately she's taken to turning on the burglar alarm in the laundry room whenever she leaves the house. I usually don't realize this until I open the door and hear a high-pitched squeal, at which point I toss my sodden clothes into the corner and rush downstairs to have a one-sided conversation with the master alarm system. I frantically punch buttons while a metallic female voice says several different versions of "Something-something-something, *please!*" I have only ninety seconds, which isn't nearly enough time to look up even one of the dozen Japanese pictographs under all those buttons, let alone figure out the proper disconnect sequence.

Eventually the alarm falls silent and I go sit by the phone with sweaty palms, practicing my most humble Japanese apologies and trying to remember this week's alarm code for when the security company calls. I'm quite sure that if I were in any other country, the security guys would look up the house number and say, "It's that crazy foreign woman doing her laundry again," then just ignore it. But this is Japan, and they always call within five minutes. If I hide the telephone under a pile of pillows, then an hour later someone in an official uniform shows up to check on it personally. They tell Yukiko, and she tells Genji, and he calls me upstairs to explain myself while he chuckles over his gin and tonic. Yukiko thinks this is hilarious. I do not.

But despite our differences, I really want us to be friends. So I discipline myself to do whatever it takes to fit into Yukiko's household and her priorities. If that means picking up the tiniest speck of lint on my bedroom floor, ironing my socks and sheets and underwear, separating my trash into seventeen different recycling categories, and becoming an expert in the culinary arts, then so be it.

To be honest, a part of me is actually looking forward to filling this long-neglected housekeeping hole in my life. For the past fifteen years my definition of a good meal has been one that takes less time to eat than it does to microwave, and less time to microwave than it does to download my e-mail.

Of course, I don't tell this to Yukiko. She doesn't even do e-mail, and her dinner preparations begin as soon as the breakfast dishes are in the drying rack. For the last half century she has dedicated herself to the ideal of Japanese womanhood, rising through the ranks with the discipline of a Tokyo salaryman eyeing the supreme spot of CEO. But then, she started at the young and impressionable age of eighteen. I, in contrast, am a squeaky old house, with ingrained habits that have to be torn down and a highly suspect foundation.

So she has taken it upon herself in the nicest possible way to turn me from an uncivilized barbarian into a proper Japanese woman.

And, for the first time in my adult life, I'm afraid.

∽

Genji, my host father and judo instructor, stands well over six feet tall. He is two hundred pounds of solid muscle, with broad shoulders and a ramrod carriage. At sixty he is catlike in his agility, with the effortless elegance of a lifelong athlete. He has, in a rare moment of un-Japanese informality, suggested I call him Gas. I could no more bring myself to say this than I would name a Bengal tiger Muffin.

Despite his size, he is the most gracious man I've ever met. He has the kind of face that you would ask directions of in the train station and the generosity to immediately drop everything and take you where you want to go. His hair is starting to gray and his character beginning to show through his features—the embedded lines around his eyes and an intelligent, watchful expression. But the thing I like best about him is his laugh. He throws back his head and his entire body dissolves with mirth, instantly exploding those Japanese stereotypes of dour businessmen sitting stiffly around a conference table.

Until recently, Genji ran one of Tokyo's largest corporations—a position that requires the ability to spread vast amounts of oil on troubled waters and regroup fleeing armies with the wave of a hand. And he does it without ever having to say no. This is the hallmark of all truly elegant Japanese communication. Genji listens quietly to my latest ridiculous proposal. He nods his head as though impressed. He says, "Yes, but . . ." He allows the pause to hang delicately in the air. I immediately realize that my idea has been vetoed. No need to be blunt or confrontational. Subject closed. It's a form of Japanese ESP, and Genji has it down to an art.

And yet beneath that gentle disposition lies an almost religious faith in the twin Japanese virtues of obligation and obedience. He takes care of you, and you do as you are told. For all his gentle manners, Genji is not a man to cross.

Like most successful Tokyo businessmen, Genji attended private school, successfully navigated high-school examination hell, and merged seamlessly into the best private university in Tokyo. By the time he turned twenty-two he had acquired not only a degree in economics but an astonishing sixth-degree black belt in judo. Faced with a difficult choice, he didn't hesitate. He accepted a coveted job with one of Tokyo's oldest and most prestigious insurance companies. Judo fell by the wayside.

For the next thirty-five years he scaled the steep cliffs of corporate hierarchy, playing golf on weekends, drinking on weeknights, and catching an occasional glimpse of his patient wife and sleeping children. His single-minded devotion to duty was finally rewarded by a short trip to the summit—a two-year stint as president. Now, on the back side of the mountain, he has accepted a largely ceremonial role running several smaller subsidiaries while he waits to turn sixty. He has, in fact, only one more duty to perform before he can peacefully contemplate the first block of free time he has had since kindergarten. He still has to find a husband for his only daughter, Junko.

My host sister is extremely stylish, self-confident, even a little brash. Technically she's my "little" sister, being somewhat younger than I am. But since she can read and write and speak and navigate and do just about everything better than I can, we have a very lopsided relationship. That irks me, in small ways. There are a few places where I can hold my own against her, though they're not particularly relevant in suburban Japan. I can fly a hang glider, for example. I know how to sheer a vicuna. And my judo is far better than hers, since she's never set foot inside a judo club. The biggest difference between us isn't our present or our past, however, but our expectations for the future.

In the olden days—meaning up to and including present times—a daughter was expected to live with her parents until the day she could be handed over to some earnest and ambitious young man: her husband. Occasionally she took a job, not so much for the salary as a search engine to help her track down a gray suit with the proper samurai-salaryman attitude and tons of earning potential. Her own income was largely superfluous since her life was paid for, soup to nuts, by her devoted dad. But, just in case she got too comfortable with her single lifestyle, the Japanese built in a catch.

Not too long ago, when a young woman turned twenty-five she was only half-jokingly referred to as "Christmas cake"—a product that plummets in value if not sold by the twenty-fifth. Lately the sell-by date has been extended by a few years, but if a woman isn't within spitting distance of the altar when she turns thirty, her frantic father almost invariably beats a path to the door of the local *nakoudo*, or matchmaker.

Now, this is the twenty-first century, and Japan is the world's second-largest economy. One would naturally assume that matchmakers are about as sought after as typewriter ribbon. Nothing could be further from the truth. One-third of all marriages in Japan are still arranged. Unlike feudal times, the bride and groom are no longer introduced at the altar. Both parties are allowed to turn up their noses at the first candidate or two. But the matchmaker can still expect a seat of honor at the wedding and a fat envelope of cash from the newly unburdened dad.

Junko is twenty-seven, meaning her father is in a mental state somewhere between actively concerned and utterly panicked. Japan has a way of enforcing its moral code: Junko's company, off the books, will only employ her until she turns thirty. She was, after all, hired principally as potential marriage material for the up-and-climbing young men who are working fourteen-hour days and don't have time to look for a wife. Though "single" isn't written into her job description, the day she marries she is out of a job. If she should—heaven forbid—get pregnant without a husband, then she had better find a new line of work. Finally, to ensure that the company's future CEOs are exposed only to upstanding young women of good moral character, she is required to live at home, under the watchful supervision of her parents.

But in a country where woman's liberation and equal rights haven't made much headway, Pierre Cardin and Calvin Klein are blazing a wide trail. This is the first generation of Japanese who have not suffered through a war or its aftermath. Baffled parents who've lived their lives by the twin codes of discipline and sacrifice stare helplessly at children raised on Hello Kitty and cell phones. Junko's entire generation has been labeled the New Human Beings. Young women with $40,000 earnings and virtually no expenses have become a major force in the marketplace. The newspapers have dubbed them Parasite Princesses. They are a designer label's dream come true—many have even taken on nicknames after the brands they favor: Ms. Chanel or Sano Laurento. They have single-handedly driven Gucci sales up 600 percent while the Japanese economy struggles to climb out of its fourth recession.

Junko has few expenses, fewer responsibilities, and little use for a system that will give her a taste of freedom before abruptly zipping her up in a tiny apartment with nothing to do but clean and watch TV.

Still, her mother does her laundry, and her father pays the $200 taxi fare when she misses the last train home. It behooves her to at least pay lip service to the party line. Genji is planning to put out the word through the same university network that washed me up on his doorstep. Perhaps one of his fellow alums has a son in need of a wife.

And what will happen if Junko waits too long and suddenly finds herself facing the yawning abyss of spinsterhood?

Traditional Japanese inheritance laws leave everything to the eldest son. He gets not only the house but all the fields, ostensibly to keep them from being subdivided to the point of nonexistence. Second-born and below are expected to hit the road and fend for themselves. There's just one catch. The elder son—or rather his young wife—must in return provide social security for his parents, who fully expect to move in with them for the last ten or twenty years of their lives. Unmarried daughters who have, over time, morphed into bat-eared aunts are inherited along with the pots and pans. Hopefully, by then the elder son has a couple of impressionable daughters of his own who might benefit from the example of watching such errant behavior come to a bad end. In other words, young women can expect to be taken care of, cradle to grave.

Doesn't sound like such a bad deal.

CHAPTER 2

Fujisawa is on the old Tokkaido Road, a famous postal route that once carried messages, spies, and armies between Japan's two bustling urban centers of Edo and Kyoto. When I first heard that I would be living here, I foolishly imagined a scene straight out of a nineteenth-century woodblock print, with weathered wooden houses and goldfish sellers hawking their wares along hand-laid flagstone streets.

Unfortunately, Fujisawa's coveted location—backed up against the beach and a mere hour's commute to Tokyo—long ago sent property values through the roof. Virtually every inch of ground has been asphalted, with barely a window planter's worth of space between suburban dwellings. Land is in such short supply that residents are not allowed to register a car until they can prove they have a parking space. Vending machines spill out onto the sidewalks, stocked with every essential from cigarettes and liquor to sacks of rice. Each morning a tidal wave of earnest salarymen heads dutifully for the train station, hair carefully combed into the standard 7/3 part. Young surfers in black and neon body suits dash off in the opposite direction, their boards lashed securely to their bicycles. Dogs are tiny, cats are leashed, skateboards are in, and Rollerblades are out—and the beach is ankle-deep in garbage.

Despite the flashing neon signs and suburban sprawl, Fujisawa feels like a village. Diligent housewives plant ivy to cover up unneighborly walls and compete to see who can hang their entryways with the brightest flower baskets. The parking lot at the corner grocery store is packed—with bicycles. An endless stream of young mothers come and go with infants lashed securely to their backs or tucked into front bike baskets. They purchase just enough fresh fruit and vegetables for the day's meal, reload kids and produce, and casually pedal off to their next stop at the tofu store or fish seller's.

∽

It's ten thirty in the morning and I'm standing in the local supermarket, trying to figure out if the bag I'm holding is filled with salt or sugar. I've smelled it, I've surreptitiously licked the plastic, I've examined the grains from every angle, and I'm stumped. The problem is, I can't read Japanese. It's an oddly uncomfortable feeling, like wearing a skirt in public without underwear. I've got a Japanese-English dictionary in my back pocket, but even if I wanted to spend the rest of my morning leafing through it, the chances of my stumbling across the pictograph for *sugar* are about forty-two thousand to one, since Japanese writing is not alphabetical.

This is my third visit to the market since I got up this

morning: I've already mistakenly carted home butter that looks like cheese and yogurt that feels and smells like milk. I've spent an hour among the frozen foods, carefully examining the ground beef for the low-fat, no-pork-added variety that is on Yukiko's list. The manager has taken up a post in a direct line of sight to make sure that I'm not fingering the fish. I've leafed through the seaweed aisle and made a surreptitious visit to "bad mom corner" to gaze longingly at the three dusty bottles of Coca-Cola behind the cough drops. Yukiko is tapping her foot in the kitchen, waiting for a few simple ingredients so that she can start dinner. It is, after all, almost eleven o'clock in the morning.

I present my purchases to Yukiko and spend the next few hours learning to put the correct amount of white miso into a wooden ladle and let it gradually dissolve in hot—not boiling— water. We make a batch of seaweed-and-bonito-shaving sauce, a key ingredient in many Japanese dishes. I've seen several bottled versions at the supermarket, but Yukiko is a chef in the purest sense and makes almost everything from scratch.

At three I escape to my room for a few hours of language study before the final push to load up the dinner table. My apartment is huge by Tokyo standards—the kind of place a young couple could hope to afford by the time they're just sending their youngest child off to college. It has a single bedroom and a living room with a small cooking alcove hanging off one end. The bedroom is traditional Japanese, with two-inch-thick tatami mats of woven rice straw—as springy as moss and smelling vaguely of sour hay. Soft orange light oozes through translucent paper screens, and all the doors slide sideways on wooden tracks rather than opening on hinges. It is also, like virtually all Japanese architecture, almost completely empty.

Those airy walls are not built for nails or hooks, so there is no place to hang a picture or a pair of Rollerblades. The tatami mats are likewise too soft to carry the weight of bureaus, bookshelves, or chairs. The only closet is reserved for bedding, so there's no place to hide a jigsaw puzzle, a sewing kit, or camping gear. My dirty laundry migrates to the top of the refrigerator, and I use a flashlight to read in bed.

My Western living room, on the other hand, has built-in hardwood floors and sturdy walls. My host family has clearly developed a taste for Western furnishings, but they haven't yet quite figured out what to do with all that stuff. My living room is crammed with five heavy chairs, a full-size sofa, a dining-room table, a coffee table, a television, and a china closet—all jostling for space like Venetian gondolas on market day. But even in this room there are neither closets nor bookshelves, and my belongings are piled up in little termite hills that spill out of various nooks and crannies and lurk behind the sofa. I am a creature of expansive gestures and the living room just does me in. I live in terror of the moment when I bang my shin on the coffee table, trip over a superstuffed chair, and, in one of those nightmare slow-motion finishes, fall through a paper door.

Dinner is promptly at six, the culmination of four hours of shopping and three hours of cooking. The table groans under the weight of half a dozen elaborate dishes. Each setting is artfully arranged with delicate porcelain bowls and tiny cups for assorted garnishes. The meal unfolds like a carefully choreographed ballet—the sesame tofu goes into the blue bowl with the soy sauce and fish shavings but never with the pickled ginger. Mayonnaise belongs on the squash; butter most definitely does not. It is only proper to raise the bowl of rice to one's face and unutterably rude to lower one's face to the bowl.

There are no napkins because, as Yukiko informs me, well-mannered folk don't need them.

～

It's nearly midnight when Junko knocks on my door. I've spent the entire evening studying Japanese, and my brain feels like it's been marinated in bug spray. What little good sense I may have had has long since evaporated.

Junko tells me that she went to a sumo party a few days ago and met a *yokozuna*. "A *yokozuna*," she repeats impatiently when I don't react. One of the top three sumo wrestlers in all Japan. She even chatted with him for a few minutes.

Afterward, his patron pulled her aside and suggested she send him a letter. The young wrestler is, he told her, in the market for a wife. Since the yokozuna was originally American, Junko wants to write it in English. For that she needs my help.

Secretly, I'm thrilled. Perhaps I'm not entirely useless after all. I whip out a piece of paper: Salutations. Thank you for a wonderful evening. Inquiries after recent injuries. A paragraph of hopeful, flattering nonsense. We wrap it up and Junko signs it. She's clearly pleased. Perhaps I've made a friend tonight.

"Don't tell my parents," she says as she's leaving.

"Okay," I agree, stupidly.

It's not until noon the next day, while peeling shallots, that the hammer falls. "Junko," Mama-san confides in a weighty whisper, "has become interested in a sumo wrestler. A yokozuna." She's quite surprised when I know what this is. Genji is extremely concerned about the situation. Yukiko is sure, of course, that I would do nothing to encourage Junko's interest.

16

It's the moment to fess up. The truth is, it's not Genji I'm afraid of—it's Yukiko. I hesitate. The window closes. I decide to play dumb. "Of course not," I say, shelling shallots as fast as I can.

But afterward I'm left wondering: What's so terrible about sumo wrestlers? In Japan, the top sumo are not only famous and enormously rich but regularly on the country's Top 10 most-sexy lists.

Of course I'm not about to ask Yukiko, but I can find out for myself. All thirty-two of Japan's sumo stables are in Tokyo. Their daily training sessions are open to anyone, even foreigners, who are willing to get up at four thirty in the morning to go watch them work out.

Sumo and baseball have been battling for years over the coveted title of Japan's national sport. Both cater to the Japanese mania for sports statistics, though sumo stacks the deck by allowing its wrestlers to change their names several times in their careers, to celebrate a victory or promotion, or even when they cut their hair. What ultimately tips the scale in favor of sumo is its homegrown origins. Sumo appears in Japan's earliest written records and by 700 AD had already been a part of court ritual and entertainment for some three hundred years. In other words, sumo has always been *uniquely Japanese*.

Then, in July 1972, a Hawaiian named Jessie Kahualua became the first foreigner to win a sumo tournament. It took twenty-one years before his protégé, Chad Rowan, was grudgingly awarded the title of Yokozuna, or Grand Champion.

But by then the foreign floodgates had opened wide. More Hawaiians followed. Nobody in Japan paid much attention to the devastating drought and savage winter in the Altay Mountains north of China until a tide of young Mongolians with gladiator bodies and panicked, desperate eyes invaded the sumo ranks. Apparently word had gotten out that a sumo wrestler in the top division, no matter what his record, earned more than the president of Mongolia. All an aspiring Mongolian sumo wrestler had to do was acquire a taste for raw fish and—if he was called Tsolmonbayar Munkhbat or Ariunbayar Unurjargal—change his name.

∞

I arrive at the sumo stable just as the street cleaners are giving way to the first scattering of briefcased drones hurrying to greet another fifteen-hour workday. The sumo wrestlers have beaten them all, starting their workout at five in the morning on a deliberately empty stomach. Sumo is one of the most rigid hierarchies in the world, an island of feudalism in a sea of glassy skyscrapers and high-speed trains. Apprentices are the first on the training floor, followed by an hourly rotation of successively higher ranks. At noon they break, and the novices attend to their seniors in the bath, patiently scrubbing yards of sandy buttocks and fleshy backs. The midday meal is also served according to rank, and juniors are made to stand at attention while the higher castes indulge. After lunch the entire stable retires for a long nap, which they believe helps convert their meal to fat. The younger members remain at the beck and call of their seniors, who require frequent massages and send them off on errands throughout the afternoon.

Apprentices are, in fact, not unlike fifteenth-century European serfs, receiving little more than room and board for their labors. Privileges, when they are awarded, would seem trivial in modern society—the right to carry an umbrella, to wear a silk belt, to store clothes in a bamboo trunk. These young men have only one goal: to win enough tournaments to rise "above the curtain" and join the higher ranks of their profession. Everyone aspires to be sumo grand champion. Only one in seven hundred will succeed.

From the looks of the unobtrusive bellies and short hair, I've caught the tail end of the apprentice practice. The training area is surprisingly modest—no larger than a one-car garage. To prevent contamination of the sacred earth, women are not allowed to set foot on the packed-dirt floor. There is only one ring, so two wrestlers fight while sixteen stand around and watch. Sumo rules of combat are quite straightforward: no part of the sumo's body, aside from his feet, can touch the ground, nor can he step out of the ring. In theory there are some seventy throwing techniques, though the daily workouts focus mostly on shoving your opponent out-of-bounds, with a little fisticuffs thrown in.

I'm sitting on a raised wooden platform, far enough away to ensure I don't accidentally contaminate the arena with my unsacred self. The practice is almost over, and the entire stable settles down to stretch. Even the full-size wrestlers are surprisingly graceful, like ballerinas inside stacks of tires. They spread their legs and lean over beach-ball bellies to touch their noses to their knees. When they're finished, they stand to recite the sumo code of honor. I sidle up to a gray-haired businessman who has been sitting cross-legged, alternately staring at a book of statistics and watching the wrestlers, since I arrived. He obligingly translates the code for me.

Having just watched five hours of fleshy mountains coming together in tectonic collisions, I'd come to the conclusion that successful sumo depends on balance, strength, and vast caloric intake. This, I am told, is dead wrong. Good sumo, the code states, does not place much weight on the physical at all, in the same way that the Japanese archer completely ignores the target in order to become one with the arrow. The sumo wrestler will win only if he is considerate, sincere, courteous, and just. The sumo code is emphatic on this point: only morally correct athletes can excel.

This belief, the businessman tells me, goes back all the way to sumo tales of yore, to Akashi, a young wrestler who was on his way to the city to make his fortune when he came upon a young lady caught in a sudden rainstorm while taking her bath. Averting his eyes, Akashi picked up both the lady and her bathtub and carried them inside. Modesty and muscle—now there's a combination that could turn even Junko's head.

More recently there was Shiranui, who happened to be present when Commodore Perry and his black ships sailed into Tokyo Bay in 1853. Shiranui put a 140-pound sack on his head and three more over his shoulders, and stumped around to show those foolish Americans what they were up against. The ship shot off a few cannons, and the Japanese promptly signed a peace treaty. No wonder the Sumo Federation isn't fond of foreigners.

But of all the sumo legends the businessman describes to me, I like Kokuna best. Kokuna must have been chock-full of sumo spirit, because when a horse kicked him in the stomach, the horse fell down.

The senior wrestlers have finished their workout and are filing into the bath, followed by their attending juniors. I'm about to slip out the door when the stable owner's wife invites me to join them for lunch. She is a tiny woman, made more so by the surrounding human real estate. She has kind eyes and a gentle, unassuming manner. I accept, more for the chance to speak with her than for the coming meal. Just because I respect sumo ethics doesn't mean I want to end up looking like the wrestlers.

Where the stable owner is the aspiring wrestler's stern and demanding father, his wife is their mother—a firm but gentle hand to help guide the frightened young apprentices back into the eighteenth century. She deals with zits and girls—or lack thereof—and delivers the unwelcome tidings that none of them will be allowed to get their driver's license until they retire at the age of thirty-five or so.

But at the moment she has several more pressing concerns. One young member of the stable is already undergoing knee surgery after only three tournaments, and his future in the sport is questionable.

Another boy, just turned sixteen, recently cabled his parents for some spending money. The moment it arrived he packed his few possessions and fled home to distant Kyushu. The stable has already sent someone to bring him back. The parents will almost certainly agree; to have a son in a Tokyo stable is considered a high honor, particularly in rural villages where career opportunities are limited. And if he should absolutely insist on quitting before he makes a name for himself and earns back the owner's investment in his training? Well, society doesn't have much use for a human battering ram with a junior-high education and an excessive appetite. Most stay.

A hairdresser arrives and sets up shop near the door. He pries open a can and scoops out a thick wad of what looks like earwax. He kneads it between his palms, then massages it briskly into a handful of the first sumo's shoulder-length hair. He combs and smoothes and nudges it into a gleaming upswept helmet with a ponytail that looks exactly like a radar antenna.

21

By now it is well past noon and I'm hungry enough to eat the wax. I watch the young apprentices slowly set the low-slung table, then haul out a huge cauldron of sumo stew. With minor variations, this dish is eaten at almost every meal. It's more than just a stable favorite—it's also the key to most post-sumo retirement plans. Sumo stew is not only famous but extremely popular, and many sumo wrestlers quit and open restaurants once they start losing in the ring.

The stew's contents are surprisingly healthy and nutritious: cabbage, onions, and assorted vegetables in clear broth with small cubes of fried tofu and chicken chunks. It's not until they bring out a second enormous vat that I realize how the wrestlers pack on so much weight: rice. Bowl after heaping bowl, put away with the same unsmiling concentration with which they manhandle each other around the ring. When it comes my turn to eat, the lower-ranking wrestlers stand behind me, hands clasped behind their backs, silently attentive to a half-filled glass of beer or yet another serving of stew. I can only imagine the ache inside those cavernously empty bellies, those muscles that have been burning calories since dawn. And yet they stand, impassive. It's the sumo code.

As I am leaving, the owner's wife gives me a full-size sumo calendar showing bellies, loincloths, and monumental collisions. One photo shows the wrestlers dressed to the nines in full-length evening gowns, too much makeup, and blowsy wigs. It's a yearly ceremony, she tells me. They look like they're enjoying themselves.

I give the calendar to Junko when I get home. It lasts exactly one week on her bedroom wall. When it disappears, I know the hoped-for reply from her yokozuna never arrived.

CHAPTER 3

The sumo scare, it seems, is over but not forgotten. Yukiko sets aside her housework to compose lists of acceptable bachelors of their acquaintance, and Genji follows up with one of his old schoolboy buddies, a Tokyo noodle-shop owner. In due time a hand-written personal history arrives from the young man's mother, carefully scrutinized by Yukiko and studiously ignored by Junko. Pressure is applied, and Junko reluctantly agrees to a meeting "just for a look." A date is chosen: Sunday brunch at a Chinese restaurant in town. Both sets of parents will attend with their respective offspring.

Genji, with consummate courtesy and not a trivial amount of courage, invites me along. I don't want to jeopardize the delicate negotiations so I reluctantly decline, but I pounce as soon as they get home.

"What's he like?" I ask breathlessly.

23

Genji slips out of his shoes. "Well," he says thoughtfully, "he's a good man."

Oh dear. "That bad, huh?"

Yukiko comes in, carrying a box of chocolates the size of a microwave oven. Junko is still out having coffee with her prospective husband.

"He didn't say much," Genji explains over green tea and scotch in the kitchen. The box squats in the middle of the table. It's the color of teak and has dozens of little drawers with tiny silver handles, like a jewelry chest—a $300 token of her suitor's serious intent.

Apparently the young man was more than reticent—he didn't open his mouth the entire evening except to eat, allowing his mother to speak for him on almost every topic. Genji and Yukiko aren't too sanguine about his compatibility with their outspoken Junko. But, they insist, a good time was had by all.

Junko comes in an hour later, annoyed and somewhat out of breath. She'd insisted he drop her off at the supermarket down the street so that he wouldn't know her address. The nuptials are clearly off to a rocky start.

"He talked about himself the entire time!" she announces, dropping into a seat and jerking open several drawers of the chocolate altar. "And he was so arrogant! He told me he's absolutely essential to his company—that they would fail without him. That he got perfect scores in mathematics in high school and his teacher said he was a genius." The chocolates are disappearing at an alarming rate. "And he has *so* many friends from all walks of life and they're all crazy about him. Ugh!" Apparently Junko was so bored that she'd nodded off several times, her chin sliding off her hand until she jerked herself awake. He didn't seem to notice.

Far worse than what the young man said was what he didn't say—he hadn't asked Junko a single question about her life or interests. He'd broken the primary rule of first-date dating.

Okay, the wedding's off, but at least we get to keep the box of chocolates. We cut a wide swath through several tiers while deciding what to do next. Junko and her father are convinced that the young man has no interest in her. I am equally sure that all of his blustering was an attempt to impress her, though I'm certainly not going to admit how many guys I've dated to come to that conclusion. Genji thinks we should wait and see what the suitor's response is. I think it would be more humane to catch him before he declares himself so that he can change his story to "Oh, I didn't like her either."

We drink tea and try out various excuses on one another.

"You're so essential to your company that I'll be lonely at home," Junko says.

"Perhaps that Junko is too busy to date right now," Genji tries.

"How about, 'You're arrogant and dull,'" I suggest.

Then we polish off the chocolates, agree that he is a good man, and go to bed.

The next evening we're all at the door to greet Genji and shake him down for news. "Not good," he says—the Japanese equivalent of a verbal atom bomb. Apparently the day had started out just fine, with his usual seat in the first-class compartment of the train and a copy of the *Financial Times*. But when he got to his office, before he even had time to glance through the morning's mail, disaster struck. The phone rang.

The voice on the other end of the line was expansive, joyous. The date had gone swimmingly. His son was thrilled. It was a done deal, really.

Genji had no idea what to say. He hadn't worked anything out in advance and besides, he hadn't even had his morning coffee. He hemmed and hawed, and in the end limped off the phone with the excuse that Junko had come in late and he hadn't spoken with her yet.

Junko is surprised and vexed. Having to turn the young man down herself was not part of the arrangement. Genji, to my astonishment, agrees to go to the noodle shop and work things out on her behalf.

I always thought of dating as something you do despite your parents, not because of them. I wouldn't ask my dad to find me a young man any more than I would seek his advice on what brand of tampons to buy. But then, my father never offered to write a Dear John letter for me either. This matchmaking business comes with some unexpected benefits.

Genji has gradually talked himself around to the conclusion that he has, in fact, already given the noodle-shop owner something of an answer. Clearly, if Junko really liked the guy, she would have told her father right away. Genji has only to wait a few days and the whole issue will resolve itself.

A week later he visits the noodle shop just before closing time. He offers a hearty greeting and invites the young man's father out to a nearby bar.

"It's too bad about the young ones, eh?" Genji says with a rueful shrug.

"Yes," the noodle-shop owner agrees over a glass of whiskey, "but what can one expect of today's generation? They insist on having their own minds."

The two fathers commiserate on the complexities of the New Human Beings, down a few more doubles, repledge their friendship, and stagger home.

∽

I must admit I'm fascinated by this latest crop of young Japanese men and women. Their world is a cross between the set of a futuristic movie and the pages of a teen magazine. It's a place where new fads appear and disappear in hours, and keeping up with them is a full-time occupation; where everyone is obsessed with what everyone else is wearing. It's also a place so cutting-edge and creative that its inventions regularly take the world by storm, from anime cartoons to manga (comic books) and Tamagotchi (virtual pets); where foreign marketing representatives arrive on bended knee to interview fourteen-year-old girls about the next global trend in consumer electronics.

It's a world within a world—the hidden face of Japan that exists alongside ordinary businessmen and housewives on bicycles. It's almost an alternate reality, like the geisha and the sumo; a subculture that is part of society and yet lives by its own rules and frame of reference. Yukiko mutters darkly about some secret alien invasion and tells me to stay away from them.

I was secretly hoping to get to know this world through Junko, but I rarely catch more than a brief glimpse of her on weekends. She spends almost every night out in Tokyo, returning home on the last train at midnight and hauling herself out of bed for work at six thirty.

I eventually give up on my host sister and start looking for another way to meet Japan's New Human Beings. Rumor has it that they tend to congregate in the neon-bright boutiques of downtown Tokyo on Sunday afternoons. They carry designer-label shopping bags and Starbucks lattes grande. They download their horoscopes onto I-mode cell phones and chatter to each other like a flock of sparrows. In nearby Harajuku, aspiring young musicians set up cheek to jowl along the sidewalks and play as loudly as they can.

One Sunday morning I catch the train to Tokyo under the pretense of visiting the famous Meiji Shrine. Two hours later I get off at Harajuku and follow the sound of 1970s disco music competing with ten-year-old rock and roll. I catch a glimpse of pinkish bangs, then a row of eyebrow rings; hair gets increasingly tufty and Muppet-green, and shoes sprout clunky nine-inch heels. I must be getting close.

Six guys in bright-orange jumpsuits are dancing John Travolta–style to the Village People. They're actually quite good. The three young men nearby are wearing dark glasses, one white glove between them, and pacifiers around their necks. They've bleached their black hair blond, then covered it with frizzy black wigs.

I settle in with one frenetic band that has more enthusiasm than audience. The lead singer is wearing the top end of a bear suit, with a fluffy jaw and furry ears. His guitarist is a Viking conqueror with horns that flop back and forth whenever he nods his head. He does a pretty good impression until he hits a complicated chord, then sticks out his tongue and ruins the effect. They finish off their song, swing their mikes around like urban cowboys, and take a break.

"Do you like my music?" The bear-headed fellow asks me in perfect English.

"It's terrific," I lie.

"How about the costume?"

"Fabulous," I say with complete sincerity. He looks just like the teddy bear that sat on the shelf above my bed when I was little.

He survived high-school examination hell and is now a freshman economics major at Tokyo University. He has the next four years to enjoy himself before stepping back onto the treadmill for the term of his corporate life. He's got a streak of weekend purple in his spiky black hair. He'll do the shoes, the wigs, the makeup, he tells me, but no tattoos or body piercing—nothing permanent. On Monday morning he'll look just like everyone else, but today belongs to him.

∽

On my way back to the station, I pass a dozen shops that cater to the Harajuku crowd. Several of them are selling shoes. A small devil takes hold of me and I slip inside.

I walk right by a prominent display of mammoth yeti boots. I barely glance at a shiny pair of patent leather shoes with artistic splatter that looks like bird droppings. I don't even pause at the cliffhanger pair of bejeweled evening shoes with ice-pick heels. I make straight for the absolute tallest, thinnest, wobbliest pair of platform shoes in the entire store, guaranteed to make me well over six feet tall. The clerk rushes over and does his level best to unsell me on them. When that doesn't work, he calls two coworkers over to back him up with a Greek chorus of nodding heads and sucking breaths. Wouldn't I rather try on some hair extensions instead?

"No," I say. "I really want the boots."

After much opening of boxes, they find a pair that might

possibly fit my boatlike feet. They wave me into a leather chair and give me the royal treatment; three of them are working in tandem to put on one shoe. I pray that my sock doesn't have a hole in it and that I've remembered to shave my legs. They use smooth wooden lozenges to lever in my heel while my toes slide screaming into the needle tip. Things go rapidly downhill from there.

I can't zip them up. I pull and tug, but they're made of unforgiving leather and there's still at least two inches of skin peering out between the metal teeth. The young men stand around and suck more air in through their teeth and mutter to one another under their breath.

Up until this very moment I've always been proud of my calves. They've carried me faithfully through several marathons. They've suffered my heavy backpack without creaking or complaint. They've even earned me the occasional compliment from fellow riders when I'm on my racing bike. But right now they just feel like huge, unwanted, globular appendages.

Eventually one of the salesmen solves the problem by tying the tops closed with several loops of purple shoelaces.

The time has come. Two of the men position themselves on either arm, while the third takes up his post directly behind my shoulder blades. They lift me out of my seat like a ninety-year-old woman and center me atop my suddenly unstable legs. They're attentive to my slightest wobble, their hands hovering barely an inch below each elbow. They act just like my parents did when I was eight years old and got a pair of stilts for Christmas.

I take a step. My nine-inch heel scrapes along the floor. One of the salesmen demonstrates how to kick my foot forward to get some momentum on the five-pound boot and carry me into the next step. I feel like I've suddenly grown an extra joint, pointing in the wrong direction. I lumber forward like a giraffe, kicking up and out and following my toes with my knee, my chest, and finally my bobbing head.

I'm halfway around the store when I lose focus for an instant and step down on the edge of one foot. I lurch forward and go into a slow-motion, windmilling fall, then suddenly feel my human scaffolding kick in. They prop me back up, then tactfully suggest that I return to my seat before I hurt myself.

I take off the shoes and buy a hair extension. I promise to go on a diet, to break both legs if necessary to atrophy those vulgar, bulging muscles into stick-thin submission. The three salesmen line up to bow me out with relief scrawled across their faces. As I'm leaving I notice a woman buying a pair of purple shoelaces. Perhaps I've started a new trend.

On my way home I have the sudden vision of a future CEO with thinning hair and the secret memory of wearing a fluffy bear suit and playing bad music. Older Japanese may not understand Junko and her generation, but maybe Japan's future is in good hands after all.

CHAPTER 4

Judo is made up of two basic principles. The first is to pull your opponent off balance. If he happens to be huge, then it is best to annoy him so badly that he will, in a moment of berserk rage, throw himself off balance as he lunges at you. Once this happens all you have to do is put something in his path—your body, a banana peel—for him to trip over. The victory dance is a little extra that I've come up with on my own. It looks very much like that tippy-toe ballet thing that football players do when they cross the end zone with the ball. In Genji's dojo, almost everybody has a black belt and outweighs me by at least fifty pounds. I don't have much use for the victory dance.

I catch a quick flash out the corner of my eye and feel an almost casual pressure on my thigh. Suddenly the world is spinning crazily, the fluorescent ceiling lights blurry and upside down. My body hits the ground with a sound like a wet frog thrown against a piece of tile.

I pretend to be examining the mat while I struggle to catch my breath. Someone once told me that Japanese judo mats are made of a thick pad of rice straw covered by woven reeds. At the time I imagined a room filled with warm yellow light, smelling of spring and piled high with bundles of freshly cut hay, like an Amish barn at harvest time. With my cheek pressed against the floor, I notice a certain amount of false advertising. The mat itself is plastic—a thin layer of vinyl covering heavy plywood boards. Not a wisp of hay in sight, nor any other type of padding. It looks and feels exactly like my parent's kitchen floor.

"Could be worse," Genji says. Apparently when he was a boy the workout mats were covered in real woven rice straw, which meant dozens of needle-sharp splinters and a lot of sprained toes. I am, he points out as he eases himself off me, lucky.

Genji moves on to a more interesting opponent—the wall. He leans against it gently, focusing his energy. His leg suddenly shoots out in a fishhook arc and his stomach slams into the wood. It trembles violently, as though a grenade has just gone off on the other side. He steps aside. I gather my energy. I throw my entire body against the wall, jackknifing my leg out of the way. Nothing. No grenades, no firecrackers, not even a popgun. Genji is watching, hands on his hips. After fifteen minutes the door is still standing defiantly and two angry red bruises have ballooned up around my hip bones. For the first time in my adult life, I stick my stomach out as far as it will go to cushion the impact. I blank my mind against the pain. Lean. Drive. Swivel. *Slam*.

Somewhere around my 118th swivel, I feel something tear wetly across the ball of my foot. I've twisted off all the skin halfway back to my heel. Hallelujah! I compose my face into a false expression of disappointment and hobble over to Genji.

"Tape," he says, and points to a dirty white surgical roll on a nearby windowsill. A thick swath of my sole is curling over itself, like a strip of old parchment. I carefully stretch it back into place and tape it down, then stand up and pivot. It feels soft and squishy, like I'm stepping on a week-old slice of ham.

The wall is no closer to caving in. I start praying for an earthquake.

Afterward I wait outside for Genji. I remember my delight when Murata-san first described him to me back in the States—a sixth-degree black belt, a competitor known for his martial-arts techniques throughout Japan. I had imagined a tiny, weathered old man with a thick accent, disheveled gray hair, and a gruff demeanor. I daydreamed complicated scenarios in which I performed almost inhuman feats of discipline in order to win his respect and the right to be his student. Eventually, by dint of a half dozen mysterious tricks, he would teach me to fight like Bruce Lee, or at least win the Olympics.

The real Genji couldn't be more different. Tall, powerful, and polished, he is also—thankfully—enormously patient with me. Each week I head into town for a two-hour practice at his old university. In between we make regular visits to various judo academies all over Tokyo. Each workout is a six-hour round-trip ride from Fujisawa, but it comes with an unexpected benefit—the chance to talk with Genji on the train.

We get home just after nine o'clock. I stumble into my room and collapse onto the sofa.

"Karin, come up in fifteen minutes!" Yukiko's voice, calling me to eat with them.

At the risk of sounding both rude and ungrateful, I don't

want dinner in fifteen minutes. I don't want dinner at all. My body feels like an overripe watermelon on a hot day. A black thunderhead headache is building just under my hairline. I need forty-two aspirin and six hours in a hot tub, then three days in bed. But this is Japan. *No* is not a word to be used lightly, and it is never used by the newest member of the household. I climb the steps, one at a time.

∽

Over dinner I casually ask the Tanakas if there are any temples or shrines in the area where I might volunteer and perhaps get to know the people who live here. Yukiko immediately wrinkles her nose—she has little use for Fujisawa and still does most of her shopping in distant Kamakura, despite having moved here over ten years ago. She's barely on speaking terms with either of our neighbors. On one side lives a woman who cuts hair out of her kitchen—an unseemly thing to do—and gossips relentlessly. On the other side the owners refuse to spray their hedges that border the Tanaka's property, and the resulting bumper crop of tiny caterpillars each spring invariably gives Yukiko an angry rash.

"Shrines . . . " Genji says thoughtfully, rubbing a finger along his chin.

"How about the Seven-Eleven?" Junko suggests through a mouthful of food. That's the closest anyone can come up with to a neighborhood landmark, and we move on to other things.

But there is no such thing as a casual conversation in Japan. Two days later I get called upstairs to the hearty announcement that we are all going to join in a *matsuri*, a traditional Shinto festival in Tokyo.

This doesn't sound too promising. Tokyo seems anything but traditional. It's one of the world's most populated cities, home to more than thirteen million people, with another twenty million living in its suburbs. It's ringed by an elevated super-toll road, a modern Great Wall of China that regularly turns into a high-priced parking lot because the streets below cannot possibly accommodate the off-ramp traffic.

Surprisingly, Tokyo began its life as a humble swamp in the early 1600s. Within a hundred years its population had grown to over a million inhabitants—the largest pre-industrial city in the world. Over the past century, it has been twice reborn; once after the catastrophic 1923 earthquake and subsequent firestorm, and again in 1945 after the devastation of Allied bombing. Each time it has risen like a phoenix from the ashes. By 1990 the ground that the Imperial Palace in Tokyo sat on was by some accounts worth more than all the land in California. In the high-fashion district of Ginza, the area beneath a single shopper's feet has been valued at an astonishing $20,000.

Despite, or perhaps because of, the exorbitant cost of living, residents of Tokyo have turned showy overspending into a badge of distinction. Eight-hundred-dollar meals and hundred-dollar shots of whiskey are carelessly tossed back in a game of ostentatious one-upmanship supported by seemingly unlimited corporate expense accounts. Those Japanese who are not Of the City, who are still inculcated with the frugal values hammered home in the aftermath of the war, cluck their tongues and mutter darkly of foreign influences. But Tokyo is to Japan what New York is to America, and, like New Yorkers, Tokyoites don't care what anyone else thinks of them.

But as hard as Tokyo plays, so does it work. More than a

million businessmen stream through its train stations every morning. Once the sun goes down, Tokyo crackles to life in a burst of neon energy. Two-story television screens flash endless MTV advertisements at a capricious clientele. Scrolling signs slither down the sides of skyscrapers. Beneath them, tuxedoed Svengalis urge you into darkened bars of financial doom. At midnight it's still standing room only aboard the trains, and the last run at 1:00 a.m. is so full that the conductors are often forced to put their shoulders to the masses like fullbacks at the Super Bowl.

And yet there is another side to Tokyo, a place where roasted-sweet-potato sellers still advertise their wares out of boxy trucks, using megaphones that blare out fifteenth-century tunes; a place where corner grocery stands haven't yet been asphalted over by lavish department stores. Asakusa, nestled deep in the heart of Old Tokyo, is a village that became a city but remained a village, with old-fashioned values and a strong sense of community. People in Asakusa still leave their doors open at night. They live in wooden houses that have sheltered six, or ten, or twenty generations of a single family line. Several of Asakusa's streets still don't have names, from a time when people knew every nook and cranny of their world. Old-fashioned cottage industries move out onto the back porch on a hot summer afternoon and fill the neighborhood with the scent of fresh-cut tatami or the sour tang of fermenting soybeans.

The yearly Asakusa festival has changed little over the centuries. The shrine itself is home to a local *kami*, a term often translated as "god" but more closely resembling a spirit associated with some local ancestor or natural landmark. Once a year the kami—Asakusa's spiritual landlord, in effect—is transferred to a portable shrine and taken for a spin around the premises.

"Portable" is another one of those relative terms; the *mikoshi*, or shrine, weighs upward of a thousand pounds and requires at least twenty sturdy young men to carry it.

Over the years, one mikoshi became two, and two became five, and nowadays more than a hundred ornate shrines spend three days winding a serpentine path through Asakusa's boulevards and back alleys. Every couple of blocks hosts its own shrine, and competition is fierce to display the most lavish offerings, paint the shrine in the most extravagant hues, and field the most strapping young men with endless stamina and matching uniforms.

Which is why I'm surprised that Genji is able to talk our way onto one of the teams. But then I haven't factored in *kashi*, that web of obligation that connects every Japanese to everyone he has ever had contact with. A favor owed in Japan is as tangible as a financial obligation in the West. They are rarely forgiven, never forgotten. Most Japanese spend their lives spinning so intricate a web that if they pluck at the proper thread, the rippling wave of reciprocated obligations reverberates to the farthest corners of Japan.

Of course, the game of kashi rarely proceeds in straight lines—which is why our first step is to have dinner at a fancy restaurant owned by a family friend. We have ostensibly come for their special menu, composed entirely of hand-gathered wild weeds—a locally celebrated spring cuisine. Our real purpose is to meet a client of our friend the owner. He is, it turns out, also a frequent patron of an exclusive bar in Asakusa that hosts a neighborhood mikoshi team. In other words, we are four favors from shouldering the sacred shrine.

We're well into dessert—salty pickled squid—when our contact finally arrives. He's inebriated. Genji slips seamlessly into a similar state; not sloppy, but delicately harmonizing. Extended introductions. Drinks all around. A toast or two. Bad news, the man says. The festival is very difficult. It's just around the corner, and arrangements take time. We should have contacted him earlier. Perhaps next year.

"Yes, of course," Genji agrees with a sympathetic smile. "We understand completely. How could we have been so rude? We're happy just to be spectators to this great event."

The man sucks in his breath. "But then, perhaps an exception can be made. I'll do my best for you."

"Wonderful! Fantastic. Please, don't put yourself out. We are truly indebted to you. Such a kind man." Another round of drinks, and the man rises to go.

"Doesn't look good," I mumble morosely.

"That went well," Genji says.

Several minutes later, pandemonium breaks loose— Japanese pandemonium. No bar stools skittering across the floor, no bottles broken against tables, just a concerted intake of breath and the sudden silence of interrupted conversation. The restaurant owner rushes over to our table. It seems our contact slapped a woman from his office, and she fled in tears to fetch her husband. In the meantime, he is sitting alone at the bar while his drinking buddies mill about with frightened, deer-like eyes. It's an absolute disaster for the reputation of our friend's restaurant during this festive event.

This is the moment when I find out why Genji made it to the very top of the corporate pyramid. He slips smoothly from his seat and maneuvers the man upstairs, while giving Junko a silent signal to sweep his entourage out the door for a dedicated evening of barhopping. She doesn't show up at our hotel until nearly three in the morning, having done her duty and drunk them all under the table. Meanwhile, Genji is hard at work on the source of the problem. He never even bothers to ask the man why he slapped the woman in the first place. His interest is purely damage control.

"A public restaurant is such an unfortunate place to have a disagreement," he says over scotch. Her husband will hear her side, of course. He'll feel he has to do something about it, just so his home life isn't hell. And the poor owner—she'll worry herself to death over her customers, though they barely heard a thing. . . .

Genji soothes. He commiserates. He exudes friendly camaraderie. And then he moves in for the kill.

"Perhaps," he says in a conspiratorial murmur, "if we put our heads together, we can think of some way to help everyone out of this unfortunate predicament."

By this time the husband has come storming in downstairs. Genji orders our man another drink and smoothly shifts floors and gears. "Terrible, just terrible! Such a pleasant evening and the owner is beside herself with worry that her guests have been put out of sorts. Of course, everyone understands completely how your wife feels, but . . . alcohol was involved. You understand, I'm sure. A sincere apology will certainly be forthcoming in the morning. And the lady? At home, alone? She must have a bottle of the best sake immediately to help her through these trying times. Will you bring it to her? She has my deepest sympathies. If she needs anything, *anything*, she has but to ask."

An hour later, our man has reluctantly agreed to an apology. The owner, our contact, his coworker, and her husband have all acquired an obligation. The festival? Yes, of course, it would be their pleasure to get us on a team.

Bingo. We're in. All because a man I'd never met slapped a woman for a slight I never figured out.

∞

It's six thirty on a Friday evening and we're standing in a gaudy tourist store in Asakusa looking over gaudier clothing. Even Junko has taken a reluctant break from her evening's liquid entertainment to attend to the weekend's couture. I'm following her around as she examines racks of *hapi* coats—long, square-sleeved tunics that we will be wearing under our team uniforms. I point out one in muted red with what looks like tailless stingrays on them.

"They're birds," Junko says.

"They look to me like stingrays," I repeat, a little stubbornly. Somehow being told exactly what to wear bothers me less than being told how to interpret it.

"They're birds."

I want to tell her, like my kindergarten teacher taught me, that we should each decide for ourselves what we want it to be. But this is Japan. There is right, and there is wrong. Right is what most people think it should be. We buy the birds.

Scarves are next. The *hachimaki*, I'm told, is far more than a square of cotton, it's a symbol of intent—like pinning your New Year's diet to your sleeve and wearing it to brunch the next day. Political demonstrators wear hachimaki when protesting. Students tie them on before sitting down to study; pilots wore them when setting off to war. The hachimaki tells the world that you are committed, *determined*. When twisted into a tight rope and knotted firmly at the back, the pain focuses your mind on the job ahead. It feels rather like a cerebral chastity belt.

41

But that's nothing compared to the penance of my pants: two tube-shaped legs connected tenuously across the crotch. The whole contraption is fastened with a bit of string wrapped around my hips. With neither zipper nor seams, it gradually slithers down my legs like a pair of oversize kneesocks.

And shoes—worker's shoes, with inner-tube soles and thin cloth tops. The big toe is separated from the rest, so for the first time in my life I can demonstrably pick up a pencil with my shoes on. Yukiko is not amused.

At last we go in search of our most important fashion accessory: the shrine itself. We find it on a back street under a hastily constructed wooden awning, getting a last-minute tune-up. Twenty of us are positioned along the heavy wooden poles like an anxious dogsled team. A priest claps his wooden sticks three times, and we're off.

The first thing I notice is the shafts. They're square. Why on earth hasn't anyone bothered to round them off, I wonder, given the hundreds of hours that must have gone into the exquisite carving of the shrine itself? Then I notice that they're four by four, and solid. Heavy. I become quite certain—not knowing a stick about carpentry—that two-by-twos would have done just as well and might even have a bit more spring to them. My teammates' heads are popping up between the shafts like mushrooms, each properly girded with a scarf of purposeful intent. The shrine itself is ringed by a second, higher rank of teammates dressed entirely in green. It is their job to watch us—to ferret out slackers, maintain the proper level of enthusiasm, and make sure there is no airspace between our shoulders and the shafts. Their decisions are final and without appeal.

Only four minutes have gone by and I know I'm in deep

trouble. It's Friday afternoon and the shrine won't stop moving until Sunday night. Thankfully, our ranks are swelling as salarymen and secretaries hurry home to slough off suits and stockings and tie on their scarves. The additional human capital gradually lightens the load. As more and more enthusiastic carriers put their shoulders to the shafts, my personal universe contracts until I find myself draped over the back of the woman in front of me and wallpapered to the fellow at my back. Someone else's sweat is running down my neck and my hands have long since lost their perch on the shaft. But the real problem is happening below my knees. There are just too many feet per square foot. Newcomers are accommodated with a certain amount of good-natured jostling and a few bruised ankles and trodden toes. Like a cranky old engine, the shrine stutters and catches, backfires, and spits, then settles into the gentle purr of a well-tuned machine. All cylinders are firing smoothly, with one exception: me.

I keep telling myself to relax—that hateful word one hears most often at the gynecologist's office and in a dentist's chair. I've already purpled three unknown toes and run a dozen laps around every form of Japanese apology I know. Things don't improve until we reach Asakusa's main gate. It's an impressive structure, an elaborate roof on steroids, supported by two columns that house the Buddhist gods of wind and thunder, both glowering angrily down at us. I don't blame them—this gate was clearly never meant to fit a Shinto shrine. We make a determined run on it and squeeze through like toothpaste, scraping off layers of green men on both sides.

The few that are left push hard on a corner of the mikoshi, and we rotate beneath it like human ball bearings. We're entering the long, straight corridor that leads up to the temple itself, lined with tiny shops selling all manner of tourist trinkets, wooden toys, and pounded rice balls. Racks of clothes and other merchandise spill out into our path. The alley is barely wider than the temple gate. It's like threading a camel through the eye of a needle. We lurch forward.

The crowd parts. Racks are pulled back into stores and older folk are helped up onto cement flower pots. The men in green go into overdrive, positioning themselves on either side of us like tugboats maneuvering a barge. One side shoves a bit too hard, and we slip sideways into a rack of hats. The owner, a tiny woman, smiles serenely and makes no move to gather up her merchandise. *"Gambatte!"* she says. "Go for it!"

∞

It's nearly midnight before the shrine is temporarily parked and we drape ourselves wearily over stools at our sponsor's bar. We haven't eaten anything since breakfast, and I'm ready to chew the leather covers off the seats. The owner is serving sake, but the thought of getting back between the shafts with an early morning warm-wine hangover is enough to keep me in tonic water. The bartender is a quiet man, always ready with a light or a drink, listening hard but saying little. He takes one look at my hopeless face and reaches under the bar. Five silver-wrapped Hershey's kisses appear magically on the countertop. I'm sitting next to Junko and I know that while she favors Godiva, she's not averse to slumming in a pinch. She ignores the chocolate. So do I. We've reached a serious impasse of Japanese etiquette.

What's really at stake is *iki*. As far as I can tell, iki is what my mother would call good breeding. In her case that meant not killing spiders that had wandered into the house and

44

treating library books better than our own. In Japan it's much more complicated than that. It's a dense morass of seemingly unrelated rules and regulations, a handbook of behavior edited by countless generations of women who have themselves been forced to struggle their entire lives to master its myriad details. Most important, like wa, iki is something I haven't got but want. I suspect it's something you're born with, though Genji has made valiant attempts to explain it to me over the dinner table, and Yukiko carefully points it out when I fall short.

Even I recognize the first iki-hurdle between me and the blessed taste of chocolate on my tongue. In Japan it is the height of rudeness to attack your food like a junkyard dog. Japanese cuisine is rightfully called a feast for the eyes. This is at least in part because you spend so much time looking at it before you are allowed to touch it. And in the rigid hierarchies of Japanese society, who eats first assumes monumental importance. On formal occasions this impasse is resolved by having the host pick up his chopsticks first, then wait for the most honored guest to take the first bite. In less formal settings things get even trickier. I'll be damned if I'm going to take the first Hershey kiss and prove myself a worthless barbarian. Junko has no such qualms. She casually unwraps a chocolate and pops it into her mouth. I follow suit.

Four kisses quickly disappear—two apiece. One remains squatting on the table. As I expect, Junko makes no move to pick it up. Not to be outmaneuvered, I also let it lie. Dreadful, interminable, tortured moments crawl past. I sit on my hands. I promise to buy myself three—no, six—candy bars as soon as I get home. I smooth out the old wrappers, fashion them into tiny silver turtles, and surreptitiously lick my fingers. More time crawls by. Finally the bartender, noticing our lack of interest, sweeps the kiss back under the table. I'm reminded of the time my brother and I fought so hard over our Halloween candy that Mom took it away.

∞

It's Saturday afternoon, and it's been raining since the crack of dawn. My festival shoes are made of thin cloth, and my feet inside are corpse-white and wrinkled, like dead pieces of brain coral. I've gained an inch at the shoulder in the form of an angry purple bruise the size of half an apple, which is at this moment supporting at least fifty pounds of reclining Shinto spirit. I've broken the prime rule of shrine carrying—I've let myself be positioned directly behind a fellow who is only five foot one, forcing me to lumber along with my legs splayed and my knees half bent, like a sumo wrestler tiptoeing to the fridge. Breakfast was not on this morning's agenda. Everyone around me is still chanting with undiminished enthusiasm: "*Yashoi, yashoi!*" I desperately want to know where they're getting their energy. I'm sure they have no idea where we are going or how long it will take us to get there—questions that have been plaguing me all weekend—and yet it doesn't seem to bother them. Even Genji seems immune to cold and hunger and sore feet. His face is lined with exhaustion, yet he cheerfully offers to once again jackknife his six-foot frame between the shafts. We eat when and where we're told and instantly jump to the orders of the men in green. But while I am plagued by the need to have some control over my circumstances, everyone else seems to take comfort from just being part of the team.

I'm gradually starting to realize that being born Japanese is not unlike signing up for a lifelong stint in the military: good benefits, great job security, but not a lot of room for renegades. Which isn't all that surprising, since the very first references to Japan in the ancient Chinese chronicles call it the Land of Wa. *Wa* means harmony, a concept that is still deeply rooted in Japanese history—in its isolation from the outside world, its tradition of small, crowded villages where anybody's business is everybody's business, and its lengthy feudal heritage. Not too long ago, a moment of wa-lessness could get your head removed by the nearest samurai blade. Nowadays it's just considered in extremely poor taste. In Japan, sacrificing personal desire in the best interests of the group is a sign of maturity.

Eventually I give up and go to a place inside my head that's at least a million miles away, a place that's warm and comfortable and filled with candy bars and hair dryers. Then I come back to my body for a minute for no particular reason, just to make sure that I'm still breathing, and I notice an extraordinary thing. Everyone is moving in absolute synchronization, like a centipede—*including me*. Heels are up, knees bent—my body is in perfect working order, right down to the smile. I just can't believe it's mine.

⌒

It's Sunday, three thirty in the morning. We've been doing zigzaggy laps around the temple grounds for forty minutes. We finally come to roost in a thoroughly unpleasant spot: a broken cement courtyard hard up against a chain-link fence. Shadowy forms flit past, trailing the pungent odor of sake and too many cigarettes. I see a shiny, tattooed scalp. *Yakuza*, the Japanese mafia. The very word strikes fear into the hearts of law-abiding Japanese. I've heard whispers about them all weekend, and once or twice a teammate's sleeve slipped back an inch too far, revealing a glimpse of a grinning dragon or flowering cherry tree.

It might seem odd for an illegal organization to so blatantly finger its own members, but the yakuza and tattooing share a long history. In Edo times, criminals were branded across the cheek or forehead to mark them for life. Once the yakuza came into power, they deliberately turned the punishment into a badge of pride, and tattooing became an art. Dense and ornate, the designs are meant to swirl around the shoulders and flow down the back. They're wrought with such delicacy that when muscles flex, the images appear to spring to life. And they don't come cheap—the more elaborate tattoos can cost $15,000 and over a hundred hours of unanaesthetized pain. It's not unusual for a particularly beautiful design to be framed after its owner no longer has a use for it.

Unlike the American mafia, the yakuza are an accepted part of society. Many corporations hire yakuza to "administer" their shareholder meetings—to visit troublesome stockholders and ensure no unexpected difficulties at voting time. Yakuza also play a large part in many festivals and public events. The government sometimes even encourages the relationship, in the hopes that by partially absorbing the yakuza into mainstream society, they may be able to exert a measure of influence over them.

The Sanja Matsuri is, in fact, a favorite of the yakuza throughout Japan. For the first two days they modestly cover their tattoos and join in the festivities. But on this, the third and final day, they shrug off their costumes and get ready to enjoy themselves. Two super-size mikoshi are preparing to parade around the temple grounds, each carried by rival, all-mafia teams. The area has been fenced off, and more than five hundred white-coated policemen form a barrier of solid human flesh along its edges.

The gate opens at six and the yakuza pour through. I climb up into some scaffolding along the far wall. Most of the men are riddled with tattoos, sodden drunk, and naked but for dirty loincloths. "There's going to be some good fighting today!" snarls a heavyset fellow. Another participant quickly obliges with a poorly aimed swing, and scattered fights break out. The first shrine arrives just in time to avert wholesale fisticuffs. A second shrine shows up a few minutes later. I expect instant battle to break out, but the two teams keep a wary distance apart. Instead of going at it, they wage war by proxy, lavishing attention on their shrines. These mikoshis are at least three times the size of our neighborhood models and so heavy that even with a full contingent of fifty men, they can be carried for only a few minutes at a time. A downed shrine is clearly an object of contempt, and both teams struggle mightily to keep theirs afloat and, if possible, bobbing up and down hard enough to cause the shrine bells to ring. A vast throng of half-naked young men swirl around each mikoshi, sweeping away everything in their path.

Several men stand atop each shrine, exhorting their teams with gilded fans. One fellow recognizes some unfinished business in the crowd and instantly hurls himself off the platform. For three hours the thrust and parry continues unabated, the anger of ten thousand violent men miraculously siphoned off into symbolic battle as the shrines shuffle around the temple grounds.

Eventually I get tired of my uncomfortable perch atop the scaffolding and decide to make a dash for the gate.

A space opens abruptly in front of me and the mikoshi appears. Three tattooed yakuza stand on top of it, treading on hapless fingertips and exhorting followers with screeching whistles and jabbing fans. The inner guard surrounding the shrine are fanatic, imperious, and as dangerous as samurai warriors. Anyone who tries to slip past them is made to see the error of his ways and then summarily expelled.

A heavy hand grabs my shoulder and twists painfully. "Foreigner?" a sake-roughened voice slurs. I nod dumbly. "Carry?" I'm pushed past bare chests covered with delicately tattooed geishas and face a solid wall of thirty carriers. One man is yanked from the middle of the line and I am thrust forward to take his place. The hole instantly evaporates as other carriers readjust themselves to fill the space. I drill an arm between two men. My heavy-handed patron puts a shoulder against my ribs and lunges forward. Gradually my body is absorbed into the huge amoeboid mass. I catch the rhythm of the chant and my feet adjust of their own accord to the mincing gate. I'm solidly connected, flesh to flesh, from my shoulders to my knees. Time slows, expands, then stops. A minute passes, perhaps an hour. Then a hand upon my arm and I am jerked free. The swirling crowd catches me and I am carried away.

The human tide flows briefly past the gate, and suddenly I am alone.

CHAPTER 5

Something is definitely going on. After two months in Japan, I still can't read a newspaper, but I can certainly follow the pictures on TV. The same story has been leading the national news every evening for over a week: serious-looking men in suits pointing at topographic maps, where blobs of color are gradually making their way south toward Tokyo.

Cherry blossoms. Japan is the only country I know where a flower can bring an entire nation to a state of near-sexual excitement. Cherry blossoms last for little more than a week and are symbolic—as any Japanese on the street will tell you—of the impermanence of life, the sadness underlying its exquisite beauty. Cherry blossoms fall in their prime, like samurai warriors were meant to do. Throughout the bars of Tokyo, gray-haired businessmen moon about, dreaming of shedding career and kin to follow the blooming flowers down the backbone of the Alps. Any stand of more than two cherry trees becomes a must-see attraction, mobbed day and night by pale-faced city dwellers enjoying their one yearly flirtation with nature. They sit in tight knots, hugging their karaoke machines and propping themselves up against barrels of sake. They compose spontaneous haiku to the breathtaking scene unfolding before them, imbibe copiously, and weep freely. Once they're gone, the blossoms gradually drift down to cover up the litter left behind.

By May the breaking news is back to the occasional blowfish poisoning and the rash of newspapers stolen out of mailboxes in downtown Kawasaki. But the air no longer has that sharp, unpleasant edge of winter, and the breeze coming off the ocean tastes of salt and freedom. Spring has finally arrived. Once the dinner dishes are dry, I excuse myself to go for a long run on the beach.

The asphalt path that skirts the shoreline is deserted but for the occasional seagull picking indifferently through the detritus of high tide. Ripples of windblown sand squeak softly under my sneakers. I pick up the pace, pushing hard and lengthening my stride. The white cement markers flash by in the darkness and I start to sweat. I feel a loosening in my chest, like a corset that has been drawn too tight and is finally tearing a seam.

It's the tiny spaces—the six-inch gap between the dining-room table and the wall, the one that I have to sidle through every evening to get to my chair. No matter how carefully I inch around, I almost always bump the corner of the table and make all the dishes rattle. I'm not used to being clumsy like that. Then there are the dozens of fragile bowls I wash and dry each night. I live in terror that I will drop one or put it away where it doesn't belong. And the bewildering array of rules: How to Roll up the Garden Hose and the Proper Way to Fold Shirts. I've never felt so lost and incompetent.

But out here no one's watching. I can vault the cement markers, dance in the moonlight, chase the seagulls. For this one, precious moment I can do exactly what I want, with no consequences and no one around to tell me I'm wrong.

I arrive home two hours later. My hair is damp and wind-blown, my shoes are full of sand, and I am ambling—loose-limbed and relaxed for the first time since I stepped off the plane. I've decided to make jogging a part of my evening routine. It will be good for my judo and even better for my peace of mind.

Yukiko greets me at the door. I stop ambling.

"Karin, you cannot run at night," she says.

I know I'm not supposed to ask. I live in Yukiko's house and I should just accept that she knows best. But I can't help myself.

"Why?"

The corners of her lips tick down. "It is dangerous," she says.

The only thing worse than questioning a superior is to openly disagree with one. But maybe if I phrase it as a compliment. . . .

"Japan is the safest country in the world. I'm sure nobody could possibly—"

"There are Arabs and Chinese," Yukiko points in the direction of the train station. "It is dangerous."

A dozen compromises flit through my mind, but by the look on Yukiko's face, I've already overstepped my bounds. I nod. She smiles. I retreat.

Two nights later I find myself pacing my tiny apartment—around the coffee table, over a pile of books, shimmy past the sofa, into the kitchen, and back out again. I've already cleaned my cameras, ironed my underwear, and tried three times to sit down and conjugate a list of passive causative verbs. The memory of that run is buzzing around in my head like a hungry mosquito. I am desperate for the exercise and even more desperate for the freedom.

But Yukiko has made herself abundantly clear, and to ignore her wishes could have serious consequences. On the other hand, what she doesn't know won't hurt her—or me. They've already gone to bed. What harm could it do?

I lay out my futon and pile some clothes under the covers in the shape of an American, then slip out my sliding door and carefully lock it behind me. I tiptoe down the brick path that wraps around the house, then run smack into the hip-high gate that separates the garden from the driveway. I know it creaks quite loudly. I don't dare climb over it and risk bending the hinges. I'm stymied by an obstacle that a Jack Russell terrier would sail right over.

That's it! I take two steps back—all the room I have—lunge forward, and just manage to clear it. I dash around the corner, then stroll nonchalantly down to the beach.

The first three miles go by easily. I take a quick break and wander over to the waterline, playing chicken with the waves and doing a half dozen handsprings along the high-tide mark. I get tar between my fingers and make a mental note to check my sneakers before bringing them inside the house.

Two miles later, my conscience finally gets the better of me and I reluctantly turn around. I'm halfway home when I notice a dark object on the path that wasn't there an hour ago. It's a woman's purse, lying on its side. It's open and several cheap trinkets have spilled across the tarmac. I stuff the contents back inside, then wonder what to do. I can't possibly bring it back to Yukiko without telling her where I found it, and when. I should just leave it—someone will come across it tomorrow morning and hand it over to the police, if its owner hasn't already come back for it. Then I remember that there's a *koban*, a tiny police kiosk, about a mile up the path. I'll just drop it off on my way home.

A single policeman is sitting at a miniature desk, concentrating intently on his paperwork. He looks up and smiles brightly. I smile back. The police in Japan have an excellent reputation. They're far better known for helping little old ladies cross the street and rescuing lost kittens than they are for midnight shootouts and SWAT-style drug raids. Most of them don't even carry a gun.

"Good evening," he says in Japanese, then courteously comes around his desk to usher me into a seat.

"Good evening." I feel uncomfortable in my bare knees and sandy socks. He is impeccably dressed, his uniform freshly pressed, hat brim shiny, and gloves a dazzling white.

Once I'm comfortably settled, he sits back down, folds his hands over each other, and gives me his full and friendly attention.

I struggle to find the right words. I know that Japanese sentences are not really supposed to start with *I*. It's considered arrogant. Those passive causative conjugations would come in handy right now. "This . . . thing . . . was made to be found by me tonight," I finally blurt out.

He looks stricken. The smile is still on his face but he's gone corpse-white, like a shark has just bitten off both his legs under the table. His hands have suddenly tightened around each other in a death grip. He probably thought I was going to ask for directions to the train station.

He pushes his hat a little more firmly on his head and starts off gently, almost in a whisper. "Where?" Down the path. I point, then draw a quick map.

"When?" A few minutes ago. I smile again and get up to leave, having done my duty as a good citizen. Doubtless he will discover the name and address of the owner inside the bag and return it to her within the hour.

He is out of his chair in a flash, one white glove waving in front of his face like a windshield wiper. He lowers both hands, palms to the floor, indicating that I should sit back down. He's between me and the door. I ease back into my chair.

He reaches into a filing cabinet and pulls out a thick wad of paperwork. At that moment his coworker walks in, carefully closes the door behind himself, and sees me. He smiles. They confer in quick, whispered Japanese. He stops smiling. They both arrange themselves across the desk from me and finger the paperwork nervously. The first one sits with poised pen, the second asks questions.

"Nationality?" American.

"Identification?" This gives me pause. I don't have any pockets, so I'm not only penniless but identity-free. I remember reading that noncitizens are required to carry ID at all times. I shake my head and he sucks air in through his teeth like he's just hit his thumb with a hammer. I've definitely broken a law.

"Visa number?" I have no idea. I do know that my visa is on my Swiss passport, since that gives me six months in-country instead of the three they allow to Americans. I have no idea how to explain this, so I shake my head again.

"Address in Japan?" Hooray! I reel it off like a pro. "Genji and Yukiko Tanaka," I add.

They perk up immediately. "Hooostu famiry?" The first one says.

I nod vigorously, then toss in a few words about how terrific the Tanakas are.

"Phone number?" I get halfway through before sanity strikes. What if he calls them? I stumble, pretend to think about it, and then shake my head.

"How long have you lived with them?" Two months, I admit reluctantly. I feel like an idiot, but there's no way I'm giving up that phone number.

They stare at the paperwork for a while, then switch tacks. "What were you doing when you found the bag?"

I'm relieved at the new line of questioning. I was running, I tell them. I pantomime.

They confer briefly. "Who were you running from?"

I stop pantomiming.

"What is that on your fingers?" I look down at my hands in surprise. Tar. I'd completely forgotten about it. What do I say—that I was doing handsprings in the sand? Yukiko was right. I never should have gone jogging at night. One of policemen gingerly examines my fingers, then tries to scrape a bit of tar onto a clean sheet of white paper. The poor fellow is sucking in air like a regular blowhole. His coworker is going through a sheaf of papers with a foreign name at the top of every listing. Are you supposed to register your foreigners in Japan the way you register a car? He gives up and pulls out another official-looking text, then refers to his notes. *Oh my God—it's a phone book.*

"Don't call!" I shout in a panic. "They're not home! They're asleep!" I know I'm acting like a criminal. I don't care—I'd rather spend the night in jail than haul Yukiko out of bed. He dials. Someone picks up on the other end. They speak briefly. He nods several times, puts down the phone, and smiles.

Everything is all right. They bow deeply, thank me repeatedly for bringing them the bag, and usher me out the door. They even try to shake my tarry fingers with their immaculately white-gloved hands.

I walk out in a daze. I trail home, let myself in through the creaky gate, unlock the sliding door, and sit in my darkened living room. I am reminded of the time when I was sixteen and stayed out late with my boyfriend eating fish and chips on the beach. When I got home I was made to sit, red-faced, through the one and only lecture my father ever gave me on the evils of sex.

"Karin, come up!"

I drag myself up the steps like a rebellious teenager.

Genji is sitting at the dining-room table in his bathrobe, a scotch in one hand. Yukiko is standing off to one side, smiling. I apologize profusely for disturbing them. I explain what happened, leaning heavily on my desire to be a good citizen and leaving out the handsprings and other unimportant bits.

And then I wait for my punishment.

Genji laughs. He makes me repeat the sound of the policeman sucking air through his teeth, then laughs again. Yukiko is no longer smiling. Genji asks me how far I ran and nods approvingly. I am excused.

Yukiko follows me downstairs.

"Karin!"

I turn. I start to apologize again but she cuts me off.

"Do not wear shorts," she says.

I nod. I'm not about to ask why. She tells me anyway.

"You are too fat."

I am stunned. I certainly weigh more than Yukiko, but then she would make a clothesline look plump. "Okay," I say.

It's three weeks before I'm invited upstairs to eat with them again. I dress carefully, determined to work my way back into Yukiko's good graces. I wish I had time to go out and buy flowers, but I don't dare be late.

Genji has gotten home early. He is sitting at the dining-room table while Yukiko puts the finishing touches on the meal. "Come in, come in!" he says heartily. "Sit down!"

I hesitate, then sit. Yukiko shoots me a look that would drop a cockroach in its tracks. It doesn't help that she knows how much I enjoy talking to Genji. He has a vast understanding of Japanese culture and tradition and is unstintingly generous in answering my endless questions. There are few things I like better than to bring him the nuggets of my daily encounters and experiences for him to polish and explain.

He seems to enjoy our conversations as well. When he was younger he spent three years in Brazil and acquired a "butter smell"—an understanding and perhaps even an affinity for Western ways. Now, with less than two years to go before mandatory retirement, his largely ceremonial post no longer seems particularly challenging. I am an intriguing diversion; occasionally thought-provoking, often unpredictable, and almost always good for a laugh.

Yukiko brings over the first dish, and I jump to my feet to help her lay the table. The kitchen/dining room is small enough that I can walk back and forth while still listening to Genji, but I cannot give him my undivided attention. Nor can I keep up with Yukiko's muttered instructions about the proper position of the tofu vis-à-vis the chopped chives and bonito shavings. By the time the table is fully loaded with five main dishes and a host of satellite sauces and toppings, I am frazzled and they are both offended.

Once we sit down to eat, things go from bad to worse. Genji wants to talk about the banking system in Argentina, and his comments are clearly directed to me. Yukiko doesn't understand enough English to follow the conversation. I try switching to Japanese, but Genji waves off my stumbling efforts. We both know that the subject is far beyond my current vocabulary. I bounce a question over to Yukiko, but she just shakes her head and sends it back to Genji. In desperation I change the subject to cooking and child-rearing, topics that I know Yukiko feels more comfortable with, but Genji just as smoothly switches back. I am at a loss. Yukiko sits and fumes.

Toward the end of the meal, Genji casually mentions a famous sword maker called Masamune in nearby Kamakura. Apparently Yukiko's hairdresser has offered to introduce us. I turn and give her my most appreciative smile and a gush of gratitude. She glares at me.

CHAPTER 6

Masamune-san is a twenty-fourth generation sword maker. His ancestor, the original Masamune, was born in 1274—the same year the Mongols decided to invade Japan. Kublai Khan forced the Koreans to build a fleet of almost 450 ships and ferry 15,000 of his dreaded Mongol troops across the Korea Strait. The Mongols had powerful crossbows, catapults, and explosive missiles. The samurai, accustomed to formalized single combat, had only their swords. That very night a typhoon blew up, sinking the bulk of the Mongol fleet and blowing the survivors back to Korea.

But the Mongols hadn't successfully plundered their way through most of Asia by giving up at the first setback. Within six years they had built an even more massive fleet, this time carrying a hundred thousand men—the largest seaborne invasion in pre-modern times. Fortunately for the Japanese, the Mongols were excellent horsemen but lousy sailors. Even more fortunately, they chose to ignore the advice of their Korean navigators and launched their invasion in early summer, during typhoon season. Right on cue, another great storm appeared and sent the entire Mongol fleet to the bottom. The Japanese called it a divine wind, or *kamikaze*, and took it as a sign of their special status in the eyes of the gods.

The truth, although it doesn't make as good a story, is that the typhoon didn't arrive until two months after the initial Mongol attack. This gave Japan's warlords time to realize that their weapons were decidedly inferior to those of the Mongol hordes. Japanese swords in particular were long and straight, difficult to wield and prone to break. Once the typhoon had taken care of the Mongol invasion, the shogun invited the country's best swordsmiths—among them the young Masamune—to come up with a better weapon. Masamune experimented for years with ways to combine soft and hard steel within the same blade. His goal was to create a sword that was tough enough to slice through two-inch armor, yet flexible enough not to shatter. Eventually he succeeded.

In appreciation, Masamune was given great honor and huge tracts of land around Kamakura. Unfortunately, back then fame wasn't necessarily a good thing. During the frequent wars of the fourteenth century, it was common practice to send spies behind enemy lines to kill or kidnap the best blacksmiths. Masamune was one of the few who lived long enough to establish a lineage.

For a sword maker, the one thing worse than war was peace. By the 1500s, samurai battles had virtually dried up. Many sword makers went out of business. Masamune's family downsized and began selling knives on the side. Then the Americans arrived in 1853, leading to the overthrow of the military government and the abolition of the entire samurai class. The desperate Masamune clan sold most of their land to the Mitsubishi Corporation and moved into town. World War II offered a temporary reprieve, as officers were once again entitled to wear swords, but shortly afterward the U.S. occupation forces forbade the making of swords because of the association with Japanese militarism. Most sword makers got out of the business entirely. Masamune's father expanded into candlesticks and other wrought-iron objects that appealed to American soldiers. Nowadays Masamune makes most of his money selling machine-made kitchen knives with his name stamped on them and catering to tourists who stop by while visiting Kamakura's famous Buddhist temples.

But the fire tongs and sushi knives are just to pay the bills. Hidden behind his pantry-size store lies the key to Masamune's soul: his forge.

The twenty-fourth generation Masamune has a flat face, chipped hands, and workman's shoes. He would not look out of place at a construction site, except for his regal bearing. Masamune addresses Genji as an equal, looking him straight in the eye and replying to his questions with the confidence of a fellow CEO. When he steps into the pit beside his forge he gains even more in stature, becoming an artist, while Genji and I fade into the role of audience.

Masamune fires up the forge and settles down to work. He carefully chooses a large lump of half-smelted iron sand from a river way up north. He breaks it into tiny pieces, then reassembles them into a solid block. Then he reverently wraps the whole thing in a sheet of rice paper covered in Japanese calligraphy. He douses the bundle in liquid clay and thrusts it into the fire. It's early summer, and even from where I'm sitting, the forge is beastly hot. Masamune is steaming visibly and his cotton gloves are pitted from random, red-hot sparks.

His apprentices move in and out like watchful cats, light-footed, silent, and preternaturally aware of their master's needs. Even if they survive the ten-year-long training, they still have to pass a rigorous exam. Only three new sword-making licenses are awarded each year throughout the entire country.

Something feels out of place. One of the apprentices, I suddenly realize, has a barrel chest, Latino skin, and full, sensual lips. In a land where anorexic is average, he is pleasantly plump, yet moves with the lightness of a ballerina. I am stunned that a foreigner would be allowed to learn the secrets of such a traditional Japanese craft.

For the rest of the afternoon I can't take my eyes off him. At last, Masamune puts down his lump of iron and wipes his brow. There is a flurry of brooms and tidying up, and I manage to catch the foreign apprentice when no one is looking.

"Will you have coffee with me?" I whisper.

He grins. "Sure."

We meet at the one place where we are certain not to run into either Masamune or Genji—the local Burger King.

His name is Roberto. He's from Brazil, and he's twenty-five years old. He speaks five languages—not just a smattering from some half-forgotten high-school text, but flawlessly. He came to Japan by way of Europe, where he worked briefly as a professional horse trainer. After only three years he can already read and write Japanese, and he's as comfortable on the streets of Tokyo as he was in downtown Rio or the shores of Lake Geneva.

I'm impressed—and baffled. Roberto would almost certainly excel in almost any occupation. What on earth made him choose to become a lowly apprentice in Masamune's tiny shop, to spend his days sweeping ash and chopping up charcoal?

"My father's friend in Brazil was a sword maker," he tells me in a low voice that barely carries across the table. "Always when I went to his home he showed me swords—how to make them and polish them." He leans forward, his face suddenly animated. "Ever since I was thirteen, swords have meant everything to me. I traveled to many countries, but everywhere I was just thinking about swords. So I thought it better just to come here and study them." He sits back and shrugs. "If you want to make truly beautiful swords, you have to live in Japan."

The sword has an almost mythical hold on the Japanese psyche; it is a symbol of the Japanese spirit, the soul of the samurai. I must admit that I don't share the fascination for a piece of hammered iron whose sole purpose is to cut a human being in half, but if a sword can bring someone like Roberto halfway around the world—to sweep and bow and scrape for years, just to be allowed to learn its secrets—then I suddenly want to know a good deal more about the sacred blade.

It is Roberto's dream to one day be chosen as Masamune's heir—to officially become the twenty-fifth-generation descendent in the famous line of sword makers and take on Masamune's name. Unfortunately, Masamune already has a son. Fortunately, the young fellow wants nothing to do with swords. He thinks the forge is dirty and boring and dreams instead of becoming an opera singer. He recently went to Italy to study.

"Is he any good at it?" I ask.

Roberto drops his head and shakes it furtively.

"Will he ever change his mind about swords?"

Roberto shakes his head again, with certainty. I hope he's right. His future depends on it.

Masamune hasn't given up hope and periodically sits his son down for the "A Song Is Gone in a Moment But a Great Sword Will Last Hundreds of Years" talk. If it doesn't stick, then Masamune will eventually have to adopt one of his apprentices and designate him as heir apparent. By all rights it should be Roberto—he is not only the best sword maker among them but already a skilled polisher, and gaining an international reputation for his knowledge of the ancient masters. But there are certain . . . complicating factors: the shape of his nose, for example. Even now, Roberto has been told to stay in the back of the forge when customers come by because they might not be too pleased to see a foreigner learning a traditional art. Is Japan ready to accept a Masamune with round eyes and brown hair?

"When will he decide?" I ask.

"Ten, maybe fifteen years."

"You're willing to wait that long?"

"Of course."

I can't help but watch him as he moves and eats and talks. Roberto is foreign born and bred, yet he somehow comes across as Japanese. It's in the way he holds his tray when he stands in line, the stillness of his body as he waits for me to choose a seat, the deliberate care with which he picks up a piece of pickle. But most of all, it's in the choices he has made. Although Roberto is highly intelligent and creative, he has committed his life to a system that rewards only obedience; a place where seniority is everything and innovation is not only frowned upon but penalized. How does he manage to survive?

"If you want to live in Japan for a long time, then you must be reborn. You must forget everything you know and everything you believe in, and start over. You must value age and experience over book learning. You must do as you're told and blank your mind to any other thoughts. You cannot feel resentment against the system, not even for a single moment. You cannot demand fairness or equality, or even hope for it. You must learn to believe in a society that is based on hierarchy. It is a completely different way of thinking, of living, of being. If you do not accept it utterly, into your soul, then you will not survive."

That gives me pause. Yet despite his rather daunting words, I feel more hopeful than I have in a long while. At last I've found a mentor—and perhaps a friend.

"Roberto," I ask impulsively as I climb on my bicycle, "am I fat?"

He looks me up and down. "No. Who said you were?"

I reluctantly explain my late-night jog and what happened when Yukiko found out.

He chuckles. "In that case," he says without a hint of irony, "you are fat."

For two long weeks I sit and watch the blade take shape. Masamune heats the iron, beats it flat, folds it over itself, and thrusts it back into the fire. The repeated hammering thins out the trace impurities, which give the sword its unique texture and coloring. By the time he's finished, the blade has more than two hundred thousand microscopic layers of densely forged, cross-welded, laminated steel of astonishing strength and durability.

But that's just the outer layer. The real secret is what he puts inside. The harder steel is wrapped around a softer core. This gives the blade flexibility so it won't shatter, but makes it hard enough to slice through heavy armor.

Masamune sits straight-backed as the lump of iron grows gradually longer, tapers, and curves. His face shines fiercely in the orange glow, and sweat drips like a metronome from his chin. His gaze never wavers from the blade. I have long since stopped asking him *why*: Why does he roll the iron block in rice husks after coating it with clay? Why does he sprinkle white powder on one surface before folding it over? His answer is always the same—it's what he was taught to do.

Gradually I realize the profound knowledge that has been handed down from father to son, each generation adding their own experience before passing the bundle on. A scientist can tell you that making a strong sword is about controlling the carbon content of the layered iron. Only tradition can teach you which pieces to choose when assembling your first block. Generations of accumulated expertise gradually refine a thousand tiny steps, each essential to a successful blade. But tradition only tells how, not why. I watch Roberto patiently chopping charcoal into perfect, one-inch squares. I'm beginning to understand why he's here.

Roberto spends most of his time in Yokohama, halfway to Tokyo, though he maintains a tiny apartment just around the corner from Masamune's shop. Three years ago he married a Japanese woman, the daughter of a famous sword polisher. Roberto now lives in the home of his father-in-law, the 89-year-old Nakamura-san.

But Roberto's only twenty-five. The numbers don't add up.

He sees my confusion and smiles gently. "She's a little older."

"Do you love her?"

"Yes."

Unlike Masamune, Roberto's father-in-law has no male offspring of his own. He almost certainly agreed to let Roberto marry his daughter in order to pass on the family name. In return, Roberto has been admitted into the inner circles of Japan's sword-making society—but at a price.

In Japan there are few burdens heavier than that of an adopted husband. The young man's name is stricken from his own family register, as though he were dead, and he takes on his father-in-law's surname. He enters his wife's home and becomes, for all intents and purposes, the oldest son. Historically that meant taking his adopted father's side in battle, even if he had to kill his real dad. Nowadays the burden, though less bloody, is no less absolute. Roberto has acquired an *on*—an obligation to his new family. Even to the average Japanese, this burden is both arduous and complex. One has *on* to the Emperor, to one's parents', to one's teachers, even to one's name. There is no way to fulfill an *on*; the obligation is limitless and unconditional and does not lessen over time. As a matter of fact, an *on* increases over the years, earning interest just like a monetary debt. There is a saying in Japan: "One never repays a ten-thousandth of an *on*." It always overrides personal preference. One should never commit to any action, no matter how trivial, without first carefully considering the full scope of one's daily *on*.

But the heaviest burden of *on* falls upon the adopted husband. His life is ruled by it, since he must prove that he is prepared to properly fulfill the obligations into which he has been reborn.

"Do you want to meet my father-in-law?" Roberto asks. I nod. I'm thrilled—and terrified.

∞

Nakamura-san is sitting in a traditional tatami room, empty but for a Shinto shrine in one corner. His hands are folded serenely over his cane and his head is tilted slightly back, as though he were surveying his private kingdom. His daughter, a stunningly attractive woman, stands watchfully to one side. Nakamura's nails are exquisitely manicured and polished to a high sheen. His socks are an impossible shade of white and his samurai-style trousers pressed into razor-sharp creases. Even the pom-poms hanging from the front of his elaborate robes have been carefully combed and puffed.

He has long since lost his hair but still has his teeth, though they are heavily fortified by an elaborate metal scaffolding. His eyesight is excellent, but his hearing could use some help. Roberto hovers beside his right ear, cupping one hand to his mouth and shouting in high-volume yet somehow deferential Japanese.

When he's pleased, Nakamura makes a sound like a rusty hinge. He responds to no one but Roberto, no matter how loudly we yell. He speaks in disconnected thoughts, following some inner screen of long-ago memories. Everyone stands and listens respectfully.

"At twenty-one, I was in the Special Forces," he says, "fighting the Chinese. I was wounded in the abdomen. I went to war twice for my country. I should have been in combat five times, but they saw how good I was with a sword and made me stay behind and teach."

70

After World War II, Nakamura-san became a realtor. For a long time things were very bad for the Japanese. Nakamura's hands tighten reflexively on his cane. "But even after the war Japan was much better off than it is now because today's young people are all doing American things—they are no longer Japanese."

I quietly slide my Diet Coke behind a table leg.

"They play football and baseball and golf—and they do it just for fun. They don't have the time to learn things in the proper spirit of hard work and discipline. If I could," Nakamura says, "I would draft everyone at the age of twenty. Then they would learn that the Emperor is the center of everything. They would understand loyalty and learn to respect the elderly."

"Would you draft women too?" I ask, despite myself. I'm trying to imagine Junko in military fatigues.

"Women?" He pauses, momentarily caught off guard. "A man's obligation is to protect his family and his country. Women must stay home and do home things. They must serve their husband, just as he serves the Emperor. And women," he says, glancing my way for the first time, "should not have an opinion."

His daughter shakes her head. "Women have to get their place in society," she says, though not loudly enough for him to hear.

"What," I ask Roberto carefully, "does Nakamura-san think of his son-in-law?" Roberto grins but translates for me.

Nakamura makes that rusty, happy sound. "Roberto, in comparison with young Japanese, is much better. He is like the old-time Japanese. Everything he does, he does as well as possible. He studies by himself and does not ask for help. He is prodigious in everything . . ." Nakamura suddenly catches him-

71

self, pauses, then adds severely, "He also does many bad things."

I perk up. "Like what?"

"He's always thinking about swords. When he's finished eating, he just runs to the swords and doesn't wash the dishes or clean up."

That doesn't sound too terrible. Anything else?

"He should practice more and study harder. What a normal person takes ten years to learn, Roberto learns in two. He should therefore try his best in everything. And," he says sternly, "he should wake up earlier, before five, to train."

"Even," Roberto adds quietly, "when I've stayed up all night polishing swords for him."

"Train?

"*Iaido*," Roberto explains. "Sword cutting. Would you like to see?"

Iaido is the art of drawing the sword. It is not, as Hollywood movies would have us believe, about swashbuckling displays of clashing steel, with multiple flesh wounds and terrifyingly close calls. It's more like a duel. Two men stare at each other impassively. They draw. They strike. The faster man steps back. The slower man topples over dead. And despite the vaunted samurai code of honor, the real-life warrior often had to defend himself against surprise attacks, so iaido emphasizes drawing the sword from any position, including sitting down and kneeling in prayer.

The goal of iaido is to reduce the basic movement of drawing the sword and striking to its most efficient form. That means repeating virtually the same motion upward of five hundred times a day. It is a very lonely sport.

Needless to say, iaido is not very popular among young people in Japan. But it was once as essential to a samurai's survival as a fast draw was to the American west. Of all the martial arts, iaido is the closest thing to *Bushido*—the way of the warrior. Roberto has been studying it for years.

Roberto consults with Nakamura, makes a few calls, and we're on our way. He eases his father-in-law to his feet and takes up his position opposite Nakamura's cane. When they reach the door, Roberto picks up the old man's slippers and gently nudges them over his toes. Nakamura shuffles off down the narrow path. Since there isn't room for them to walk side by side, Roberto tiptoes awkwardly half a step behind, his hand still tucked firmly under Nakamura's arm.

They reach the car. Roberto opens the door for his father-in-law and relieves him of his cane. As Nakamura-san stoops to get inside, Roberto puts a protective hand on top of his bald head to make sure he doesn't bump the door frame. In that small, unnecessary gesture, I see the truth. Roberto loves this man.

Once Nakamura-san is safely seated in the gym, Roberto drags in a heavy sack that looks disturbingly like it might have a corpse inside. It's not that outrageous a thought; once upon a time, swords were tested on the bodies of live or executed prisoners and the results carved into the handle. Many famous swords still boast "six legs" or, if they're really sharp, "three torsos." Nowadays they substitute rolled-up, wet tatami mats to mimic the consistency of human flesh and bone.

Nakamura straps on his sword. He shuffles slowly and painfully to the first tatami roll. The sword appears almost magically in his hand and the tatami keels over. A hundred thousand cuts—a single motion honed over eighty years of relentless repetition. He lowers the blade and shuffles to the next roll.

Finally, it's Roberto's turn. He bows to his father-in-law. He stands motionless, slows his breathing, quiets his mind. He leaps explosively, shouts, cuts three times in an exquisite blur of sword and footwork. The tatami topples to the floor. He steps back, turns to his master, sheathes the sword, holds it up, and bows deeply.

Nakamura smiles.

As we are packing up to leave, Nakamura addresses me for the first time.

"The only thing that hasn't changed in ninety years," he says, "is the Way of the Sword."

I watch him shuffle off, one hand resting comfortably on Roberto's arm—an old man who fought two wars for the Emperor and the young foreigner who will one day carry on his name. And I think, *No, Mr. Nakamura. Nothing has changed more.*

∞

Roberto's warrior resolve has rubbed off on me. I head back to Fujisawa determined to bear any burden, to submit to any task. If Roberto can be reborn, then so can I.

"Karin, come up!" Yukiko calls down the stairs. Genji wants to speak with me. I scamper up, bow to both of them, and stand at attention.

"Tomorrow," Genji tells me with genuine enthusiasm, "is the big day. Masamune is going to temper his sword."

I know this already from Roberto, but I express surprise and joy.

"I've bought two bottles of very special sake to thank Mr. Masamune for everything he's done for you," Genji adds.

The blood drains from my face. Special sake costs several hundred dollars. I can't possibly afford to spend that kind of money on everyone I film. I'm in a quandary—if I let Genji buy these gifts, then I am tacitly agreeing to the role of daughter—with all the obligations that come with it. But if I insist on paying for them myself, I will go through all my savings in a few short months.

Genji isn't finished. "Chibo"—Yukiko's hairdresser who initially introduced us to Masamune—"also gave Masamune two bottles of special sake," he adds delicately. I suddenly feel like sitting down. "What should I do to thank him?" I ask carefully.

"Well," Genji replies, "you should take him out to dinner." I do a quick calculation. A fancy dinner in Kamakura—I would have to invite the Tanakas, of course—could top a thousand dollars. The last of the blood puddles queasily in the pit of my stomach. Genji, for all his social graces, doesn't have much of a handle on how the other half lives.

I swallow hard and thank Genji for his wonderful generosity on my behalf. *One ten-thousandth of an on.* There's no turning back.

∞

It's nine in the morning and we're sitting beside the forge, waiting for a sword to be born. Masamune got up early to pray to the Shinto gods, though from his puffy eyes and grayish skin he probably also stayed up late toasting them with a bottle of Genji's special sake.

He will need all the help he can get today. It's not enough that he's spent two weeks combining the hard and soft steel in precisely the right proportions. The most difficult step still lies

75

ahead: to temper the cutting edge. In that instant, Masamune will create a masterpiece or destroy the blade.

If you heat a sword, then plunge it into cold water, it gets very hard. But it also loses its flexibility and becomes brittle. How do you keep the blade itself somewhat elastic while giving it a razor-hard edge? The secret, as Masamune's ancestors discovered, is to use clay. Over time they came up with just the right formula, a closely guarded family recipe of slip, polishing-stone powder, fusible salts, and other secret ingredients. Masamune meticulously coats the entire blade. This will insulate the red-hot steel so it doesn't cool down too fast when it gets plunged into the water bath—and remains a little flexible. Then, inch by inch, he scrapes the clay off the cutting edge so that *it* gets as great a shock as possible and becomes extremely hard. Then he sets the sword aside to dry.

Roberto drags in a rotting wooden trough and fills it with cold water, then superheats a heavy iron bar and drops it in. Once the water is just the proper temperature, he scurries around outside, covering all the windows with plywood boards. Then they fire up the forge and turn off all the lights.

Masamune's face glows an eerie red in the reflected fire-light. His concentration is intense. He pulls the sword halfway out, thrusts it back, pours on charcoal, pumps the air blower. He judges the temperature of the fire by the color of the flames—he uses no thermometer. It's a risky undertaking; if he makes even a small miscalculation, the sword will crack. Four out of five swords are lost this way.

Without warning, he pulls the blade out of the fire, swings it high over his head, and plunges it into the waiting bath. Steam billows out of the boiling water. The lights go on. The magic fades. Masamune feels around in the dirty bath, withdraws the mud-encrusted piece of steel, and examines it. A cry of despair. There is a hairline crack an inch from the tip. He must have let it get too hot. It's fixable—he can cut the blade down and reshape it—but he has let down both the gods and his ancestors.

∞

Roberto carefully selects a button-size piece of polishing stone, centers it on his fingertip, and gently rubs it back and forth along the blade. "If you do a good job you can see a little bit of yourself in the sword," he says. "A perfect sword means that you have patience and you have respect for the work you do."

He's been sitting in the same small room for eight long days, endlessly grinding down the blade with tools that belong to the Middle Ages. He uses nothing but his eye to guide him yet manages to create perfectly parabolic arcs and a mirrorlike finish. The surface of the blade is so sensitive that moisture from a human finger will create a rust stain. It is so sharp that the sword must be unsheathed upside down or it will cut through its own scabbard.

"When people see a sword you've polished, they will feel exactly what you were feeling when you worked on the blade," he tells me while his finger moves endlessly back and forth.

"What do you think about?" I ask.

He grins. "I listen to Brazilian music," he admits, and pulls back a curtain to reveal a boom box and a pile of tapes.

"Roberto, what would you do if you weren't allowed to make swords anymore?"

His finger falters. "I would go back to Brazil," he says, after a long silence.

He polishes up a few microscopic imperfections, then dries the blade and holds it up for me to see.

For the last four weeks I've watched a lump of iron sand gradually transformed into a priceless work of art. I've tried to understand why the sword is such a powerful symbol of all those values that the Japanese hold dear—honor, courage, and discipline. It's not until I catch a glimpse of Roberto's reflection in the polished, blue-gray steel that, finally, it all makes sense to me.

CHAPTER 7

I love the garden. I sit in it for hours while I'm studying, listening to the trickling fountain in the corner and watching the dark-green leaves nod gently in the occasional breeze. I'm even more thrilled when Yukiko asks me to take over the daily chore of watering it. I immediately send an e-mail to my judo instructor in the United States, gushing over the lovely flowers and my new role in keeping them properly irrigated. Toward the end of the letter I mention—a casual aside, nothing more—that I might try to plant some vegetables along the back wall as a contribution to the dinner table.

I haven't quite gotten around to asking Yukiko how she feels about a few friendly tubers among her magnolias when a package shows up, rattling ominously.

Radish seeds.

And carrots. Tomatoes. Cucumbers. And pumpkins. Good Lord, what am I going to do with pumpkins? They aren't even edible, and carving one up at Halloween would probably earn me a visit from the local police.

The next thing I know, I'm sitting at the table with the seeds, an accompanying note, and a stone-faced Yukiko, who looks like she's attending her own funeral—or mine. She is explaining in a slow, careful monotone that my U.S. judo sensei is Genji's *sempai*, or senior classmate, from their long-ago university days. His American wife, by association, is Yukiko's senior as well. Never mind that the two women have never met and don't even speak the same language; the implied relationship has all the authority of a general ordering a private to the battlefield. Now even if Yukiko were willing—which she's not—to have eggplants infesting her lilac patch, the tomatoes in the garden down the street are already thigh-high and, "*Karin, what were you thinking when you sent that e-mail?*"

I point out that the accompanying letter clearly tells me not to bother if it's too much trouble. Yukiko stares at it for some time and decides that this is really secret code for "I expect a weekly report with photographs." Her expression sours even more. "We have no choice," she says.

Secretly I'm pleased. The endless hours carrying Yukiko's groceries as she chased down just the right brand of silk-strained sesame tofu have been a bit wearing. Some time spent grubbing around in the dirt is just the antidote.

Half a day and an absurd amount of money later, the seeds are resting comfortably in thick beds of High-Yield Power Grow potting soil. I wander out every half hour or so to see if they've broken ground yet.

In between, I reluctantly crack open yet another grammar text. In my experience, language books the world over will try to seduce you with the good news first. Hallelujah, I'm told, Japanese has no future tense. Verbs are not only extremely regular but have no plural, no grammatical gender, and no person. "Man walk to store." Presto! I'm practically fluent.

But every language has its darker side, and Japanese is no exception. Over the centuries, the country's rigid social hierarchy has given birth to several parallel languages based on the speaker's birth, gender, social status, and education. Or, as my relentlessly cheerful little volume puts it: Japanese is like ice cream—it comes in a variety of different flavors. There are male and female Japanese, regular and humble and honorific Japanese, insider and outsider Japanese. The Emperor, of course, gets his own sacred flavor, though having your very own language seems about as useful as owning the world's only telephone.

But in the end, Japanese isn't really about communication—it's about maintaining harmony. Negation, for example, always comes last. This allows you to look your listener in the eye and gauge his level of agreement while there's still time to change what you're saying. "What a terrible cook that woman—your wife?—is . . . not." Personal pronouns are the height of arrogance, to be avoided at all costs, and the passive tense is encouraged. The result is a curiously detached form of Vulcan-speak, as in, "There exists a car that was bumped by the mailbox this morning." Despite what my parents might say, in Japan this is not an attempt to avoid responsibility—it is just good manners. Clarity and directness, my book insists, are to be deliberately avoided.

My Japanese is clearly going to be a train wreck.

There's a loud, unfamiliar ringing coming from the living room. It's my telephone. I instantly break out into a sweat. Answering the phone is the linguistic equivalent of staring down a fire hose.

I pick it up gingerly, like a short-tempered rattlesnake. To my relief, it's Roberto.

"Can you ride a horse?"

"Sure."

"Would you like to go to a *Yabusame* training?"

Samurai mounted archery! An ancient and extremely difficult art of accurately shooting arrows from the back of a galloping horse. Until the Middle Ages it was considered an important military skill. Nowadays the tournaments take place in Shinto shrines and draw upward of a hundred thousand spectators. Losers no longer commit *hara-kiri*, but the sport is still taken very seriously. Of course I want to go.

The training ground is in Tsuruoka, a three-hour train ride away. By the time we arrive, the Yabusame riders are already leading the horses out of their stalls, slipping on their four-hundred-year-old saddles, and trotting them around the ring. Kaneko-san, the thirty-fifth generation Yabusame master, stands at its center, gyrating slowly as he inspects each rider in turn and occasionally calls out a gruff correction.

Eventually Kaneko is satisfied with his team's performance and motions them into a nearby cabbage field to set up the target. We intercept him as he emerges from the ring. Kaneko is eighty-five years old, with a ramrod spine and a habit of clicking his teeth together sharply when he looks at you. He has the presence of a much taller man.

Roberto introduces me. I bow. I know just how low to go because Roberto's hand is pressing discreetly on the small of my back. With my face to my knees, I suddenly notice how muddy it is. I also notice that, despite slogging around in the sloppy ring, Kaneko's socks are still snow-white. What is it about the samurai arts that makes these men impervious to dirt? The pressure eases off. I bob back up. Kaneko nods and clicks his teeth.

"He's a great man," Roberto says as Kaneko walks away. "A kind man."

"How so?"

Roberto hesitates. "Once I did something to make him lose face, and he forgave me."

"What did you do?"

He doesn't want to say.

"Something big?" I prompt. I can't imagine Roberto offending anyone.

He shakes his head, then reaches down and picks a tiny bit of dirt off the path. "One small grain of sand," he says, "can blow in someone's eye and cause a lot of trouble."

We watch the riders thundering down the narrow trail between the cabbages, shooting at a plastic bull's-eye. A Yabusame archer, Roberto explains, must hold himself absolutely steady so that he has a stable platform from which to shoot. To do this he stands on the stirrups and uses his legs like pistons to absorb the motion of the galloping horse. He is, in effect, balancing his entire body on the balls of his feet while manipulating a six-foot-long bow, all without frightening the horse into a bucking fit. It takes at least three years before new riders are allowed to use a bow, and five before they can join in the tournaments.

There's no shade in the open field and no soda machine. I've eaten nothing since dawn except a few dirty leaves pilfered off the cabbages when no one was looking. To distract my rumbling stomach, I take up a position a foot below the target, trying to get some footage of the archer shooting directly into the camera lens. The arrows have two-inch, bulbous wooden tips, more than heavy enough to take off the top of my head. The horse streaks by. The arrow punches into the target six inches away. I feel like William Tell's son.

"Karin!" It's Roberto's voice. Oh dear. I must have done something to annoy Kaneko. What could it have been? *A grain of sand* . . . "The sensei asks if you want to ride!"

I toss my camera into the cabbages and dash down the trail before Kaneko can change his mind. They hand me a horse. I climb aboard warily. They're all retired racehorses, and they don't hesitate to buck off a rider if they think they can.

Kaneko instructs me to ride Yabusame style, but without a bow. The horse kicks into a gallop. I rise off the saddle, drop the reins, and stretch my arms out horizontally. I feel the powerful surge of muscles between my legs. The target whips by. Twelve seconds later it's over. I bump gracelessly to a stop. I dismount. I'm hooked.

Once all the riders have had their turns, we walk the horses dry, then wash them down, oil their hooves, clean their feet, wipe off their saddles, lay the blankets out to dry, and settle them back into their stalls. I've been assigned to combing out their manes and tails. My face is stinging from a long day under the relentless sun and my legs are rubber. I can barely wait to stagger into the train, then topple onto the soft cushion of my bed.

Roberto pokes his face over the horse's withers. He's grinning from ear to ear. "Kaneko-san has invited us to his home to see his saddles!"

My muscles go mushy with dread. "Great!" I say and paste a smile on my face.

Kaneko's house looks like a forgotten temple set back against the hills of Kamakura, surrounded by ancient trees and thick beds of moss. Inside it's a virtual museum. Entire walls are lined with fearsome samurai armor, helmets, and row upon row of arrows, saddles, and stirrups. One long hallway is hung with photographs of all the great Yabusame masters—Kaneko's ancestors.

He pulls out an armful of old photo albums, and we slowly trace his family history. It reads like the Old Testament, with lots of begats and an official Yabusame rulebook that bestows an almost mythical authority on anyone who gets his hands on it. I struggle to connect the words, to fill in the blanks where my vocabulary fails, to de-conjugate the verbs, and sometimes just to follow the gist of what Kaneko is saying. My brain feels like it's been run through the washing machine. The conversation, thankfully, moves over to the far side of the hall, where Kaneko pulls out several swords and Roberto avidly examines them. I slide backward a foot or two, lean against a wall, and close my eyes.

Roberto shakes me awake almost immediately. A whispered, surreal conversation ensues.

"You must have the discipline of a samurai warrior in battle," he says. "If a samurai sleeps, then he will be killed. His friends will also be killed because he is lazy and has no self-control. A person who sleeps cannot be trusted because he will always let his friends down."

"What if he is so tired that he makes a mistake in battle and gets killed?" I ask groggily.

"It's okay to die because you're tired. That doesn't show a lack of discipline."

A vivid memory suddenly pops through the cottony embrace of sleep. It's a story Genji told me over the dinner table shortly after I arrived.

"It was during our judo winter training," he said with a rueful laugh. "I went into the coach's room late one night to ask him a question. He was sitting at his desk, writing a letter, and he didn't even look up when I came in. I sat down on his bed and waited for him to finish. I was exhausted from the workouts, so without realizing it I leaned over and fell asleep. Afterward he was so angry that he wouldn't speak to me for the rest of the training."

A grain of sand. I sit up abruptly and apologize, though I'm sure it's already far too late.

When I leave, Kaneko invites me to a tournament. I have been forgiven. Roberto is right. He is a great man.

I get home so tired that I can barely make it up the front steps. I'm woozy from the sixteen-hour day, the blazing sun, a single candy bar, and the thousand grains of sand. Yukiko is waiting for me at the door.

"The maid was here today."

I do a quick mental inventory. Before I left I put away my futon, vacuumed every horizontal surface, washed and dried my dishes, lined up my shoes, watered the plants, and thoroughly scrubbed the bathroom. What could the maid possibly have complained about?

It's obvious the moment I walk into the living room. My cards.

After several days of agonizing over Genji's special sake, I finally came up with a solution. Gift-giving is carefully calibrated in Japan based on the status of the giver, the recipient, their relationship, and the favor involved and can be calculated to within a very narrow price band. Since there's no way to change my status, I had to find a cheap source of expensive gifts. Then I remembered how much the Japanese value anything, from pottery to paper fans, that's made by hand.

I hurried over to the *washi* store in Kamakura, bought an armful of their exquisite handmade papers, and began to fold. Two days later I finally had an acceptable prototype. Each card took close to three hours to make, with several layers of intricate birds and origami insects on an elaborate background. Genji was impressed. Yukiko took one look and declared war on my new cottage industry.

Since I had no place to store my raw materials, I hid them under the coffee table whenever I wasn't home. Several bright-green origami birds are clearly visible, scattered just beyond the table's edge.

"She could not vacuum," Yukiko says severely. I nod. It doesn't matter that I vacuumed this morning, nor that I'd much rather Yukiko's maid didn't clean my apartment in the first place. I wonder where I can hide the thumb-size origami so that Yukiko simply cannot find them. They eventually end up in the refrigerator, inside an empty tub of miso paste. I pull out my futon and topple into bed.

CHAPTER 8

I wake up bathed in the soft golden light that suffuses through the paper shoji screens. I make myself a cup of tea, then wander out to see what miraculous changes have happened to my shoebox garden overnight. The cucumbers broke ground today. The marigolds are struggling, but the morning glories have already burst into purple flower. The carrots will soon need to be thinned, and the tomatoes are finally catching up to their cousins in the gardening store. I pull out the hose to soak the soil and water down the bricks, then mist the leaves until they're bright and heavy in the early morning light. When I'm done I set the paper screens to catch the breeze that curls around the moist, dark plants and welcome it into my living room. Japanese architecture is delightfully airy, designed to let nature in wherever possible. The shoji screens admit light and are easily removed. The Japanese house is rather like a ship—

you trim a screen here and there or throw open a shutter, then sail it through the seasons.

Later I dig into a heavy tome of sixteenth-century Japanese history, keeping a wary ear cocked for Yukiko. Despite my best intentions, our relationship has steadily deteriorated. We play a game of cat and mouse—if I am reading on the sofa and I hear her coming, I jump to my computer, since neither reading nor sofas are on her list of acceptable activities for the middle of the day. If I've stayed up late studying and want to take a nap, I curl up on the vinyl floor in a corner of the kitchen, the only place that's not visible from a window or a door. When I go out she often inspects my apartment to make sure that that there's no errant scrap of paper in my plastics recycling bin, my shirts are folded evenly, and my cutlery is lined up correctly in the proper drawer.

Her ceaseless vigilance is making an impression. For the first time in my life I feel guilty about putting the toilet paper roll on backward. Until now, I never even knew that toilet paper had a front and back. I resent feeling guilty, so I refuse—on principle—to turn it facing forward. Then I worry that Yukiko will see it, so I use it up as quickly as I can and hope the next one will end up the right way around.

But the kitchen is our real battleground. My shelves are stocked with enough tableware to host an army. All the plates are tiny and made of cut crystal and translucent porcelain. I'm terrified of dropping one, so they stay safely behind glass doors while I eat out of a few Tupperware containers I found stuffed beneath the sink. Last week Yukiko caught me using my Schrade pocketknife to eat a slab of tofu off the back of a plastic lid. She disappeared without a word and returned with a conventional Japanese kitchen knife. I thanked her and put it in the drying rack, where it will look like I use it every day. My Schrade now lives, like a forbidden pet, in my pocket, where I can get at it easily and put it away even faster.

∽

Something is going terribly wrong with my vegetable garden. I sadly examine my last surviving tomato vine. It's long and lanky and infected with some sort of creeping leaf rot. This morning I found thirty-three caterpillars on my radish plants. Since Yukiko doesn't believe in pesticides, I pick them off with chopsticks and toss them into the neighbor's yard. The few remaining radish leaves are barely keeping the plants in chlorophyll, while underneath their roots are hard as wood. My eggplants have almost disappeared behind a thick cloud of white flies. Each night an unknown insect cuts a swath through my beleaguered carrot plants. In the morning I find a trail of truncated seedlings, like trees felled by some tiny woodcutter.

It's not just the plants that are suffering. With the onset of the rainy season, the mosquitoes have arrived in force. They land on my window screens and thread hungry siphons through the holes, looking for their meal of blood. Every afternoon I douse myself in insect repellent, pull out a small hand brush, and get down on my knees to scrub another few feet of the walkway stones. I love seeing the natural oranges and yellows of the hand-fired bricks.

I don't know why the garden means so much to me. Perhaps the plants, no matter how bedraggled, offer a measure of companionship. The garden feels like a place of peace—a sanctuary.

"Karin!" Yukiko's voice. I put down my scrub brush, wash my hands, and climb the stairs.

"Please cut the lawn," she says, handing me a pair of rusty scissors. The lawn? I take the scissors and go in search of it. The entire garden is no larger than a two-car garage. I circle the house twice before giving up and reluctantly asking Yukiko for directions. She points to two square feet of dead grass bordering a flower bed.

I kneel down in front of the unkempt grass and struggle to keep my frustration from boiling over. I feel like I've spent the last three months being fixed—the way I live, travel, think, cook, eat, hold my bowl, sleep, drink, and say thank you. It's like I'm six years old again, living by someone else's complicated and incomprehensible set of rules.

I lie flat on the ground to eyeball the lawn. The bricks are cool against my cheek, and I can smell the fresh-turned earth. I cut layer after layer with the unwieldy scissors, watching the long dead blades fall away in swaths. Gradually a trim square of grass emerges, the young shoots finally free of the long, overgrown stalks.

When I came to Japan I fantasized about training under a master for whom I could perform herculean feats of discipline in order to win his respect and the right to be his student. I always assumed it would be Genji, but it's not.

It's Yukiko.

❦

"Do you want a husband?"

Yukiko and I are sitting at the kitchen table, preparing the finely chopped filling for her signature beef-and-vegetable

91

dumplings. There is only one right answer to her question, and it leads directly to a lecture I don't really want to hear again. *Of course I want a husband.* But if I tell her that, my life will become truly unbearable. "If he really loves me," I reply carefully, "then he will not mind that I do not cook that well."

"Maybe in the beginning, but after two or three years his heart will grow cold." She speaks with absolute confidence.

"Perhaps I can find someone who loves me for my other qualities."

"No."

An hour later I hear her footsteps approaching my door. Yukiko knocks perfunctorily and marches in without waiting for an answer.

"I am going to the Netherlands for eight days," she announces, "to see my brother."

Eight days! "We'll miss you," I say.

She produces a sheet of paper with a hand-drawn calendar and lots of words in big, block letters. "You will have dinner ready for Genji every evening when he comes home," she says.

My feet go cold and my stomach flips itself inside out. Yukiko's meals are works of art. Even on an ordinary day, there are so many plates jostling for space on the dinner table that it's almost impossible to see the tablecloth. Food at the Tanaka household is more serious than the stock market.

"Yukiko, I can't do that. I can't even read the labels on the ingredients in the supermarket!"

"You have a dictionary."

"What about Junko? I'm sure she would do a much better job."

"Junko," Yukiko pauses to let the word sink in, "works."

"Can Genji eat at the office cafeteria?" I say in panic. "I'm sure the meals there will be much better."

"It's not for Genji."

Oh. It's for me—so that I might one day get a husband.

This is going to be a catastrophe.

Yukiko goes through the rest of the schedule, but I'm too dazed to object. I must be home at nine every morning for the dry-cleaning man. There are several afternoon deliveries. The upstairs plants have to be watered every other day, without spilling a drop on the furniture. Garbage day is Wednesday and Saturday, out by 6:00 a.m.—but not the night before. Tuesday morning I'm to visit her friend, who will teach me to make those meat dumplings that take six hours to cook from scratch. On Wednesday I will accompany Genji to some family friends for dinner. Their son is thinking of coming over next weekend. Where will I be?

"Out," I croak. "Working." Anywhere that doesn't have me cooking to Yukiko's standard for a dozen of her eagle-eyed relatives.

When she walks out I'm shell-shocked.

⌇

"You have to do it," Roberto says.

"But it makes much more sense for Junko to—"

"That doesn't matter. Yukiko is your senior. You must do as she says."

He's right, of course, though it goes against every fiber of my being. Nothing means more to me than freedom and equality. But in Japan, hierarchy has been a fact of life for centuries. The Japanese have learned to trust their proper place in life, to depend on the security that comes with a structured social order. Right and wrong, fair and unfair, even personal happiness are largely irrelevant. Virtue depends on recognizing one's place in the vast web of mutual interdependence that makes up their society.

The concept is deeply rooted in Japanese history. The country has always had a strong caste and class structure, but in 1603 one man succeeded in uniting the country and establishing a rigidly hierarchical society that would last for 250 years. His name was Shogun Ieyasu Tokugawa, and his rigid rule of law has molded the patterns of Japanese relationships to this day.

Tokugawa divided society into four classes. Every family had to post their class position on their doorway, and everyone was obliged to live according to that place within the hierarchy. At the top of the pecking order were the samurai, the military elite; next came the farmers, the backbone of society, harshly controlled and heavily taxed; then the artisans; and finally the merchants, who created nothing and were therefore thought of as parasites. Beneath them were the classless—the beggars, the blind, and the untouchables—groups so scorned that they were not even counted in the yearly census.

As time went on, the Tokugawa shogunate tightened their control over every aspect of daily life. Most peasants were no longer allowed to eat the rice they grew—only coarse grain and millet. Headmen might be permitted to wear rough silk, but the ordinary farmer had to content himself with linen or cotton. Neither could wear red or pink, or clothes that had been dyed into any sort of pattern. Even the size of the stitching was specified. Farmers were allowed to use a pack saddle when riding but forbidden to place a blanket on it. Sumptuary laws controlled the kind of house each citizen could live in, the amount of money he could spend on a funeral, and the size umbrella he was allowed to own.

To justify his iron grip on society, the shogun invoked the teachings of Confucius, which placed great emphasis on proper behavior and obedience. Confucianism taught that all human relationships could be classified into five types: ruler/subject, father/son, husband/wife, older brother/younger brother, and friends. Certain rules and behaviors must be observed to maintain order in these relationships. It was everyone's duty to accept his lot with good grace and to obey his superiors without question.

For the next 250 years Japan remained suspended in time. A legal ban on progress and invention froze society in place. Contact with the outside world was forbidden on pain of death. Every detail of life was fixed and predetermined. There was no liberty, but there was peace and safety in knowing what one was supposed to do. Farmers tilled the land just as their grandfathers had, wore the same clothes, and abided by the same rules. As generation followed generation, hierarchy and structure gradually wove themselves into the fabric of society.

In 1868 the shogun was overthrown and the class system abolished. The disbanded samurai cut their topknots, donned business suits, and joined the new government. They proceeded to build a modern nation on the same value system by which they had been raised: loyalty to superiors, respect for authority, hierarchical structure, highly formalized systems of behavior, one's proper place in the social order. Despite the extraordinary changes of the past 130 years, Japanese society is still based on the warrior ethic. People form neat lines when the bus arrives, and trains are always on schedule. Taxi drivers wear white gloves and keep their vehicles meticulously clean. Children are obedient, and everyone waits patiently for the light to change. And when a superior has a chore for you, you do it without complaint.

"If you want to learn to be a good Japanese, you must learn how to suffer," Roberto says. "You must learn discipline and patience."

Patience is not my strong suit, but if the Japanese can do it, so can I. I head home to start putting together recipes.

"Don't forget to write her a thank-you note," Roberto calls after me.

⌾

Perhaps it was the terror in my voice—or maybe sympathy for Genji's taste buds—but Yukiko partially relents. I only have to make rice, a simple seaweed salad, and fruit for the first night. I get up at the crack of dawn and scour the fruit stands for blemish-free produce worthy of a still-life painting. I do a test run with the rice cooker, then a second batch when it comes out just a trifle underdone. At noon I run down to the corner market to buy a bag of seaweed.

When I get home I tear it open. The stink of low tide immediately floods my entire apartment. The little packet that came with it—I had assumed it was seasoning—says DO NOT EAT in large (thank goodness) English letters. I throw it out. The seaweed itself is hideously salty and clearly inedible. I put it in a large bowl and soak it, changing the water frequently. It swells up to double its size, then double again. It tastes like something that had been lying in the bottom of a boat for several months. Maybe I'm meant to boil it with soy sauce. I put half of it in a pan, squeeze in a generous dollop of seasoning, and leave it to simmer. Half an hour later my apartment smells like the slimy, rotten corner of a prehistoric swamp. I taste the seaweed. Blech. Maybe it's supposed to go into miso soup. I put half of the pot into a larger pot—the seaweed is still growing, like some kind of marsh monster—and throw in several tablespoons of miso. Eventually the miso overpowers the seaweed and it becomes palatable. I have to admit, though, that the dish would taste a good deal better without the seaweed, and better still with some cubes of tofu.

When Genji gets home I bring up the half bowl of raw seaweed for consultation. Genji, bless his heart, has extraordinary intellectual abilities, but the kitchen is not his natural environment—it takes him several minutes to figure out how to turn on the hot-water maker. We both stare at the limp seaweed for a while until he suggests putting it into miso soup. In the end he tells me to ask Junko. The seaweed is banished to my refrigerator.

I know Junko isn't going to get home until one in the morning, and I have to be up by five. Trash day isn't until Wednesday. I can't possibly live with that stench for two more days. I light some incense, gather up all the seaweed, and head down to the beach. When no one is looking, I set it free.

On my way home I realize I have no choice—I have to ask Junko for help. Unfortunately, my host sister cooks only under duress and wouldn't dream of doing housework if her life depended on it. But then, she doesn't have to—her mother gets up early to make her breakfast, does her laundry, cleans her shoes, and makes her bed. Junko rarely gets home before midnight, rises at noon on weekends, and usually heads back into Tokyo by one. She's not likely to be thrilled by my request.

But even Junko can't ignore the man who pays her rent. On our way to judo I humbly ask Genji for his daughter's assistance, pointing out how valuable the experience will be when she gets engaged.

The next afternoon a distinctly crabby Junko arrives home on the early train. We sit at the kitchen table and pass cookbooks back and forth.

"We should make Western food," she says.

"Sure," I agree enthusiastically, thinking the recipes will be less complicated and easier to read. She smiles, and I realize I've been neatly outmaneuvered, since "Western" puts me in charge of the main dishes. I download several recipes, compare them mentally to our local market, and hope for the best.

The store is out of sour cream. Never mind, we'll use regular cream and add a dash of lemon. Fresh mushrooms not in season? The dried ones will do, if we soak them long enough. Genji sits and drinks a beer while we stumble around the tiny kitchen. I take random ingredients out of the fridge and put them back to make us look more competent.

The creamy sauce comes out too thick and the chicken is hard and leathery. Junko picks at her meal, then bolts when it comes time to clear the table. I do the dishes and trail down the stairs. Yukiko is sure to get a full report from both her daughter and her husband. Even I know what they're going to say. I've failed again.

CHAPTER 9

There's a message in my in-box. I read it three times, then dash up the stairs.

"My mother is coming to visit me," I announce breathlessly.

Genji is genuinely pleased. I am beside myself. She'll be here for eighteen days. We'll travel high into the mountains and down to the Inland sea. We'll wander for hours along deserted beaches and hurtle through the urban landscape aboard the bullet train. I'll finally make good use of all those hours I put into learning Japanese. But more than anything, I'll have a friend.

"You must take her to Kyoto," Genji says. "I know several excellent hotels. Yukiko will make reservations for you when she gets home."

I bump abruptly back to earth. "Excellent" by Genji's standards might well be $1,000 a night. "We're going to wing it," I say quickly. "Mom prefers to travel without plans."

"You should fly down," he continues implacably. "It will be quicker that way."

"Unfortunately," I lie, "we've already purchased rail passes, so we'll have to take the train."

"You should buy plane tickets anyway, so you have a choice."

Japan's prices are going to knock my mother's socks off, even without the $800 just-in-case airfare.

"And you should stay in Osaka. It has very good restaurants."

"My mother would like to see some of Japan's pottery villages," I try, hoping to shift the conversation away from crowded cities and expensive cuisine.

"Well," he thinks about it for a moment, "Satsuma porcelain is quite famous."

And very far away. I was thinking more of Tamba, which we could reach by train.

"You can go directly from Kyoto to Kyushu," Genji continues, mentally mapping out our itinerary.

"I'll talk to her and see what she wants to do," I say as firmly as I can.

Genji nods his head, but I know he isn't listening.

By midnight the euphoria has worn off enough for me to realize what a disastrous position Mom's visit will put me in. I've always done what Genji says, no matter how subtle his request. I gave up candy altogether when I saw him frowning at my post-judo Snickers bar. I switched to traditional medicine when he expressed disdain for Western quick-fix pills. But I can't possibly ask my mother to spend thousands of dollars based on his off-the-cuff suggestions. For the first time, I'm going to have to say no to Papasan.

Jinsei Annai is the daily advice column in the local newspaper, a sort of Japanese Ann Landers. I download it every morning and translate it over breakfast, ostensibly to practice my Japanese but in reality to remind myself that other people have personal problems too. It covers everything from nosy neighbors to husbands who drink away the rent. The counselors— there are several—are quite severe and rarely take the supplicant's side. Their replies most often run to "You are being selfish" or "not thinking of those around you" or the frequent admonishment, "Look inside yourself to see what you are doing wrong." Unlike the American version, where you are a better person if you can establish that it's not your fault, in Japan it seems you are a better person if you admit that everything is entirely your fault and you're very sorry about it.

"Dear Troubleshooter," the first letter begins, then goes on to describe a woman whose adult son is still living at home and racking up huge debts. "Do I have to pay them?" His mother wails. The counselor cuts straight for the jugular. "Why did you not raise your child to handle money better? Or find him a wife who could do so on his behalf? And why is he not productively working if he is no longer in school?" The last line is a grudging admission that, at least according to the law, a mother is not responsible for her grown son's debts.

The second letter is from a sixty-one-year-old whose husband installed himself in front of the television the day he retired, two years ago, and hasn't gotten up since. She wants to travel and socialize, but he's not the least bit interested. I brace myself for the poor woman to get stomped, but the counselor is unusually sympathetic. "You should discuss the problem with the person you are in conflict with, thereby winning them over," she advises. That sounds like a good idea. Perhaps I can apply it to Genji and my mother's visit. We'll have an hour on the train this afternoon, on our way to judo.

By the time I meet Genji at Tokyo station, I've thoroughly rehearsed my spiel. How much I admire the Japanese way of doing things. What a good idea it is to plan everything ahead of time. But my mother—I've decided to blame her, since she's not here—often changes her mind at the last minute, and reservations would really complicate things. I end in a rush: "I thoroughly appreciate your efforts to arrange everything for us, but I don't want to go against my mother's wishes, so I'm not sure what to do. . . . " I leave the sentence hanging, the way he does when he's about to veto a request.

The silence lengthens. "What do you suggest?" I nudge.

"Well," he says thoughtfully, "if you just do as we say, then everything will be all right."

The train is slowing for our station. I suddenly remember where we're going and shoulder my judo bag with a strong sense of dread. It's a famous judo academy known for its tough instructors, unforgiving mats, and the champion players it regularly turns out.

By the time we find the place, the workout has already started. I step over mothers chatting amiably in the hallway while their children beat each other up inside. The head sensei is built like a fire hydrant, with a bald round head and snowman's belly. He carries around a plastic baseball bat, which he applies with great enthusiasm when anyone falls short of his expectations.

I step onto the mat and immediately realize that I'm in trouble. The larger students are immensely strong and the smaller ones are fast like hummingbirds. All of them are as flexible as chewing gum.

They call *randori*: four-minute, one-on-one fights. I face off against a twenty-year-old with the whip-thin figure of a ferret and a look of steely determination. All thoughts of dinner recipes, tomato blight, and verb conjugations evaporate the moment he grabs my uniform. Randori is all-out combat. Let your mind wander for an instant and you'll be picking yourself off the ground.

He fakes, then twists and drops with catlike precision, and I slam into the mat. It's as unforgiving as the asphalt parking lot outside.

Two hours later I've only thrown one student—a fifteen-year-old girl. My muscles ache, but I'm loose and limber and I've finally made my peace with the iron-hard floor. I feel a heady satisfaction that no perfect side dish or polished silverware can ever duplicate. This is, after all, why I came to Japan.

When the workout is finally over, my frustrations have burned away like the morning mist. On our way home Genji and I stop at an informal restaurant and share plates of sautéed squid and pickled cabbage and talk about the recent takeover of Renault. And suddenly, I'm sure that everything is going to be all right.

∞

I wake up to warm sunlight and utter agony. I can't lift my head off my pillow. My calves and thighs are tight and hot. My elbows ache. My shoulders burn. Two huge bruises above my hips are gradually draining along the muscle lines in a purple spider's web. What made me think my thirty-five-year-old body could handle a twenty-two-year-old's workout? I roll over with exquisite care and crab out of bed, then slowly claw my way up the wall.

Putting away the futon is sheer agony. My legs cramp up. My head throbs painfully. I sit in the bathtub. Nothing helps.

Yukiko arrives late in the afternoon, puts down her suitcases, and immediately disappears into the kitchen. Two hours later an enormous feast is spread out on the sideboard. I am, to my surprise, invited to eat with them. I take six aspirin and shuffle up the stairs.

Yukiko seems happier and more relaxed—an entirely different person from the one who got on a plane just eight short days ago. She tells us the news from the Netherlands and laughs at our bungling attempts to keep the house in running order while she was gone. Maybe I've been wrong about her all along.

The next morning my eggplants are lying in a heap, torn out by their roots and casually tossed against the wall. The entire garden looks like it's been scraped over with a giant comb. My carefully scrubbed orange bricks are filthy with dirt and leaves. I forget my aches and pains and take the stairs up to the second floor three steps at a time.

"The gardener was here today," Yukiko says, straight-faced.

"We have a gardener?"

She nods, deadpan. "He comes by four times a year," she says.

I wander through the garden to assess the damage. Okay, so the carrots probably did look like a bunch of weeds. The tomato plant has disappeared, and the radishes are somewhere under a pile of rotting leaves. I sit on the doorstep and try to figure out what went wrong. I just wanted to help out, to give the Tanakas something to remember me by, to make myself a part of the household. But the garden belongs to Yukiko. I should have watered it, admired things the way they were, and left well enough alone.

What was that columnist's advice? *It's better if you admit that it's entirely your fault and you're very sorry.* I seek out Yukiko and apologize at length, then ask, "What kind of plants do you want in place of the radishes and marigolds?"

"I am waiting for your mother," she says.

I smile, thinking she wants to ask Mom for advice, then hesitate. "Why?"

"So she can see."

A cold wave washes over me. "That I failed?"

She laughs and slaps me on the arm. And for the first time, I realize just how angry she must be.

With Mom's arrival just a few days away, Genji sits me down to finalize our travel plans and make the reservations.

"What temples are you planning to visit in Kyoto?" he wants to know.

"That depends on how much time we have."

"Have you made hotel reservations?"

"We're not sure yet when we'll be there."

"What if they're all full?"

"We have camping gear."

Silence.

It's the sound of our relationship disintegrating.

CHAPTER 10

I catch a glimpse of her in the crowd of arriving passengers, and my entire world contracts around her beloved face. The furrowed lines and creases of her smile are exactly as I've envisioned them almost every day for the past three months. I fly into her embrace. I soak up the feeling of her cheek pressed against my face and her arms around my waist. After far too long, I reluctantly let go and introduce her to a beaming Genji.

In the car I gather bits of news from home like uncut gems, to hoard against those wee hours of the night when loneliness gnaws deep inside my chest. Are there many squirrels this year? How are the azaleas doing? Is her pottery selling well? I suddenly realize that she is sagging from exhaustion after the eighteen-hour flight. I panic. I know that Yukiko has been cooking all afternoon and that the table will be creaking with a dozen dishes. The coming meal will almost certainly be a multihour marathon.

By the time I've got her bags downstairs I've made up my mind. "Let me tell them that you're too tired to eat tonight," I beg. I know how badly this will go over—even Yukiko's eighty-eight-year-old mother sat through dinner after returning from the Netherlands—but the dark smudges under Mom's eyes have given me a backbone that I never knew I had.

"It's okay. I'll manage," she says quietly, and slowly climbs the stairs.

She's brought gifts of homemade bread and several pieces of exquisite pottery from her studio. The bread creates an instant connection with Yukiko—a rapport of sugar, rising time, and the merits of sourdough starter over conventional yeast. In minutes my mother has forged a friendship where I, after three long months of effort, failed.

And yet when I look at them sitting side by side, I can't believe that they would get along so well. Mom's hair is softly gray and falls in short-cut layers that float naturally around her face. Her weathered skin and chipped nails speak of her two chief pleasures: sailing and her enormous garden. Her forearms are thick and taut from hours at her potter's wheel, pressing clay into graceful, flowing shapes. She is several inches shorter than Yukiko and somewhat bent. Her body has relaxed into sixty-year-old curves and a less determined shape.

Yukiko, though only ten years younger, is flawlessly maintained, from the roots of her hair to the tips of her toenails. She is slender and so exquisitely dressed that if she stood still in a department store, she might be mistaken for a mannequin. I wonder if either of them secretly feels sorry for the other.

I watch them as we pass dishes around the dinner table. Mom is quiet but laughs easily with Genji. She handles her chopsticks like a professional and doesn't even think to pour soy sauce on the tofu squares. She seems to navigate the rocky shoals of Yukiko's rulebook with an almost instinctive understanding. I am both proud of her and a little jealous.

The next evening Genji invites us out to a traditional restaurant for dinner. I can feel Yukiko's eyes on us throughout the meal, weighing our easy camaraderie. I wonder what is going through her mind. Does she think I should be more respectful, or my mother more severe? Or is she thinking about Junko, who spends time with her parents only because they foot her bills?

Once we're back in my living room, Mom and I have a whispered conversation about our travel plans. Despite my seeming nonchalance with the Tanakas, I've secretly spent weeks mapping out the perfect plan. We'll avoid the crowded streets and bars of downtown Tokyo and the endless temple tours of old Kyoto that form the backbone of most tourist itineraries. Instead I want to hike up into the mountains, walk the black-sand beaches along the Inland Sea, join in a samurai festival, and spend some time in a tiny, forgotten village on the back side of Japan. I offer Mom a half dozen options, but she seems happy no matter where we go. In truth she came less to see Japan than for the chance to travel with me.

Mom was born and raised in Africa and spent her teenage years feeding a voracious appetite for exotic places, from the rolling hills of Lapland to the slopes of Kilimanjaro. She gave up her beloved backpack once she got married and had children, but couldn't completely extinguish the longing for distant lands. She passed on to me her love of foreign culture and now explores the world vicariously through my letters and documentaries. Traveling is a passion that has bound us together

108

ever since I was young enough to listen to her stories of Tanzanian crocodiles and locust plagues.

My father doesn't share my mother's love of footloose adventuring and is beside himself with worry that something might happen to her in some remote and foreign land. He prevailed upon her not to visit me in Vietnam, or Peru, or the Amazon. But Japan is the safest country in the world, and this time—reluctantly—he gave in.

∞

We slip on our backpacks, say goodbye to the Tanakas, and struggle up the train-station stairs. We're heading for Tamba, one of Japan's six ancient pottery villages, some 370 kilometers west of Tokyo.

At noon we stagger into the bright sunlight of a tiny rural station. I wander over to the bus depot. Five vehicles are parked at intervals, but only one has a driver inside. He opens his door and a wave of lovely cool air rolls over me, momentarily banishing the sweltering July heat. Yes, he goes to Tamba village. The bus departs in fifty-one minutes. No, we can't wait inside, it's against the rules. Boarding isn't permitted until twelve minutes before departure. The doors close firmly in my face. The humidity welcomes me back into its stifling embrace. I stomp back to Mom, muttering my opinion of bus drivers in particular and rule-bound societies in general. We wander around until we find some shade, where we sit as still as possible and sweat copiously.

It's strangely lifeless, this village, like the dry husk of a cicada after its owner has dried out its wings and fled. The houses are the color of long-dead wood, and none of them have window boxes—not a single patch of color to carry the eye away to brighter places. The flies are so lethargic that I can snatch them from the air with two fingers, and the only living creature appears to be an old gray cat lying in the middle of the square. The entire place is coated with a thick layer of powder the exact color of the buildings, as though invisible termites were gradually chewing the town to sawdust from the inside out.

I'm counting down the last four minutes before we're allowed to board, when the bus suddenly roars around the corner and pulls up directly in front of us. The door hisses open. The driver smiles and motions us inside. He couldn't stand to see us sitting in the heat, he says, so he bent the rules to pick us up.

Several other passengers climb on board behind us, and I realize how far we've come from Tokyo. This is Ura Nihon— the back side of Japan—where hair is allowed to go gray, belongings are carried in knotted scarves, and everyone wears sensible shoes. The women all nod and greet one another before sitting down. They pass out handfuls of tangerines, carefully remove the skins in perfect spirals, and boldly spit the seeds out the window.

We're barely under way when the driver gets onto the loudspeaker and calls me to the front. I gather up our tickets, but he doesn't even glance at them. He wants to know where we're going, what we plan to see, if we're going to spend the night in Tamba, and who is meeting us there. He proudly uses every word he can dredge up from some long-ago middle-school English lessons. He repeats my answers into his loudspeaker for the benefit of the hard of hearing and those in back. Craggy faces crinkle up with laughter, and my mother is inundated with bright orange tangerines.

After some discussion, he decides to drop us off at the

110

Tamba pottery museum. He makes sure I have the return schedule and know exactly where the bus stops. When he finally pulls away, we wave goodbye to a row of friendly, smiling faces and the smell of fresh tangerines.

The museum owner immediately offers us a cup of green tea. She's horrified at our lack of reservations. I'm beginning to feel like I'm doing something profoundly irresponsible, like trying to climb Everest with nothing more than a pair of sneakers and a cotton vest. As we look at the exhibits, I hear her talking on the phone and catch the sentence, "A potter from America is here."

In due course a young man arrives in a shiny new SUV and offers to show us around. His name is Ichinoseki-san, one of thirteen families in the area who share a prolific ancestor, a love of pottery, and identical last names. He's twenty-eight, a university graduate, and the intended heir to one of Tamba's famous pottery studios.

His shop is buzzing as it gives birth to hundreds of identical bowls and plates. Trays of sake cups line the rafter drying racks. My mother immediately comes to life at the smell of clay. Ichinoseki-san struggles manfully with reduction rates, cone temperatures, and other specialized vocabulary of the pottery world. I watch him gesturing at a kiln. His fingers are delicate and slender, with none of the crusty calluses that come from long days at the wheel, and yet he knows every detail of clay and glaze as only a seasoned potter would.

"What kind of pottery do you do?" I ask. He hesitates, then takes us to a small room off the side of the studio. Inside we discover massive, modern sculptures that glow softly with a swirling orange glaze, fire-etched onto the baking clay. After much prodding, he admits that he is entering them in two jur-

111

ied shows and has already won several prizes for his work. He is clearly making a name for himself in the world of cutting-edge ceramic art.

But Tamba is famous for its Tokugawa-period pottery, a style developed several hundred years ago. It's not the sort of place that has much use for a modern, avant-garde designer.

"When I turn thirty," Ichinoseki says without regret, "I will return and take over the shop and studio." He will put aside his modern flights of fancy and step willingly back into the yoke. He will do his duty to his ancestors and the traditions into which he was born and raised.

I admire his willingness to sacrifice his own dreams for the common good. But when I look back at those soaring sculptures, I wonder if he isn't making a terrible mistake.

Ichinoseki drops us off at Tamba's only lodging house, a traditional *ryokan*. He calls ahead to let them know we're coming. It's obvious from his half of the conversation that the owner isn't pleased to be housing two foreign barbarians. What if we forget to take our shoes off at the door, or don't know how to use chopsticks, or refuse to eat Japanese food? Or—the height of barbarian ill-manners—climb into the bathtub without first scrubbing ourselves clean?

She's in her eighties, thin and stiff as plywood, with narrow, watchful eyes. She supervises the removal of our footwear and leads us up the stairs in total silence to our tatami room. It's completely empty, moldy with neglect, and hotter than a kiln. We drop our packs and scurry out as soon as she's disappeared around the corner.

Just beyond the entrance we stumble straight into an eighteenth-century woodblock print: terraced paddies of the deepest emerald green; in the distance, mountains climb in steep, sharp lines that reach up to touch the sky.

The village streets, barely wide enough to accommodate a single car, are lined with immense wooden houses, their cedar shingles black with age. Doors and windows are propped wide open to entice the furtive summer breeze inside. Curling strips of masking tape line the doorframes where careless young fingers tore through the paper in their haste to play some long-forgotten game.

The high-pitched roofs are made with century-old tiles, fired with pine needles to a shiny, rock-hard finish. Tiny shrines, piled high with offerings of rice and oranges, have yet to be replaced by cigarette machines. Hand-built walls with uneven steps lead to hidden vegetable gardens. Flowers sprout from window baskets, along walkways, and in priceless Tamba pots that stand in nearly every doorway.

It's the Japan of my dreams.

⟲

The next morning at six the owner stalks into our room. Japanese breakfast is served downstairs, she announces, if we eat that kind of food; otherwise she can make us a plate of American scrambled eggs.

I march downstairs, determined to disprove her Western stereotypes and polish off my plate. The meal is already laid out on the table: dried grilled horse mackerel, as stiff as sawdust soaked in Elmer's glue; pickled radishes and strips of seaweed; rice and tea and soy sauce; and—my heart quails—two servings of *natto*.

Natto is a popular Japanese fast-food snack made from fermented soybeans. It tastes at once sour and bitter, like something you'd find in a forgotten Tupperware container when you're cleaning out the fridge. Natto is the perfect budget-traveler's food—inexpensive and available in any convenience store. It's so nutritious that the Russians took it along on their early *Soyuz* missions. The live bacteria in natto are supposed to be even healthier than those in yogurt and to survive in your intestines three times longer.

It's not so much the taste that gets to me, it's the consistency. It has the texture of fresh, lumpy mucous and a tendency to ooze out from between my chopsticks like a leech that's trying to escape. It ranks right up there with boiled sea slugs and fresh blood soup as one of my least favorite foods.

I can't ask Mom to eat her share. I open my mouth, close my eyes, and toss both servings down the hatch.

The owner comes in and eyes our almost empty plates. I smile smugly. She pulls out two eggs and brandishes them in my face.

"Raw or cooked?" she asks, her eyes glittering.

A raw egg cracked over a large bowl of rice and stirred thoroughly to spread the taste is my second least-favorite item on the Japanese breakfast menu. I can still feel the sour natto clinging to the back of my throat.

"Cooked," I say in defeat.

∞

By 8:00 a.m. it's already eighty-two degrees, and the thermometer is still rising visibly. Our room smells like a cross between a hunk of moldy cheese and a sewage-treatment plant.

114

The owner is perched in the hallway like a vulture, waiting for us to leave. We take a vote and it's unanimous. In ten minutes we're heading for the beach.

We set our sites on the coastal town of Uwajima on the island of Shikoku. We arrive in the early afternoon and are met by Mr. Inoue, an old friend of the Tanakas. He is somewhere between forty and sixty, with deep laugh lines around his eyes and an extraordinarily handsome face. He is the local godfather, the center of a *kashi* web that extends far out into the countryside. He hands us over to one of his employees, and the next thing I know we're in the back of a pickup truck, barreling down the coast.

We pull up at a Buddhist temple. Two dozen pairs of women's flats are lined up neatly at the foot of the stairs. Their owners are inside, sitting on the tatami floor, each shepherding a pile of sweet and salty crackers on a bit of folded paper. They wave us in as though we're old friends. It feels like a slumber party—there's not a stick of furniture, and everyone is thoroughly enjoying themselves.

These small, rural temples are more than just a place of worship, they are the heart and soul of the community, like Southern churches in the United States. They deliver rice balls and bowls of miso soup to neighbors who aren't feeling well, organize everything from festivals to funerals, and build a protective social scaffolding around the elderly. The women are as spry and active as teenagers, laughing often, listening intently, and wielding their fans with enormous energy. Their average age is seventy-six, and all but five of them are widows. And, it turns out, they make up a champion local gateball team.

"Gateball?" I ask. It's a kind of high-speed croquet, they explain, played on hard-packed sand. Each game is limited to fifteen minutes. Would we like to try?

Our driver wants to carry on. I bribe him with an iced coffee and the women tease him gently until he laughingly gives in. His mother, it turns out, is on the team.

They gather up their crackers and gleefully discard the afternoon's agenda in favor of a game. They seem profoundly content with the life they've carved out for themselves and happy to be together. They carefully pull themselves upright and lean on each other like human canes as they navigate the temple stairs. They all wear comfortable shoes and stoop to help each other slip into them.

As we pull up to the gateball court, the sky cracks open and lets loose a torrent of dense gray rain. I stare mournfully out the window, until I see the old women cheerfully climbing into raincoats and plastic pants. They wait until the worst is over, then dig ditches in the sand to drain off water and lay foam rubber on the last few stubborn puddles. They pick chopsticks to see who goes first, set the timer, and like a steeplechase, they're off.

By the time the first ball has cleared three wickets, I know I'm going to get completely clobbered. They play with the casual competence of hustlers on their day off. They give no quarter—they don't walk, they run, and when they capture an opposing ball they do their best to knock it into the next town. I'm not only going to lose, I'm going to take down my entire team.

I decide to cheat. I don't even try to get away with it. I dig a trench in the sand to help my ball around a corner. I give it an extra nudge when it threatens to slow down too soon. If I did this in front of Yukiko I'd be banished for all eternity. I peek over my shoulder to see how the old women are going to react.

They laugh. They double over, leaning on their mallets to keep from falling down. They cluck their tongues and shake their heads and hide their gold-rimmed teeth behind deeply veined hands. I look at their smiling faces, full of grace, and never want to leave.

After three games our driver pries the mallet out of my reluctant hands. He takes us high into the mountains, to a lonely farmhouse at the end of a long country road. After a brief introduction, he climbs back into his truck and disappears.

Mr. Yamashita, our new host, pulls a watermelon out of the family well and offers us an ice-cold slice. He's forty-something, never married, and this is his parent's home. His sister, also single, lives here full time, though she works five days a week as a secretary in the nearby town. Their parents—both approaching eighty—tend the surrounding gardens and the family orchard around the corner.

He introduces us to his mother, a tiny woman who barely comes up to my shoulder. She wears puffy pants and a tight, powder-blue bonnet, like a creature out of a children's story. She's constantly in motion: hanging out the laundry, digging up some onions for the dinner table, or scrubbing out the sink. Her muscles are steely strong, but her skin is thin as the finest parchment and bruises to the touch. She is the kind of person who would take in your laundry when it starts to rain, fold it, and leave it on your doorstep—anonymously.

She clearly still lives by the values of her postwar generation. Her son may own a fancy car, but she manages without air-conditioning or indoor plumbing. She hunts down every grain of rice in her tiny bowl and carefully gathers up the watermelon rinds to throw into the chicken coop. After dinner she pulls out an enormous basket of medications and carries them into the living room, where her husband is staring at a twenty-year-old television.

The next morning she's up at six to harvest peaches from their orchard on the far side of the hill. Her husband's already been there since dawn, protecting the ripe fruit from marauding monkeys that come down from the surrounding forests. He has an ancient rifle, duly licensed, though his eyesight is so poor that he is no longer allowed to drive a car.

"Do you also take a turn?" I ask.

"Oh yes! When the peaches are ripe we guard them day and night."

"Do you use a gun?"

She giggles behind one hand. "Goodness no! I hit them with a stick." She pantomimes swinging an imaginary club with all of her seventy pounds. Then she ties on her faded blue bonnet, hops on her bicycle, and pedals off.

Each peach has been wrapped in paper so that it will ripen blemish free. She chooses carefully, examining every fruit before she picks it, while her husband sits on a plastic chair and pretends to watch the woods. An hour later her son arrives, looking a good deal less comfortable in farmer's clothes than he did in his business suit. He uses a stepladder to get at the higher branches while his mother scurries back and forth, gathering up the half-full buckets and transferring them to flats. She giggles when she finds a perfect peach and shyly brings it to me to eat.

"This will be the last year," her son tells me firmly. The peach trees are getting old. They were planted twenty-five years ago; the productive life of a peach tree is at most twelve to fifteen years. They're way too much work to spray and prune and fertilize, and he has to help with the harvest because his parents can't manage the stepladders anymore. If they cut down the trees and replace them with tea bushes, they'll finally start making money on this plot of land.

I bring a bucket over to his mother. She overheard our conversation. "Maybe one more year," she whispers from behind her hand. "We haven't completely decided yet." I watch her line up the peaches in perfect rows, pausing from time to time to pick one up and smell its heady fragrance. Then she closes her eyes and slowly sets it back in place.

By noon we're all tired from the heat and flies, while she is still darting back and forth like a chipmunk gathering nuts in fall. She runs her bike down the hill, jumps on, and pedals off furiously to make us lunch.

Despite her kind smile and tireless activity, I feel a secret sadness hovering over this household, like a missing loved one who is never spoken of but in everyone's thoughts. They both rise early and get plenty of exercise. They eat well and sparingly. But there are no grandchildren to teach how ripe a peach is by the way it smells. When those trees come down, a way of life is going to end.

By the time we leave Uwajima, I dread the thought of ever going back to Tokyo.

We find a tiny bed-and-breakfast tucked behind a narrow street in the old section of Kyoto. It's run by four old sisters who move through each other's lives with an almost telepathic harmony. They bow when they show us to our rooms and kneel on bony, flattened knees to slide the paper door shut when they leave.

We've come to see the Gion Matsuri—Kyoto's largest festival—but there's something important that we have to do first. I buy a phone card and we call Dad.

I can hear only one side of the conversation, but I can guess exactly what he's saying on other end. Mom talks for a few minutes, overflowing with stories of bullet trains and gateball games. Dad is mostly silent.

"What do you miss most?" he asks.

"Chairs," Mom answers immediately. "It's so uncomfortable to sit on the floor all the time. And a good salad."

She tells him about a nearby international pottery center, with eight huge kilns and fifty foreign artists in residence.

"Will there be fifty-one next year?" he asks.

It finally sinks in.

He's afraid—afraid that he's going to lose her like a bird that has the chance to test its wings and never returns to the safety of its perch. I want to grab the phone and tell him not to worry. I've been watching Mom these past few days. Her eyes are still sharp and her curiosity undiminished, but this kind of travel no longer comes as naturally as it did when she was young. In two weeks she'll be more than ready to go home.

Our roles have changed so gradually these past few years that I barely even noticed. Once she was showing me the world. Then I took the lead. Now I think she's ready to let me venture out alone and bring home stories to tell in the evening by the fireplace with a cup of tea.

She asks Dad if he wants anything from Japan. He does, although he's not the kind of man to admit to it. But they've been married for almost forty years, and she knows exactly what he needs.

"I'm looking forward to coming home," she says.

☙

After only two nights in Kyoto, we climb wearily back on the train. We've agreed to meet Genji and Yukiko for a samurai festival in Soma, three hundred miles to the north. We arrive early at the ryokan Yukiko has reserved for us. Its $200 price tag comes with a knee-high table, a jar of moldy tea leaves, and a futon in the closet. To my mother's horror, there's only one bathroom in the building, which we'll be sharing with at least a dozen men.

Two hundred mounted warriors are already gathering on a nearby playing field, all tricked out in plastic rented armor and huge, mushroom-shaped wigs. They gallop self-importantly in random circles and shout at the hapless foot soldiers to get out of the way. I'm amazed how ugly the softly sibilant Japanese becomes when filtered through the swollen vocal chords of a salaryman-turned-warrior. They finger their swords, clearly wishing they were real so that they could lop off a few slow-moving heads.

This is their one chance—a single weekend every August—to relive their childhood fantasies. Where American kids grow up brandishing six-shooters and pretending to be cowboys, Japanese children play samurai warrior, defending their honor with plastic swords. The samurai is the ultimate action hero: unperturbed by overwhelming odds; ready to die in defense of honor, duty, and his posthumous reputation. He's John Wayne, Bruce Lee, and Sir Galahad all wrapped up in one, with a bit of Yoda thrown in.

The samurai are often compared to European knights, and indeed there are some striking similarities. Both strove to perfect their skill at arms, to exhibit bravery in combat and loyalty to their lords. They expected to be handsomely rewarded for victory in battle and were always ready to die—or kill—to protect their good name.

But the differences are even more revealing. The samurai had no code of chivalry toward women, nor were they motivated by religious ideals. Though samurai loyalty was, at least in theory, unconditional, most battles were won or lost by treachery. Most important, where the knights of medieval Europe saw mercy as a virtue, the samurai held it in contempt.

In your typical Western drama, Kurt rides into town, reluctantly shoots a dozen bad guys, incurs a nonfatal injury, gets the girl, and gallops off into the sunset. Things aren't so simple for Kayoshi and Junchiro. They are bound by duty and obligation, no matter how many innocent lives are on the line or how beautiful the wench. After much soul-searching, usually in some dark and rainy forest, they do right by their assorted obligations, and almost always die before the final credits. The girl in question obediently marries the man her father has promised her to and mourns her young non-lover for the rest of her miserable days. Or sometimes she just climbs the nearest volcano and throws herself into its smoldering pit. The underlying theme reflects the prevailing Buddhist philosophy: life is short, uncertain, and generally full of sorrow and suffering.

Suffering also seems to be part and parcel of today's parade. The foot soldiers are wearing tight, restrictive armor layered over leather leggings, gloves, and vest. The few riders are moving at quite a clip; the others practically have to jog to keep pace. The temperature is ninety-two and rising in the shade. Sweat pours from beneath helmets and drips off fingertips. One man keeps trying, unsuccessfully, to light a soggy cigarette.

Three grueling hours and no end in sight. We're about to give up and slink off to the nearest train station, when several riders turn unexpectedly into a small parking lot and their attendants mysteriously appear to help them dismount. They're apparently going to trailer the entire parade to another part of town where the main ceremony will take place. I park Mom in the shade, then dash from truck to truck, determined to get us a ride. One driver finally nods and motions to the back of a half-empty four-horse trailer. We thank him profusely and naively march inside. The metal doors slam shut behind us, and I distinctly hear the bolt slide into place. Ten minutes later the truck hasn't moved and reality is sinking in. We're locked inside a tin oven with two stinking horses on an asphalt parking lot. I knock on the back door, but the entire parade has disappeared for lunch.

"I'm sorry," I say for the umpteenth time. We take turns pressing our faces against the tiny slotted window to catch a breath of air. Mom's gray hair is sticking out in sodden tufts like a bedraggled cat. This is one story that neither Genji nor Dad is ever going to hear about.

An hour later the trailer abruptly lurches into motion. When it finally reaches the parade ground and the doors swing open, we leap out like fleeing deer and make straight for the nearest soda machine.

The senior samurai have already arrived and are sitting in full armor under the blazing sun. They seem determined to recreate the misery of seventeenth-century warrior life. Bushido—the samurai code—demanded an almost religious commitment to physical hardship. Samurai were known to burn incense in their helmets before battle so that, in the event that they were decapitated, they would present their opponent with a sweet-smelling head.

They may have been calm in the face of death, but in life the samurai were known for their quick tempers and almost pathological sensitivity to insult. This was, in fact, an essential survival trait among the warrior class. A samurai's response to even the most modest slight was considered a valid prediction of his future performance in battle. No aspiring warrior could afford to let courtesy or moderation be mistaken for cowardice. According to the ancient records, typical conflicts in the 1600s often developed out of the most trivial misunderstandings: Two samurai of equal rank pass each other on a bridge. Their umbrellas inadvertently make contact. The first samurai immediately pushes the second away. "What an insolent man you are!" he cries.

His opponent shoves him right back and says, "What right do you have to insult me?"

"What do you mean! It is you who should apologize!"

"I'm not going to put up with this!"

It sounds like a few bad relationships I've been in. Only in the samurai's case, it generally doesn't end until one whips out his sword and decapitates the other.

We've downed three sodas while the sun creeps slowly across a leaden sky. Tethered horses, as limp as old lettuce, hang their heads and close their eyes. Dried dung tumbles across the asphalt. Mom and I are obviously not made of the stuff of samurai, because we slip into the train and ride home dreamily anticipating a cool shower and a long soak in the *furo*.

There's a tour bus parked in front of our ryokan. Twenty men have taken over the bathing room, even though the sign clearly states that it's the women's turn. We march huffily back to our un-air-conditioned rooms, shove our packs against the wall, and lie flat on the floor, our faces pressed against the cool tatami mat.

There's a brief knock on the door. Before I can even think of getting up to answer it, Yukiko marches in. She's dressed in a stylish blouse and meticulously ironed jeans. Her hair is perfectly aligned and carefully curled at its tips. She takes in every detail of our appearance in polite and utterly damning silence. She and

Genji have checked into the room next door, she finally announces. She brought her own green tea, in case the ryokan's was not up to standard. We are welcome to come and join them for a drink. And then, without another word, she sweeps out the door.

I crawl to my feet and stick my head into the hallway. The men still have firm control of the showers. They look like they'll be in there for at least another hour. I feel like a piece of roadkill and as worn out a fifteen-year-old tire.

"Do we have to?" Mom asks plaintively, like a small child who doesn't want to take her medicine.

I nod. A part of me is perversely satisfied. Finally, someone else realizes what I'm up against.

∽

Mom has only three days left. I want to get her out of the heat, to someplace cool and quiet. We wave goodbye to a worried Genji and Yukiko and head up into the mountains.

We get off the train in Tsumago, an historic village full of paper lanterns, cobbled streets, and cedar-shingle houses. From there we pack a picnic lunch and climb high into the Alps. The path is bordered with giant cedar trees and paved with four-hundred-year-old flagstone. We come across an unmanned stand with fresh cucumbers heaped up beside a hand-lettered sign: *Please help yourself.*

We have a picnic in a meadow and cool off under a creaky wooden waterwheel. The sky is blue, the view is breathtaking, and we are the only ones here. It's a perfect day. I never want it to end.

And then she's gone. I don't even remember our last hug. A train to Fujisawa, a final meal with the Tanakas . . . There must have been a trip to the airport, but I can't bring up a single detail. My last memory is sitting in a grassy meadow, our hair still wet from playing with the waterwheel, eating raw cucumbers slathered with miso paste. But when I look around, I'm back in my granny suite and Mom is nowhere to be found.

I pull out my bicycle and wheel it through the creaky garden gate without a second thought. I pedal through the darkness to Enoshima Island, several miles down the coast. The shops are dark, the houses shuttered tight. The road is deserted but for a few blinking fireflies. I ride up and around the island until I reach the ocean side. When the asphalt ends I drop the bike and climb countless flights of stairs, past darkened temples with silent bells. The mist rolls off the ocean, sluggish and thick with salt. Spiderwebs drift across my face. I stop at a small clearing along the edge of a cliff. Far below, I can hear the waves casting themselves relentlessly against the rocks. There's a bench beside a tiny shrine that is, inexplicably, covered with a hundred rusty locks.

There's a raw ache deep in my chest, like bronchitis, every time I take a breath. I can't even cry. I want to climb out of my own body—anything to get away from the desolation that follows me no matter where I go. I'm so lonely that I'm suffocating.

I feel a gentle touch along my calf. I freeze. I'm not afraid; I just can't stand for anyone to see the expression on my face. I wipe it clean, force my lips into a smile, and turn. There's no one there. I wait. A shadow moves beneath a nearby willow tree—a stray cat, with a hollow body and a kink in its tail. It's watching me, half hostile, ready to take flight at the slightest provocation. And yet it deliberately brushed up against my leg. I make a soothing sound and stretch out my hand. It doesn't move. Those baleful eyes stare unblinkingly at my face. Eventually I let my hand dangle and look away. Ten minutes slip by, twenty. I feel the lightest brush against my fingertips. It sends a shiver of longing up my arm and down my spine. Again. With each pass he lingers a little longer, until his purr is steady beneath my fingertips. He leans his weight against my calf. The feel of moving flesh beneath my hand, the rumbling buzz, unleashes a yearning so powerful that it hurts.

He leaps lightly onto the bench and curls up into a tight ball against my leg. His eyes slip shut, and eventually so do mine.

When I wake up again, the moon has drifted far across the sky and the cat is gone.

CHAPTER 11

The drums have been beating for hours—*TOM tom-tom tom tom*—ominous and unstoppable, like an army marching off to war. The men are wearing off-white robes with brightly colored tassels and animal skins hanging down their backs. They chant deep-throated sutras and walk slow, plodding circles into the sand. But it's the drums that hold me motionless, their relentless rhythm reverberating deep inside my chest.

The men are Yamabushi, a fourteen-hundred-year-old ascetic mountain cult. Their religion is an ancient blend of Buddhism, Shinto, and folk mythology. They believe that they can walk on burning coals, which is why I've come to see them tonight. They've set up in a wide dirt space between a shrine and a kindergarten. I arrived early enough to see the children laughing on the swings and merry-go-round, but now the playground is silent and deserted, and the shrine itself is dark.

The grounds are gradually filling up with spectators. They're mostly older folk, farmers who grew up in the countryside and went out each spring to welcome the mountain gods and ask for a good harvest. The men have craggy jowls and untrimmed, bristly eyebrows that keep out the rain. The women are stoop-shouldered and bowlegged from years of planting rice. A few have brought along their grandchildren in a vain attempt to pass on a dying way of life.

A Yamabushi elder dips a bamboo branch into a boiling iron kettle and abruptly sweeps it across the crowd. I duck reflexively. The old people serenely raise their faces to catch the searing drops. "If you are pure in heart," a woman whispers, "then you will not be scorched." I nod and try to look relieved, though I'm not at all sure where I stand on the Yamabushi saint-and-sinner scorecard.

They pause to pass around a large vat of chrysanthemum-soaked sake (for longevity) and flick playing cards into the audience (for luck). Both should come in handy later on because tonight we'll be braving the red-hot coals as well.

I admit I'm somewhat skeptical about the whole event. The Japanese are not exactly known for taking risks. I've never seen one cross against the traffic lights, and most of them won't go to the movies by themselves. Besides, their feet are as soft as tissue paper. How can they possibly survive a stroll across a bed of burning embers?

I forgo a second splash of sacred water and tiptoe behind the shrine, where several workers are laboriously stacking wood into a six-foot pyramid. "Beech?" I ask with studied nonchalance. Perhaps it's a softwood that looks hotter than it really is.

"Nope," the pyre builder says, and raps a stick against the

ground. It makes a heavy, solid sound. "Maple." He points out, unsolicited, that they stuff all the cracks with dried pine needles to make sure it fires up like a funeral pyre.

"Are you going to walk?" he asks. When I nod he grins and offers me his hip flask of sake. I accept. Perhaps I should have fought harder for a lucky playing card.

We sit and drink until the sun goes down.

"Are you going to do it?" I ask.

He laughs and shakes his head. "No way."

I take another slug.

By eight the sake bottle is dry. He checks his watch and totters over to the pile. There's a loud whoosh as the pine needles blaze to life. The flames climb twenty feet, and the spectators look stunned as they stumble back against the unexpected heat. Several of them suddenly remember an urgent errand and walk briskly back to the parking lot.

The drums start up again. Two Yamabushi light torches and begin to dance. A dozen deep male voices chant in rhythm with their swaying steps. The burning points of light arc and loop and coil and twist through the darkness, as hypnotic as weaving snakes.

Ten minutes flow by, or perhaps an hour. When I finally look down again, the embers are twinkling a dull orange against the cooling ashes. The Yamabushi line up and march through it with calm deliberation. The spectators approach the coals with a good deal more trepidation. By the time my turn comes, the remaining embers are barely warm enough to tickle my soles. I turn and watch the few who still have to cross. A mother counts to ten before marching arm in arm with her eight-year-old daughter; their faces shine with fear and pride. A businessman, briefcase still in hand, looks straight ahead and steps out smartly, as though crossing a busy street. A grandmother shuffles slowly with a cane, as unconcerned as if she were strolling down a country lane. When it's over they all celebrate as though they've just made it up Mount Everest.

The crowd suddenly surges over to a nearby building. Several Yamabushi appear on the second floor with tattered cardboard boxes in their arms. A sea of desperate hands stretches skyward. Without another word, the Yamabushi toss handfuls of small, fluffy objects down to the seething mass. Sacred relics? Blessed charms to be laid on ancestral altars? It's several minutes before I catch a glimpse of a successful supplicant scurrying away with her prize clutched tightly to her chest: potato chips.

I think about them on the long journey home. I'm a little disappointed that they don't stub out cigarettes on the backs of their knees or climb ladders made of sharpened swords. A part of me really wanted to see the supernatural, even if I paid for it with charred insoles. Oddly enough, their very fallibility makes them even more intriguing. Tomorrow they'll put on their suits and look for all the world like ordinary businessmen, but underneath . . . I like people with secret lives.

For the next few days I can't get that drumbeat out of my head. It pulls at me when I try to study and weaves itself into the fabric of my dreams. Traveling with Mom did little more than whet my appetite. I'm desperate to go out and explore Japan, with or without the Tanakas' blessing. And after four months in Fujisawa, I'm no longer entirely dependent upon their help. I even have a clue—a single word—pried out of the drunken shrine workers: Haguro, a sacred mountain far to the north, the birthplace of the Yamabushi cult. Once a year, at the end of August, they gather at the summit to conduct their ritual fall training. That gives me just two weeks to track them down.

I call the Tokyo Tourist Information Center. They laugh at the very idea of a mountain cult in a modern country like Japan and suggest a visit to the famous Senso-ji Temple to help me clear my head. I comb through all my books, then make a trip into Tokyo to search through the Foreign Press Club's library. Nothing. Not even a footnote.

Genji has never heard of the Yamabushi and assures me that if they ever did exist, they have long since died out. He is clearly not going to use his connections to help me find out more about them. But then, I have a web as well. I go back downstairs and hop on the Internet.

And there it is. Several articles and an entire PhD thesis from 1964. It's heavy lifting, but by the time I'm through I know everything about these obscure ascetics from the time they go to bed to the color of their underwear. This time I by-pass the Tokyo Information Center and call directly through to Yamagata Prefecture. A woman answers, and my odds of finding my way into the cult suddenly skyrocket. Lynnika is not only an American but a graduate of Williams College, my alma mater. It's the first strong thread of *kashi* connecting me to the mountain cult.

A dozen e-mails, twelve faxes, and several muddy phone calls later, I have permission to film the Yamabushi's eight-day fall training in the sacred mountains. There are rules, of course. I must bring a Japanese interpreter. This sets me back a bit; a professional will cost upward of $800 a day, plus expenses—far beyond my meager savings. I speed-dial Lynnika again. Does Yamagata have student guides? No, but she might know someone who can help. Tomo, she tells me, is a thirty-something-year-old mountain man, as comfortable scaling mountains as he is translating the esoteric terms of Buddhist philosophy. He's temporarily unemployed and doesn't need a salary. I can't believe my luck.

When Genji gets home I take the Yamabushi training schedule upstairs and ask him to help me translate it. He looks it over briefly but isn't familiar with the arcane kanji characters. He shrugs and hands it back.

Something has changed in my relationship with the entire family. I still go to Genji's workouts. We chat on the way there and back. But I'm not invited up to dinner very often anymore. Yukiko hasn't bothered to try the sourdough starter that Mom gave her from the States. The Masamune sushi knife I gave her is no longer on the shelf. Nothing has been said out loud, but there's a chill in the air, like the first cold snap of fall. I do my chores meticulously, but I no longer go upstairs to ask Yukiko if she needs anything from the store. And they don't ask me what I'm doing or where I'm going anymore. It's as though I'm gradually being erased. It's a disconcerting feeling—like looking in a mirror and seeing nothing but a silhouette.

But as the trip to Mount Haguro draws closer, it temporarily crowds out any other thoughts. It's an extraordinary opportunity; no foreigner has ever been allowed to film the Yamabushi in their sacred mountain hideaway. I'll have to be extremely careful not to draw attention to myself. And since I don't really know what's coming, I'll carry everything I need with me in my pack. Whatever isn't absolutely necessary—toilet paper, extra socks, waterproof matches—I'll do without.

By the time I've assembled cameras, tripod, film and accessories, my backpack tips the scales at eighty-eight pounds.

That's three-quarters of my body weight, and I know there's going to be at least one twenty-mile hike. I split the gear between my back and a belly bag. I glue my camera to one hand and grammar book to the other. I look like a pregnant camel and waddle like a potbellied pig. I don't fit in anywhere—on trains or buses or revolving doors—and stand out like a sumo wrestler at a refugee camp. So much for blending in.

At four thirty on a Thursday morning I slip on the pack and struggle to my feet. Then I quietly lock the door behind me and head for the Dewa Sanzan Mountains, three hundred miles to the north.

My first leg is on the bullet train. I didn't bring anything for breakfast—food went by the wayside with my spare sunglasses and inflatable pillow. The train barely pulls out of the station before tray tables drop en masse and *bento* boxes materialize in a dozen shapes and sizes. Soy sauce is squeegeed over balls of cold rice and gradually decomposing fish. The *pfft-pfft* of popping coffee cans sounds like a whole pod of whales surfacing at once. Not a single face is looking out the window. Nobody is sleeping, though it's still dark outside. Everyone, it seems, is intent on eating their way across the country. My stomach rumbles unhappily.

The food cart comes by. It's outrageously expensive. Luckily, the tiny woman sitting next to me also passes on the early-morning coffee and half-stale croissants. I settle back to snatch a few more hours of sleep. Before I close my eyes I inadvertently glance over at my companion. She smiles and asks me in careful English if I am American. I almost don't answer. I'm exhausted from my early start, and it's going to be a grueling week. But I wasn't raised to ignore a polite request from someone who looks like my first-grade teacher. I smile and nod and reluctantly sit back up for a couple hours of superficial conversation.

She's traveling to Sendai, to visit her two children. Her son is in marketing for a company that customizes databases for the financial side of the real-estate sector. He's due shortly for a promotion. Her daughter is a full-time housewife, though she recently took a class in lacquerware—she's really very talented—and is thinking of trying to sell several of her pieces at a local gift shop.

The woman settles back, her résumé complete. Once a month or so, she adds, she goes down to Tokyo to visit her sister, who has no children and makes her living as a hairdresser. "Every day making other people beautiful! And what does she have to show for it after all these years except bad cuticles and a closet full of cheap shampoo. . . . "

"Terrible," I agree, with just a bit too much enthusiasm.

She turns and skewers me with a sudden, penetrating stare. "And how many children do *you* have?" she asks.

It's six thirty in the morning. I've been up for three long hours on an empty stomach. I take one look at that determined face and cave in like a house of cards. I don't even have to think about it—the words just tumble out: twenty-nine years old; engaged to a fine young man who works at IBM; the wedding's in October. We're hoping for two children—a boy and a girl. In fact, we've already decided on their names.

She smiles and nods approvingly. I slump back with relief. She rummages around inside her enormous handbag and thrusts a heavy block of brownish paste—obviously for cooking—into my lap. I have absolutely no use for it, so I say thank you and hand it back. She insists that she has plenty more and opens a huge handbag full of exquisitely wrapped gifts. She reminds me of my grandmother, who used to buy everyone's Christmas presents by the middle of the summer and give them all away by Labor Day.

I get her business card to send her a thank-you note. She takes my picture and asks for my address so that she can mail it to me. She confides that she is an *obachan*—a grandmother—and shows me a photo of her grandchild. She is both appalled at the idea of getting old and proud to have raised a son who has successfully married and fathered the next generation. I express surprise at her smooth skin and jet-black hair and compliment her on the solid family values she has obviously passed on to her kids. I am rewarded with a large bag of seaweed crackers. I explain that I just can't take it—my backpack is already bulging at the seams. She tears the package open and makes me eat them on the spot. I scramble frantically through my belongings for some way to reciprocate and come up with nothing but my super-duper emergency box of four chocolates in their bullet-proof metal tin. I hope the contents haven't melted—it's been a while since I checked. And then, in desperation, I excuse myself, roll over, and pretend to go to sleep.

She wakes me up to present me with a hand-stitched puppet made of antique kimono cloth. I have nothing left to give her—I'm down to my camera gear, used toothbrush, and some spare tripod clips. The cart comes to my rescue, and I splurge on green tea for both of us and packets of dried squid. By now she knows I live in Fujisawa and that I have a host family. When I drop my guard just for a moment, she slips a package of spun-sugar cookies into my hand. They will survive about ten seconds among the heavy camera gear inside my pack. "You have to take it," she tells me placidly. "It's not for you—it's for your Japanese family."

Our train is slowing for a station. It's not my stop, but I thank her and get off anyway. We smile and wave to each other as she pulls away. Then I sit down and wait for the next train.

∞

Tomo is there to meet me when I finally arrive at the right station. He is tall and flat and stringy. When I shake his hand a little too effusively, he stiffens up into a stick of wood. During our two-hour drive to Haguro, he never cracks a smile.

The parking lot in front of the main temple is already filling up with trainee Yamabushi. A man pulls up beside us in a fancy silver car. He extracts a duffel from his trunk and walks jauntily inside. There's a check-in line just past the door, like freshman registration. All new arrivals are issued rule books and little pamphlets and copies of the sutras they will need to memorize.

Mr. Yamaguchi, the head priest, waves us to a table in the corner. I sit beside Tomo as we go through the inevitable list of do's and don'ts and the weekly schedule. Tomo doesn't offer to translate, and I pick up what I can. I'm thoroughly distracted by Yamaguchi's fingernails. They're long and curved, like talons, filed into perfect parabolas and buffed to a high shine. He has a watch the size of a hockey puck and an equally outsize belly.

Horseflies buzz lazily around our heads, looking for a place to land. One slips under the table and bites Yamaguchi on the ankle. He lashes out with unexpected speed and vehemence, then calmly picks up the corpse, tears it in half like a scrap of paper, and deposits it in the ashtray.

The trainees, he informs us, are not permitted to bathe, brush their teeth, shave, or change clothes for the duration of

137

the eight-day training. They'll be fasting for the first forty-eight hours, though they are allowed to drink green tea and, if they must, watered-down orange juice. There were five hundred applications for the hundred fifty available slots. The costume is rental only. The management is not responsible for accidents or injuries.

He starts to explain the various ascetic stages and quickly loses me in a tangle of specialized vocabulary. I watch the new arrivals nervously fingering their costumes and the smugly superior returnees. The newcomers eventually ask for help, then proudly tie on their baggy pants, careful to cross the strings over at the midriff and tuck them under at the ankles. They don't realize how desperate they will be to take those same clothes off a week from tomorrow.

For those who came ill-prepared, there are jockstraps for sale at the counter, along with Saran Wrap raincoats for $30. Socks are sold only in packs of five—four more than they're allowed to wear. Cigarettes are available by the carton and the pack. I'm surprised that the acolytes are not allowed to brush their teeth but are allowed to smoke. Mr. Yamaguchi shrugs and stubs out his cigarette. "Rules change," he says.

∽

The neat rows of Yamabushi suits are almost gone. Everyone is assembling for a quick parade through town before they disappear into the sacred mountains. Mr. Yamaguchi takes his place at the head of the procession, under a large red umbrella carried by an acolyte. His second-in-command wields an enormous wooden axe to clear the air of demons so that the trainees can safely pass.

We reach the entrance to Haguro just as the bloated sky finally bursts open in a torrential downpour. The trainees pull on their flimsy raincoats and mill around, waiting for instructions. I notice two dozen well-dressed women watching us intently from a nearby path. They look distinctly out of place, huddled under umbrellas and trying to keep their fancy footwear dry on the uneven asphalt. I make a few discreet inquiries. Yamabushi wives. Most of the trainees are close to sixty, Japan's mandatory retirement age, the time when men who are accustomed to a position of authority suddenly find themselves at loose ends. Their wives, who have had sole possession of the house for thirty years, are faced with a brooding semistranger who is constantly underfoot. From the women's stony faces and grim expressions, they haven't come to bid their husbands off but to make sure they leave.

The stairway beckons. It leads directly to the temple on the mountaintop, 2,446 steps away. Through this gate there's no turning back. The triton blows. A long white caterpillar winds its way slowly up the stairs. The men look proud and scared. The women look relieved.

The path is ancient, its hand-carved steps worn smooth by countless generations of straw-clad feet. Giant cedars tower over us, their massive trunks thrusting toward the heavens, their roots plunging deep beneath the springy moss. Dense green branches snatch away the sunlight, leaving us in perpetual twilight. A heavy mist rises from the moist black soil, as though the earth itself were exhaling after the life-giving rain. The Yamabushi's shoes, softened with pads of rice husks, barely whisper on the moistened stones.

By the time we reach the top, everyone is tired, wet, and bored. The acolytes are not supposed to speak to us, but they

139

nod at my soggy clothing and smile in shared misery. I am already learning to tell them apart by the color of their pom-poms. First-year participants wear white to match their uniforms. If they stick it out for two more years, they graduate to non-fast orange. The truly dedicated rise slowly through the ranks to blue, red, yellow and, after twenty years, purple.

Yamaguchi is surprised that Tomo and I walked all the way up the stairs. This does not, however, earn us an invitation into their sacred lodging temple. We head out to a nearby campground, and I set about the thorny task of getting to know my interpreter.

Tomo's story comes out in bits and pieces. At twenty-four he went to America on a sightseeing tour, then came home to work for five years as a salesman in his father's corporation. He hated the corporate treadmill, deliberately and almost angrily opting out of the train-commuting, business-suiting lifestyle of the corporate rat race. "Not for me," he says with unexpectedly strong body language, crossing his hands in an X in front of his face and shaking his head vigorously. At thirty-three he quit and went to New Zealand for a year. He camped and backpacked with a pair of Kiwis and a Swedish woman. He spins a long tale of living off the land, working his way around the country on a pittance, and camping for months on end, and yet he had trouble setting up his tent and has no idea how to light a Coleman lantern. He describes with pride and repulsion a week spent on a sheep farm. Blowflies had laid eggs on the sheep and he had to pour medicine on them and watch the maggots wriggle out.

"Have you ever done anything like that?" he asks aggressively.

"No," I lie.

He smiles for the first time and nods his head.

∞

It's one of those scorching August days, so stifling hot that even the crickets have fallen silent and the birds fluff out their feathers and open their beaks wide to pant.

We've been climbing up a steep mountain trail since early morning, pausing only long enough to chant sutras in front of misshapen trees and rocks. "These mountains," Yamaguchi tells me, "are where one's Buddha nature can be found." But first the trainees must throw away all worldly connections and purify themselves in body and soul. By sacrificing cleanliness they take themselves back into the world of animals, where they can then reforge their spirits into a more enlightened form. "White," he says, pointing at the Yamabushi uniforms, "is the color of purity, and death." They must all die symbolically so they can be reborn as mountain ascetics.

The path is steep and treacherous, and their baggy sultan trousers are already beginning to suffer from repeated falls. Each man wears a *Tonkin*, a round black cap the size of a small Camembert. It's secured with a thin elastic strap that only occasionally holds it in place. It is smooth but for a small, concave triangle. A real Yamabushi knows to turn that toward the front.

In the olden days the Yamabushi carried short knives to kill themselves the moment they achieved enlightenment and a pouch with just enough money for a proper burial. Their modern counterparts have instant cameras to capture the big moment and cell phones to alert their friends and family.

Today they are allowed to speak to me but not to reveal the

secrets of their late-night sessions in the temple. It's so hot that they're also permitted to carry bottled water, though many— used to a life of air-conditioning and elevators—didn't bother. Halfway down the trail I come upon an older man sitting on a log, his body slack, his face a thick and blotchy red. I offer him my extra water bottle. Tomo makes a slashing gesture. *No.* I pretend not to see him, but half a mile down the trail he turns on me in fury. "We are not supposed to interfere with their training," he tells me sharply.

"But they're allowed to carry wa—"

"They must help each other. That's the only way they'll learn."

I don't agree with him, but he is so angry that I nod my head.

On our way back we catch up with a half dozen trainees, and I listen in on their conversation. They're tired and miserable, hungry and focused on themselves. They talk mostly about food and beer and television and their favorite La-Z-Boy chairs. No breakthroughs yet.

We reach the parking lot and wait several hours until word filters back that one man has collapsed somewhere down the trail. No one makes a move to help.

☙

It's been dark for several hours, and the air is finally cooling down. I'm waiting outside the temple for Mr. Yamaguchi to arrive. The crickets are making up for their slow day, pulsing through the darkness, their song punctuated by the plaintive bleat of lonely tree frogs trying to attract mates. The stars are bright and hard, and the night crackles with energy.

And then, from inside the temple, a single bell rings twice. A lone voice begins to sing. A hundred follow, stumbling at first, then gradually catching on—rich baritone and bass, in a great wave of sound that seems to be coming from deep inside the earth itself. How can those exhausted men, these disparate and untrained voices, harmonize so seamlessly? After a few moments I slip off my headphones, close my eyes, and just listen to the angelic voices blending with the rhythms of the night. It is the sound of enlightenment.

At ten, the temple goes abruptly silent. Windows slam and doors are locked. I grab my gear and scurry backward. Silence. I put my headphones back on and unashamedly eavesdrop. Shuffling. A stifled cough. Another. Good Lord, it's *namban-ibushi*—ritual death by asphyxiation. I've read about it, but I assumed it had long since gone the way of live burials and all-night exorcisms.

Namban is red pepper. *Ibushi* means smoke or fumigation. The Yamabushi seal up the temple and toss a mixture of red pepper and rice hulls into several large braziers. Bluish smoke quickly saturates the room. It burns the nose and eyes and creates an almost uncontrollable choking sensation. It's meant to mimic death and prepare the participants for rebirth into the natural world. It also drives off mosquitoes, covers body odors, and keeps everyone awake. Occasionally, if they're overzealous, the men keel over and pass out.

The doors slam open without warning and the trainees stagger out. Smoke billows all around them. They stand in knots, tears streaming down their faces, coughing up great clouds of pepper smoke as though it were tear gas. They'll do it twice a night for the remainder of the training. No wonder the head priest doesn't mind the trainees smoking cigarettes.

Mr. Yamaguchi arrives just as they're shuffling back inside. Tomo has agreed to ask my questions for me, to be sure that I get a completely accurate reply.

"Why," he translates dutifully, "do these men want to become Yamabushi?"

Yamaguchi explains at great length while Tomo listens intently, occasionally breaking in to clarify a point. After twenty minutes I tug on his sleeve and beg for a translation.

"They want to understand more about life," he says.

"That's all?" I ask.

"Nothing important. Just details."

Later, when we're back in camp, I pull out my notebook and ask him if he might be willing to elaborate on a few of those unimportant details. "I don't remember," he says shortly. I ask him if, in the future, he might be willing to translate every other sentence. He immediately goes on the defensive, aggressively accusing me of calling him a failure. I frantically backpedal. I take full responsibility for my less-than-perfect language skills. I promise to be more careful in the future. It takes an hour to put out the fire, and he is still as prickly as a chestnut seed when we finally finish dinner and head off to bed.

∞

The trainees are still haggard and hungry, but at least they've learned to carry lots of water, and they fall less often when scrambling from stone to stone. I am impressed by their speed and stamina, and they are impressed that I keep up with them despite my camera gear and heavy pack. Tomo is upset that they compliment me so often.

They've gotten past their fantasies of food and sleep and are

144

starting to take an interest in one another. The sweat and dirt and long, hard days have already bound them together. They no longer require elaborate introductions. They don't pass out business cards. They refer to each other by name, not rank, and they use an informal language that's usually reserved for childhood friends. Even the color of their pom-poms—their status in the hierarchy—seems less important than when they first arrived.

Groups have formed based on shared interests and fitness levels. Ours has a professor at a Nagoya university, a sailor, a masseuse, two businessmen, a scaffolding manufacturer, and a professional pachinko player. Several musicians like to hike together toward the front. We can hear them singing rock and roll whenever they go downhill and breathless disco on the way up. There's a clique of born-again Yamabushi—all newcomers—who follow every rule to the letter and have taken it upon themselves to make sure everyone else does the same. They shut me up when I ask questions and obviously don't want me around. The youngest group is known for the salves and bandages they apply each evening to their knees and ankles and wear proudly the next day like military decorations. And there's one man—he could be thirty-five or sixty—who's mentally disabled. He is childlike in his simplicity and always forgetting his hat or staff. I don't understand a word he says. When we stop at a scenic lookout, he often throws his arms into the air and cries aloud in joy. I like him the best of all.

Gradually, as I get to know the trainees better, they include me in their conversations. Everyone, it seems, has a different reason for signing up. Some want to rediscover nature; others, to experience the strict discipline. One man saw a famous Japanese pilgrimage on television and was inspired by it.

Another has a daughter who had problems in the womb but turned out whole and healthy. He comes back every year in gratitude. An older man tells me somewhat sheepishly that his wife gave him the training to get him out of the house. And one plump fellow stares forlornly at his lunch of vinegar-and-rice balls and says he thought it would be a good way to kick off a diet.

Surprisingly, though we have a scattering of both Buddhist and Shinto priests, only one in five of the trainees is here because of his religious beliefs. Most, it turns out, have recently retired and have no idea what to do with the rest of their lives. They've put forty years into their jobs, rising early to catch the train and coming home just in time to crawl into bed. They never really had time to get to know their children, and now their children no longer have time for them. Their wives treat them like knickknacks, something to dust around.

One man retired less than a week ago. He began working for his company at twenty-one. His commute was two hours and thirty-four minutes each day. I do the numbers. Five days a week. Fifty weeks a year. Thirty-nine years.

"You've spent twenty-five thousand hours on the train," I say. "That's nearly . . . three years, night and day."

He gets very quiet. I leave him alone.

❧

In the middle of the fourth day, the professional pachinko player confesses in a whisper that he's here to cure himself of the game.

Pachinko is a cross between pinball and a slot machine. You feed it some money and watch a bunch of oversize ball bearings filter down through various bumpers and pins. When one falls into the proper hole, it starts up the digital slot machine. If it stops on a winning combination, you are rewarded with a handful of fresh ball bearings. Absolutely nothing you can do will affect the outcome, and the odds are stacked against you. "How," I ask, "can you possibly make a living at the game?"

"It never used to be that way," he quickly explains. Twenty years ago it was completely manual—there even used to be men whose job it was to stand behind the machine and pour the balls back in. After everyone was gone, the *kugushi*—the nail men— would go around and adjust certain key pins to change the odds in each machine.

By now there are a dozen Yamabushi listening attentively. In Japan, pachinko is a national obsession. The other trainees have almost certainly put in their time bellied up to the machines.

"Professional players," the man continues, "usually ex-*kugushi*, knew how to 'read' the nails and jockey the lever before playing." Lately, however, the machines have all gone digital. Nowadays the only way to win is by hooking a piano wire through the hole, or using a modified cell phone to override the computer and open up the gate. "You can't make an honest living at it anymore," he complains. Nevertheless, he's still in there from noon to midnight, seven days a week. It's eating up all his retirement savings.

"If you can't win, what keeps you going back?" I ask quietly.

"The alternative," the man says quietly, "is unbearable."

Several of the men are nodding. "Home," one of them says matter-of-factly.

"Why not go out with friends or coworkers?"

"Then you have to maintain face."

147

"Pachinko," one of the trainees explains, "is *nothing*. No stress. No thought. No responsibilities. It's even easier than watching a sitcom you've seen a dozen times." The lights are deliberately kept low and the noise unbearably loud in order to inhibit social interaction. "That's why you go. So you don't have to pay attention."

"The pachinko parlor," the soon-to-be-ex-player says quietly, "is the only place where you can be yourself."

∞

On the sixth day I make a terrible mistake.

We're halfway through our daily hike, traversing a long saddle between two sacred peaks. The path winds off into the distance, backed by layered mountains and an extraordinary view. I step off the trail to film a group of Yamabushi as they walk by in single file. I'm kneeling on a gentle, sandy slope that gradually sheers off into a cliff. One of the Yamabushi catches sight of me, and they all stop dead. I hear a curious buzzing noise, like a hornet's nest that's just been kicked. It's the sound of thirty men sucking air in through their teeth.

"Come back from there," one of them says gently, as though he's talking to a jumper on the fifty-second floor. I glance behind me. The drop-off is twenty feet away, and I'm solid as a rock. "No problem," I say gaily. "I'm fine." Then I notice that he's wearing purple pom-poms—a twenty-year Yamabushi veteran. Despite Yamguchi's legal caveats, these men are still my seniors and therefore morally responsible for my safety and well being. In other words, my body may not be in jeopardy, but I'm dangerously close to committing political suicide.

I get off the slope. I apologize, profusely. I am forgiven, barely. After that, when I want an unusual angle, I climb a tree or hide behind a rock.

Six hours later the trainees disappear into their temple, and I go sit by a crackling fire with Tomo. He insists we build one every evening, despite the sweltering summer heat. I think it reminds him of his carefree days in New Zealand, before he had to come back and face an uncertain future in Japan.

I've been trying to get behind Tomo's inscrutable exterior ever since we met at the station. I already know that he likes to jog and once almost finished a marathon. That he failed his university exams and took a year of *ronin* study. That he is terrified of bugs. Every time a moth is attracted to our campfire he flees in panic, shaking his head like an angry bull and covering up his neck. He cooks—I like that about him—and even takes a turn at the dishes. He's loved dried figs ever since he read about them in *Arabian Nights*. And he requires more feather-smoothing than a twelve-year-old Pekingese with asthma. There's an intense fury of wills hiding behind that thin veneer of civility. When he giggles, it's a wild, unhappy sound. I really want to ask him what he thinks of the pachinko player, but that's sure to set him off again.

He tells me about an office job he interviewed for at the Tourist Information Center. The position was way beneath him, given his gender and education. When the Board asked him why he was willing to consider such a lowly situation, he told them he wanted the experience. They hired a twenty-two-year-old girl instead.

"What are you going to do now?"

"I have a doctor friend in Bangladesh," he says with sudden animation. "We're thinking of starting a trading company."

Unfortunately, the doctor is very busy at the moment, so maybe in a year or two . . .

"Trade what?"

"Bangladeshi things. Japanese things." He shrugs.

∽

It's our last long hike: a thirty-two-kilometer mountain pilgrimage. The difficulty is etched in the trainees' faces and the bruises on their legs. Their hunger pangs are fading. They walk more confidently and seldom use the ropes or metal railings. Their baggy white pants are filthy and their straw sandals are in tatters.

Soon we are above the tree line, following a trail through waist-deep grass. The line has spaced out and looks like a string of white pearls floating on a grass-green sea. From time to time the three-toned triton—a Yamabushi calling to the spirits—drifts over on the breeze. I fix every detail in my mind. I know this day will never come again.

We crest the hill and head down and down, through shrubs, then trees, then a muddy trail strewn with boulders, and, finally, a river. The path emerges on the far bank and disappears into the woods.

It's wide but shallow. One man steps boldly forward, using his staff to feel his way and leaping from stone to stone. Others quickly follow. The first few have already reached the other side when someone in the middle slips and tumbles in.

He comes up spluttering. The water is only hip deep, but he seems in no hurry to climb back out. He starts bobbing up and down, rubbing at a dirt stain on his pants and trying to rinse it out. The idea catches on like fire, and within minutes the water is filled with splashing Yamabushi, stripped down to nothing but their underwear. They wallow gleefully in the shallows, scouring the creases behind their ears and the spaces between their toes. They carefully scrub every inch of clothing and spread them on the rocks to dry. Of all the austerities they suffered this past week, not bathing must have been sheer misery.

When they finally put on their newly whitened uniforms, I am reminded of the tentative and frightened city slickers who showed up at the Yamabushi headquarters only a week ago. But these men emerging from the river are nothing of the sort. They're sunburned. Self-sufficient. Rugged. Mr. Yamaguchi was right. They have been reborn.

An hour later I'm following the trail along a river valley when I see the first white-clothed figures emerge at the summit far above. The disabled man is with them; they must have helped him up. He turns and looks back down the valley, then throws back his head and spins around and lets out a shout of unadulterated pleasure. The others burst into applause.

I'm beginning to understand the power of this cryptic cult. It's not their *mudras*—the nine-fold secret gestures that they practice late into the night—and it's certainly not their pepper-powder death. It's not even their weeklong brush with nature, though a good hard sweat and plenty of fresh air certainly didn't hurt.

It's the silence. The time away from their web of obligation, from the voices that have ruled their lives and influenced their every thought. For some, it's the first full week in forty years that they've had nothing to do but think about their future: to imagine possibilities, to find out who they are, and to talk to others who share their situation. They may not have discovered the truth about the universe, but they're finally discovering themselves.

Tonight there will be a ceremony. They will kick up their knees and skip around the purifying fire and chant the ancient Yamabushi songs. It's their official graduation. But as I look up at the distant figures high atop the mountain and hear their voices rising in exquisite harmony, I know it's really just an afterthought.

They've already earned their place among their Yamabushi ancestors.

CHAPTER 12

I stand inside Tsuruoka station and watch three trains go by, all heading back to Tokyo. I can't bring myself to get on board. The very thought of going back to Fujisawa makes me want to sneak back into the mountains and hibernate until spring.

It's not the lack of privacy—I've lived in crowded situations before. I can handle the complete absence of human contact— no hugs, no handshakes, as though I had a skin disease. I don't even mind having my housekeeping skills held up to public inspection. It's that I feel so utterly unwelcome, like a telemarketer or an intestinal parasite. The truth is painfully obvious. No one wants me there.

I should go back and try to set things right. If I were a little stronger, I would march onto that train and do whatever it took to make up for my many failures these past few months. Instead, I do what I always do when a relationship goes bad. I bolt.

Ten minutes later I'm walking backward down the road, holding up a hand-printed sign. *Direction south and west. Will share chocolate cookies.* I'm heading for Oguni, a remote farming village on the back side of Japan. Two months ago an acquaintance of a friend asked me to join her for the local rice harvest. Her name was Yuka. I'm not at all sure that the invitation is still open or that she even remembers me.

All around the fields are turning crisply golden, the drying yellow stalks nodding under the weight of their heavy golden heads. Soon the colors will be turning on the mountaintops. Already the breeze is softening with the scent of fresh-cut grass.

A truck approaches. I hold up the sign and smile. He pulls over to pick me up. He doesn't even want the cookies that I offer once I'm settled inside.

His English and his manners are impeccable. He looks to be about thirty, prematurely gray. He tells me he studied computer graphics design at university.

He is friendly and polite and deeply cynical, though his anger doesn't seem to have anything to do with me. I put away the cookies and start asking careful questions.

"So you want to understand Japan?" he repeats. "There's only one thing you need to know." He grips the steering wheel and stares straight ahead. "The nail that sticks up gets hammered down."

He looks over at me briefly. "There is no Bill Gates in Japan. Such a person would be hated here. The Japanese deeply resent the arrogance of a self-made man. When wealth is achieved outside the system, public opinion turns against it. Look at the powerful people in society—they've all gone to the right university, the right corporation. This is how the country works. There are no mavericks or entrepreneurs here."

He falls silent for a moment, then starts up again, as though talking to himself.

"But there's nothing that the Japanese hate more than the *narikin*. You call them nouveau riche, but in Japan the word means a pawn that has been promoted to a queen. It is a peon rampaging around the board as a big shot. It has absolutely no right to do such a thing."

He glances down at my camera gear. "Do you know how to use the Internet?"

"Of course."

He nods. "In this country almost everyone under thirty has at least one cell phone. You can call up your daily horoscope, download the most efficient train connections, send a photo of your new girlfriend to your college roommate. And yet most senior Japanese managers don't know how to access their own e-mail. They have their assistants print it out, then dictate a response. In Japan, if you want a consensus, you pass a piece of paper around the office. Everyone signs it with their *hanko*—their personal stamp. The system hasn't changed in two hundred years! The decision makers—all over fifty—have never used the Internet and don't see the need for it. And even if they did, most Web designers are under twenty-five—too young to be taken seriously in the business world."

His face is absolutely without expression. The rumble of the engine fills up the cabin like the roar of an oncoming train.

"What happened?" I ask quietly.

He tried to start an Internet design company when he was twenty-two. He failed and went bankrupt. Now he drives a truck.

He goes forty minutes out of his way to drop me at a train station near Oguni and insists on giving me the *bento* box that would have been his lunch. I wrack my brains for something that won't sound like a cliché.

The nail that sticks up gets hammered down.

"I understand," I say.

I make a phone call inside the station. Yuka isn't there, but a friendly voice tells me that someone will come pick me up, then hangs up before I can respond. Within an hour, Osawa-san pulls up in a beat-up old pickup truck, gets out, and introduces himself. He's a carpenter working on an office building in nearby Yamagata City. "I escaped Oguni almost sixteen years ago," he says. He's only going back to help his friends with the harvest over the weekend.

"What's Oguni like?" I ask.

He shakes his head. "It is conservative"—he makes a fist—"like iron." Everyone watches everyone else: how thoroughly you shovel the snow off your sidewalk in the winter; how many begonias you plant in the spring. Traditional events like weddings and funerals are enormously important. "You don't elope to Thailand if you ever want to come home again." Osawa spent seven years in Hokkaido—Japan's equivalent to wild Alaska—and wants desperately to go back. He liked the cold and, even more, he liked the freedom.

We pull up beside a steeply wooded hillside where his friends are cutting poles to make the drying racks. These are real mountain men, casually confident with their chainsaws and their grappling hooks. They pick their way down the mountainside with twenty-foot saplings balanced on their shoulders and heave them effortlessly into the back of the truck.

They nod by way of introduction—no elaborate greetings, no business cards or bows or hours of small talk.

They all grew up in the surrounding countryside but, surprisingly, it was an American who turned them into friends. Her name, as near as I can figure out, was Cristober. She spoke almost perfect Japanese and was obsessed with organic farming. She convinced them that 45 percent of Americans are vegetarian and that New Yorkers are an alien species. She left behind a dozen bags of organic beans with indecipherable English instructions, a floppy hat, and a pair of knee-high waders. She seems to be the benchmark by which they measure all other foreigners. No, I'm not a vegetarian. Yes, she has a point about New York. And thank goodness, we have the same shoe size. I pull on her boots, grab a scythe, and wade into the rice paddy.

We cut the stalks an inch above the mud, then lay them in neat piles all pointing in the same direction. It's nose-to-knees, hamstring-stretching, back-aching toil. I'm beginning to understand why so many older Japanese women are shaped like bobby pins. No Western farmer would ever dream of bending over every plant. But then, America's endless, amber fields of grain don't exist in Japan. The average Japanese farm is tiny, less than three acres, and nearly 90 percent of farmers have to take a second job just to pay the rent.

Our field is about the size of a basketball court. It will yield about ninety kilos of organic rice, enough to feed two people for a year. Yasunori-san, the owner, could buy that at a supermarket for a few hundred dollars. I put my hands on my hips and straighten up like a rusty folding chair. "Is it really worth all this effort?" I ask. Even with volunteer labor, he must be earning less than a dollar an hour.

"It's rice," he replies, equally baffled that I would even ask. Rice. The sacred grain. It has played a pivotal role in

Japan's history ever since it was first introduced from China nearly two thousand years ago. Until recently it was the country's official currency. Peasants were required by law to cultivate their rice fields and often had to hand over their entire harvest just to pay their taxes. They survived on millet and toasted barley; to eat rice was cause for celebration.

Once the bundled stalks are neatly tepeed over the drying racks, we pull off our boots and head inside for dinner. Yasunori's wife is already cooking sukiyaki, a traditional Japanese feast. I pretend to chop vegetables and make small talk while keeping a worried eye on the front door. Yuka, the acquaintance of my friend, will be arriving any minute, and I'm still not sure she's going to remember who I am. The connection was tenuous at best and the invitation two months out of date. Now that the harvest is over, I don't know if I'm welcome to spend the night.

Ten minutes later Yuka comes barreling through the door. Her hair is brown and her breasts are huge and her smile is wider than the Mississippi River. She plucks her English out of thin air and strings it together like exotic beads. She immediately wraps me up in a great bear hug, and I melt like an icicle on an August afternoon.

"Everything okay?" she says.

It's more than okay. It's wonderful.

Dinner is a rural feast. Meat and cabbage and mushrooms cooked in a huge pot right at the table. Pickled vegetables, fermented squid, sugared chestnuts—all made by hand in someone's living room. And my favorite: boiled crickets—sautéed in sugar, soy sauce, and a dash of sake, and served cold and sticky with a glass of beer. The Japanese may not use much pesticide, but at least they get to eat the pests.

Over dinner I get to know everyone a little better. Yasunori owns a propane-gas delivery company. His wife, Yasue, is eight months pregnant. They climbed Kilimanjaro for their honeymoon and spent several years in Tokyo but returned to this tiny village to raise their family. Their house is a study in contradictions: tatami floors and an ancient tile roof over a kitchen stuffed with modern gadgetry. A rotary phone beside a forty-six-inch TV. A surround-sound stereo system and a pit toilet.

Gaku is a professional carpenter and avid mountain climber. Ito-san teaches middle school. Yuka works in an office and moonlights as a professional *taiko* drummer. Her fingers are as callused as a sumo wrestler's feet.

They want to know about my life in Fujisawa and my host family. I describe Genji in some detail: his social graces and his judo; his extraordinary knowledge of Japanese culture and history.

"Your sister?"

I look at Yuka's irrepressible grin. "Not like you."

Her eyes twinkle. "And your host mother?"

I hesitate for a long moment. "She is very kind to let me live in her home."

Yuka bursts out laughing. "I call Yukiko-san while you were with Yamabushi," she says. She pretends to shiver. "Brrrr. Cold like ice."

I reluctantly admit that my host mother may not be so fond of some of my less savory character traits.

"Like what?" I shrug, but Yuka won't let it go. She parries my attempts to change the subject and wiggles at my evasions like a loose fence post. Before I know it, I'm swallowing back the tears, trying to explain to a roomful of strangers how things went so terribly wrong with my host family. When I'm done, I look up to see Yuka's normally cheerful face crinkled with concern. "Karin, you must come here and live with us. We will find you a place."

Everyone is nodding in agreement. I'm stunned. *Leave Fujisawa.* That perfect, polished house where I'm always falling flat on my face. I'm mentally packed in thirty seconds. But wait . . . Winter's just around the corner, and Oguni is virtually snowed in for five months a year. It would be the end of my documentary.

"You stay here until you know your heart's feeling," Yuka says firmly and pours another round of sake.

I do a quick calculation. The Tanakas just left for Europe for the next three weeks. I don't have to decide until then. . . .

I drift off to sleep to the sound of raucous laughter as everyone toasts the first rice of the season and argues baseball teams. It's bright and noisy and my pillow is brick-hard, but that night I have my first untroubled dreams since I arrived in Japan.

∞

The days slip by in a blur of snapshot images as I am passed from hand to hand through the web of Yuka's friends and acquaintances.

∞

Watanabe-san is a full-time farmer. He grows a variety of produce—tomatoes, mushrooms, and other vegetables in low-slung plastic greenhouses that sprawl across his fields like fattened caterpillars. He uses the most technically advanced fer-

160

tilizers and pesticides to coax the highest possible yield out of every inch of his carefully tended acreage.

"Just fifty years ago," he tells me over green tea and sugar cakes, "over half of all Japanese were full-time farmers. Today we're only 3 percent." After the war, Japan put all its resources into modernizing its manufacturing and exports. The rural sector was completely ignored. Eventually the government established farming subsidies, just to keep them from going broke. Tariffs were set up to kept out foreign competition. Farmers prospered, but they got less and less competitive: rice in Japan now costs 600 percent more than it does in the United States.

"If the tariffs were lifted," I ask, "what could you grow to make a profit?"

He sits silently for several minutes. "Gravestones," he finally says.

∽

The buckwheat-noodle maker begins work promptly at eight in the morning. He kneads a large bowl of flour and water, squeezing the granulating mixture between his blunt fingers until it becomes a dry, springy dough. He pulls off a lump the size of a Danish and uses a simple wooden dowel to roll it flat. The blob becomes a plate and then a pizza, flipping, twisting, spreading out across the table. Ten minutes later it's a perfect three-foot circle, barely thicker than a credit card. He folds and folds again, then pulls out a knife and cuts the dough in precise, two-millimeter increments. He weighs each single portion before twisting it into an artistic figure eight and setting it aside to boil. By noon—three hours later—he's made enough noodles for thirty-five servings.

The wild mountains all around Oguni are home to antelope and deer, wild boar, and sheep. Bear hunting is both big business and a local passion. Almost every house has pelts hanging off several walls, and local shops and restaurants proudly display their best specimens at the front door. A bear hide sells for $1,000, the gall—a sought-after traditional medicine—for $7,000, and the meat for $500.

The produce in the local market is sold fresh from the earth or sometimes gathered wild from the forest. In the spring there's *takenoko*, the tangy sprouts of bamboo shoots. In the fall it's the giant matsutake mushroom that grows in the local pinewood. In winter there are twenty kinds of pickled vegetables in plastic baggies, each hand-printed with its maker's name and home address.

⌒

Ito-san pulls into the parking lot of the largest building I've seen since I left Tokyo. It's the local school.

"We used to teach reading-writing-abacus," he says as we make our way to his first class. "Now it's bookkeeping, PC, and English." He doesn't sound too happy with the new agenda. He's a serious young man with a compact body and flat face who coaches the school Ping-Pong team and hunts on weekends. He tells me he was too shy to talk to girls in fifth grade and so stuck his nose in books, then one day looked up to find that he had become a teacher himself.

Which, in Japan, is not a bad profession. Teachers are the shining public example for the next generation, the very center of the web of human relationships. But they must comport themselves accordingly. A small-town teacher cannot cross the street against the lights or drive a foreign car. He shouldn't chew gum in public or buy a case of beer without a proper explanation. He cannot neglect to mow his lawn or let his hair grow an inch below his ears. Ito-san's most important responsibility is neither the computer nor the abacus—it's teaching his students how to become good Japanese.

Ito drops me off to spend the night with Yuka's mother. I recognize her immediately—she has Yuka's rosy cheeks and ample figure. Her buck teeth keep popping out in a broad smile like a sweater that's been buttoned on too tight. She feeds me rice and sweet-fleshed *ayu* fish and gallons of green tea.

The next morning some fifteen village women are waiting out on the driveway, talking quietly among themselves. They're comfortably dressed in frocks and aprons and house slippers. There's not a smear of lipstick among them, and they're all well over fifty. I assume they're here for a cooking class or perhaps a Buddhist ceremony. Yuka's mom bustles out to unlock the basement door, and we step straight into a miniature assembly plant. Large plastic containers are stacked ceiling-high against the wall. The cement floor is covered with fake putting grass. Twenty-foot-long schematic diagrams span every room, fixed to slanted tables bristling with metal pegs. The women march briskly over to their stations, grab rolls of wire and electrical tape, and set to work. They're assembling Nissan electrical harnesses destined for the United States.

They cast expert eyes over the complicated electronic diagrams, stretch out lengths of wire, and hook them over the proper pegs. They snap open their measuring sticks like seasoned carpenters and wrap the tape in perfect spirals. They work with the serene efficiency of grandmothers making apple pie for a Thanksgiving feast.

When I ask them why they're here, they giggle shyly. "To get out of the house," one replies on behalf of everyone. They like the relaxed environment and the chance to be with friends. But it's more than that: they are the postwar generation, brought up on the twin values of sacrifice and discipline. Amid the 1950s belt-tightening, work became much more than just a means to earn a living—it was a moral imperative. These women are here, not just for the friendship and camaraderie, but because it's how they were raised.

��

At last, I pile into Yuka's tiny car for the long drive to her taiko drumming rehearsal. I've barely seen her since our first evening together—she usually stops by just long enough to flash her enormous grin before staggering home to bed. The steady march of recessions has thinned the ranks of her coworkers until she is doing the work of her entire department, at lower wages than when she first got hired. She faces presentations at least twice a day, preparations late into the night, and marathon meetings almost every weekend. The stress is obvious in the exhausted creases across her forehead and the raccoon smudges around her eyes. But lately she's got bigger problems than too much work and too little rest.

"Karin, what you have with your host family, I have here too," she blurts out as we barrel down the highway.

Three times a week she drives two hours to her team's studio and drums the night away, often not tumbling into bed until two in the morning, to rise before dawn to go to work. She would like nothing more than to quit her office job and play full time, but taiko doesn't pay the rent on her minuscule apartment, and Renzan, her drumming master, is too busy grooming his two sons to pay much attention to anyone else.

Despite her best efforts, the situation is coming to a head. Renzan's team is scheduled to perform in distant Aomori in ten days. Yuka's boss has forbidden her to go. Renzan insists that she attend. The creases between her eyes deepen into clefts.

"Renzan is like a father to me—my family. But I have to pay the rent . . ."

A teacher who doesn't understand her financial situation. A career she would love to pursue full-time but bills that have to be paid. And Yuka's only twenty-three years old.

"I talk with Renzan so that we would understand each other's hearts, but . . ." she stares out the rainy window and shakes her head.

"What will you do?"

"I don't know." She glances over at me. "And you?"

"I have no idea," I say.

∞

The taiko studio is tiny and packed with drums of all shapes and sizes. Practice is already under way. Yuka picks up drumsticks and settles down to play.

It's like being inside a great, multichambered heart, each section moving to its own rhythm yet perfectly synchronized. The enormous *odaiko* thunders deep inside my chest. The smaller drums tap out a complicated melody. The flute wafts through the waves of sound like wind through swaying pine trees. Tiny cymbals flit in and out like swallows. If nature were

165

ever to conduct a symphony of the elements, this is how it would sound.

At the very epicenter stands Renzan. He is tall and athletic, with rippling shoulders from years of forging his skill at the drums. He is more than merely handsome; he has the kind of animal magnetism that no plastic surgeon can replicate. He plays with the joy of a child and the precision of an Olympian. He's a natural entertainer, spinning and snatching the drumsticks out of the air and flashing his irresistible smile. When it comes time for his students to learn a new routine, he steps up to the drum, snaps out an enormously complicated rhythm, and says simply, "There, like that."

Four hours later they finally take a break. Renzan announces that he'll be teaching a multiday taiko seminar at a nearby school the following weekend. I take one look at Yuka's radiant face, the stress completely erased, and sign up on the spot.

I spend the two-day seminar watching Renzan when I should be paying attention to my drum. He is that rarest of Japanese—an unapologetic extrovert. He sits off to one side like a benevolent monarch, arms crossed, only rarely stepping forward to make a correction or demonstrate a technique. Yet even in repose, he throws off energy like a red-hot light.

Students bandage blisters and layer tape over the bandages until they can hardly wrap their fingers around their sticks, but still they drum and drum. Even those waiting their turn on the instruments keep time with clapping hands and tapping feet. Every now and then they throw surreptitious glances in Renzan's direction, hoping that he'll notice them.

In the evening he sits at the head of the table while half a dozen volunteers vie to make sure his sake glass is always filled to overflowing. He is the perfect host, insisting that the students from Fukuoka province demonstrate their famous flower dance and that the shiest girl in the group sings a karaoke song. He points to the glasses of the nondrinkers and orders them filled. He is the patriarch. We drink.

When he leaves the room the whispering begins. Low-voiced conversations among the older men in business suits: *That Renzan, he's very loud, isn't he? Not a team player . . . always making decisions without consulting anyone else.* The same men who compete to sit beside him at the dinner table, who laugh the loudest at his jokes, who bask in the reflected light of his personality, quickly fade back into the grayness of their business suits and carefully combed hair when he goes away. And the whispering begins again. Renzan laughs and takes a drink. He doesn't care.

Once the seminar is over, the team packs up the drums and we head north to Aomori, a twelve-hour bus ride away. Renzan gives one of the drummers a brisk massage, then props his feet on Yuka's shoulder and drifts off to sleep. *Renzan is like a father to me. He is my family.* I'm absolutely certain that if Yuka got pregnant without a husband, Renzan wouldn't hesitate to take her and her baby in. If another player was permanently disabled in an accident, Renzan would arrange for his lifelong care. Absolute obedience in return for security and rock-solid relationships.

The performance is extraordinary—an extravaganza of 200 colored lights, $400,000 drums, a hand-carved dragon rigged with glowing eyes and steaming mouth, and even a magic show at halftime. The audience is mostly older, though there's one boy of seven or eight sitting in the front row. Everyone claps politely as the curtain rises. The taiko drums roll over them like a giant, cresting wave. They begin to tap their shoes and nod their heads despite themselves. It's not the extraordinary rhythms or the dazzling technique that draws them in; it's watching the players so thoroughly enjoying themselves. Renzan's arms ripple in the pulsing light. His smile is enormous and absolutely genuine. Even his teeth glow a luminescent white, as though lit from within. When the final drumbeats fade away, the applause is thunderous. Renzan spreads his arms and accepts the flowers and flasks of sake as his rightful due. When the curtain drops for the last time, I catch a last glimpse of the young boy, eyes huge and fixed on the towering figure in the center of the stage.

The audience leaves the theater twenty years younger than they went in. Their steps are light and springy and their shoulders square. They're practically swaggering.

Renzan is neither meek nor modest—in many ways he's very unJapanese. But that's precisely what makes him so appealing. He embodies everything the average Japanese cannot afford to be. Tomorrow they will wake up, put on suits, and climb aboard the train to go to work. But tonight they'll dream.

I say goodbye to Yuka soon after the performance. I haven't known her for very long, but I am sure of several things: she drives like a maniac, can drink three men under the table, and would give her last yen to a stranger on the street. She helped to heal the yawning cracks that threatened to tear apart my life. Five minutes after meeting her I was ready to pull up stakes and move to her tiny town up in the mountains. Getting to know her was like coming home. I am heartbroken to go.

CHAPTER 13

The Tanakas return from their three weeks in Europe exhausted and thoroughly relieved to be out of the others' sights, at least for a little while. Their Italian itinerary was stuffed with far too many castles, all at the top of tediously long hills, and the Spanish toilets were frightfully unclean. All three of them got awful head colds four days into the trip and gained at least five pounds from too many fatty European meals.

Yukiko immediately puts everyone on a draconian diet and makes an emergency appointment with her chiropractor. He pricks her finger, takes a drop of blood, and examines it under the microscope. He then informs her solemnly that she has bacteria and pieces of dirt floating among her red blood cells, and declares that her large intestine is not functioning properly. He prescribes a bag of absurdly expensive white powder that turns out to be soybean starch.

Yukiko insists on my opinion. I can't think of a single positive thing to say about either the man or his medicine, so I lob the question over to Genji. He clearly doesn't believe the chiropractor either, but he doesn't stop his wife from going and meekly downs any medicine she brings home for him. In Japan, house and health are the woman's exclusive domain. If the kitchen counter is dirty or her husband has a hangnail, she is to blame. Yukiko decides whether they need colonoscopies (never), spinal adjustments (several times a month), or dental checkups (only when it hurts). When in doubt she consults their trusty eighty-nine-year-old family physician. Most important of all, she keeps a record of everyone's blood type.

In Japan, your blood type defines your personality. It is used to assess potential employees, to choose friends and business partners, and to target customers. Back in the 1920s a series of articles entitled "The Study of Temperament through Blood Type" kicked off an avalanche of interest in the subject. Type A, it said, is supposed to be cautious, genial, intelligent, peaceful, reticent, fond of formalities and structure. These people are also—if you read the footnotes—highly strung busybodies, with a tendency toward constipation and high blood pressure. Type B is caring, selfish, and sociable. Type O is extremely generous and honest, and dislikes authority.

Within ten years, a space for blood type had been added to most job-application forms. This supposedly allowed for a balanced work environment—too many A's created an overly passive atmosphere—and ensured that people were assigned to jobs compatible with their blood dispositions. Type A's were best as salarymen and shop clerks. AB's made good schoolteachers and foreign diplomats. O's were better off as geishas and army chiefs. On the downside, white-collar crime was largely an A offense, though they were also more likely to be highly educated. O's had a tendency toward violence. B's were bums.

In 1971, "What Blood Type Reveals about Compatibility" was published, and has since gone through more than two hundred printings and spawned nine follow-up texts. Its influence is so pervasive that even vending machines now sell condoms based on the user's blood type.

Yukiko is an A. "What is your blood type?" she asks me suddenly. As it turns out, I am also an A. She is not at all happy about this.

"If you ever need a transfusion, you know where to come," I say and offer her my arm. She wrinkles up her nose as though she just got a whiff of something dead. I nearly point out that she's the one with dirt in her blood, but sanity prevails. Type A's are, after all, supposed to be reasonably intelligent.

I had hoped that the month apart would smooth things over, but if anything it's made them worse. Everyone is studiously polite, but there is a palpable distance whenever we meet. Nobody asks me questions about where I've been or what I'm doing. Genji is still his usual friendly self when we get on the train to judo, but once inside the house he immediately disappears upstairs. I want so badly to make things right between us, but I have no idea where to start. Maybe Roberto can help.

He listens silently while I list a catalog of cooking and cleaning failures, but it's not until I describe our dinner conversations that his face turns truly grim.

"You should have followed Yuikiko's instructions for preparing dinner instead of talking with Genji," he says. I know he's right, but it's a moot point by now. I am no longer invited upstairs to eat, to talk, or even to do the dishes.

Roberto thinks Yukiko is very jealous of my relationship

with Genji. I hasten to assure him that there has never been a whiff of impropriety about the man. "It doesn't matter," Roberto says, shaking his head. "It is very dangerous." He suggests extreme caution on my part.

"What can I do?" Surely he too has made mistakes at some time or another and found a way to patch things up again.

"You must apologize until she forgives you," he says slowly. "Bow your head and accept whatever punishment until they are ready to take you back."

His advice reminds me of a Mark Twain story about a blue jay that tries to fill up an empty house by dropping acorns through a small hole in the roof. "That could take thirty years," I say.

He nods. "Then you must be very patient."

I go home and carefully wrap up my favorite silk scarf and brooch. I write a note to Yukiko on a handmade card, telling her how sorry I am and that I miss speaking with her. I leave both on the bureau near the front entryway. They vanish without a trace. Next time I go to town I bring home special food that I know they both enjoy. It disappears as well.

Then one afternoon a fat manila envelope arrives on my doorstep. I rush it to my room and quickly tear it open. Ever since Junko's brush with the sumo wrestler I've been fascinated by the whole Japanese approach to love and marriage. A few months ago I put together a survey on the subject and arranged to have several English teachers distribute it as homework to their students—mostly forty-something-year-old housewives with grown children and not enough to do. I skim through the sheath of papers and quickly compile the results. This is just the sort of thing that would interest Genji and Yukiko, and perhaps even angle me an invitation to sit down for a friendly conversation.

Over the past few months they have both become increasingly concerned about finding a husband for Junko. She's now creeping up on twenty-nine without the shadow of a boyfriend or an eligible mate. Lately Yukiko has browbeaten her into once-a-week cooking classes, though she never brings home any samples and I suspect she doesn't go as often as she says. Junko knows her company won't employ her past the age of thirty but doesn't seem concerned. When pressed about her future plans, she says she wants to travel around the world for a year—without her parents—or maybe attend pastry school in Paris. Yukiko perks up at the thought of Junko whipping up French delicacies, while Genji wilts at the image of his daughter loose in the Paris shopping districts. They both agree that the three-year foreign apprenticeship is far too long for her to be away from home and that she needs to marry Japanese.

I can't help but sympathize with Junko's efforts to put off the inevitable. She clearly has no desire to exchange her current lifestyle for what looks to her like long days cooped up in a tiny apartment, trying to make the price of one Armani handbag cover a week of living expenses, changing endless diapers, and waiting on her husband hand and foot. It's a role few Japanese women can escape; not even Princess Masako, a tennis-playing Harvard graduate who gave up a bright future in the foreign service for a straitjacket of twelve-layered kimonos and endless ritual and etiquette.

Japanese pop culture doesn't do much to ease the transition. Unmarried women depicted on television and in advertisements are the very picture of postmodern infantilism. Carefully packaged teen idols—role models for millions of attentive prepubescent girls—wear pom-poms on their socks, glossy pouts, and, sometimes, Mickey Mouse hairdos. They embody the

173

kawaii style—cute, childlike, adorable, innocent, vulnerable. Human saccharine. Even when they're well into their twenties, women are expected to be dependent, feminine, and utterly nonthreatening. Female office workers take on an almost child-like personality. They answer the phone with artificially raised voices and defer to every man, from errand boy to CEO.

And what happens when a young woman finally finds her Prince Charming and dons a wedding gown? Overnight she goes from cute and adorable to a "flat top"—an aircraft carrier—the butt of office jokes. She is suddenly responsible for the house, finances, children, and education. As a mother, she is expected to be the epitome of strength and good judgment. If money runs short, she is at fault for not economizing properly. If her child does poorly at school, she has failed to teach him proper study habits. If her husband gains weight, she is to blame for allowing him to overeat or drink. More often than not she acquires a spouse who has never lived away from home and has been thoroughly pampered by his mother. It is then her responsibility to mold him into the proper shape. Suddenly she is judged not on whether she is wearing the correct shade of lipstick but by how much she is willing to sacrifice to create the perfect home for her husband and children.

According to my survey, many newlyweds don't even have the illusion of love to ease their way into married life. Matrimony, I am told, is far too important to be based purely on sexual attraction. Marriage is less the search for a soul mate than it is the correct thing to do at a certain age and time of life. Love marriages are not uncommon, but even those often start with a go-between. Society does everything it can to establish the difference between infatuation and marriage. Teenage love

174

songs dwell on lips and eyes and slender legs but hardly ever mention happily-ever-after. Television love stories almost never have a cheerful theme. There's almost always a woman crying quietly—tormented by inner desires that can only lead to misery and disgrace—and long, yearning looks in the pouring rain. If the young lady in the throes of passion doesn't turn away, she inevitably comes to a bad end. For many Japanese, the only true romantic love is impossible love.

As if that wasn't difficult enough, dating is generally discouraged until the end of high school. Very few teenagers can afford a car, and given Japan's strict auto-emissions laws, fixing up an old clunker is not an option. No drive-in movies, no parking by the lake; Japanese teenagers—and their parents—may not go through the bumps and bruises of a typical Western adolescence, but they also don't get to learn from the experience. When they finally do get married, it often feels like they're stepping off the steep cliff of childhood and trying to survive the impact of wedded bliss.

I finish pulling together the fifty-odd responses to my questionnaire. *What is the worst vice in Japan? Kijinshugi*—Individualism. It's almost a curse word here. No Sense of Shame and Not Being Diligent come in a close second. *Greatest virtue?* Noble-Minded Character and Courageous Spirit. Good Sense of Shame. Wearing a Kimono Properly. Matchmakers are generally considered an effective way to meet potential mates, with the exception of one woman who detests her husband and holds the matchmaker responsible. Young women living at home should help with the housework, though they shouldn't have to pay rent. Mothers must teach their daughters to cook and clean or else they will be useless. Older, unmarried women are blights upon society. It's a woman's job to stay home with the baby and, if necessary, take care of aging parents. A good education in a woman is bad for the marriage.

I whisk my surveys upstairs and knock cautiously on the living-room door. Genji is inside, watching CNN. I briefly explain my research and offer to show him the results. He immediately switches off the television to give it his full attention. Even Yukiko leaves her cooking to listen in. They call Junko from her room to see how she responds to my questionnaire.

"What's the most important thing in a marriage partner?" I ask after she slumps into a chair.

"*Takai, takai, takai*," she quips. It's a common cliché that plays off the three meanings of the word: Good income, good school, and tall.

I try a different tact. "What if you had to choose between love, earning power, and similar socioeconomic background?"

"Earning power," she says, without hesitation.

Genji doesn't say anything, but his eyebrows climb up his forehead in surprise.

"Is love necessary to marriage?"

"No." Earning power is the single—perhaps the only—important factor in marrying a man. "If a young man has good prospects," Junko explains, "then I would marry him and hope that the love would come later."

"And if you didn't find him attractive?" I ask quietly, fascinated despite myself.

"If I wasn't attracted to him then I'd do everything to get around it."

Genji's eyebrows are still hovering just below his hairline. My survey is about to backfire into a major family conflagration.

176

I glance through my notes for a way to change the subject. Often, when an engagement looks imminent, the parents will hire a detective to make discreet inquiries with coworkers, friends, and neighbors about the prospective mate. Retardation in the family, even bankruptcy, can torpedo an otherwise successful match. It's one of the reasons Japanese are so reluctant to seek professional help for alcohol addiction or depression. It contaminates the marriage prospects of their children.

"Would you investigate the background of your potential son-in-law?" I ask Genji. He's not sure. Yukiko is already nodding her head. She'd be talking to his kindergarten teacher to see what grade he got in crayon class.

"Would you veto the marriage if the father has changed jobs?"

"It's up to Junko," her father says.

All eyes turn to Junko. She nods vigorously. "Of course. The father is the role model, so the son would be the same way." Yukiko looks pleased.

I take a huge gamble. "Were you in love when you got married?" I ask Genji.

"Well, she was in love with me!" He grins. Yukiko elbows him in the ribs. He laughs.

I edge further out on the limb. "How did you meet?"

He thinks about it for a moment. "I don't remember."

Yukiko gives him The Look. But he's just teasing her again. He describes exactly where they met, and who introduced them. She smiles.

I love to watch them together like this. They clearly adore each other, and even more important, they really get along. They each fulfill their respective roles within the system and respect each other's skills. They are living proof that the system works. Maybe Junko should reconsider.

By the time the conversation's over, I practically float down the stairs. I've missed them more than I realized. Perhaps the hole I dug isn't thirty years deep after all.

∽

Two days later I get called up to the kitchen. It's dinnertime. Genji is sitting at the table in his slippers, nursing a scotch. He wants to talk. Yukiko is slicing ginger next to the stove.

"Come in! Come in!" Genji says heartily. He waves me to a seat. "Sit down!"

I surreptitiously check his drink. It's only a third full, but sometimes he has two. I glance at the sideboard. Dishes are piling up, but the ingredients are so beautifully laid out that I can't tell if they're ready for the table or the cooking pot. "Are you sure?" I ask.

"Sit!" He really wants to talk. This is exactly what Roberto warned me about. I should be helping Yukiko lay the table, but I don't even know if I'm invited to eat with them. And ignoring Genji is not an option, no matter how mad Yukiko gets. I slide into a chair.

We discuss the evening news. Genji is expansive. It must be his second scotch. He describes the latest happenings at Renault, which just got taken over by French management. I could listen to him forever. I've never been that close to my own father, and these conversations are the highlight of my week. But I can hear Yukiko pacing back and forth in the tiny kitchen, just a few feet away. After fifteen minutes I get to my feet, mumble an excuse, and thank him for the conversation. When

I turn to say goodbye to Yukiko she sends me a look that stings my face like a dose of radiation. I flee.

She must have been ready to eat dinner. I never should have sat at the table. I feel like I invested all my savings and the stock market just crashed. I sit in my room and try not to listen to the clink of cutlery upstairs.

Yukiko no longer greets me in the garden or when she hands me my mail. Her face puckers with distaste whenever she glances in my direction. I survive it for three days, then pack up my cameras and escape.

I step off the train in Kyoto without any concrete destination. There's a Tourist Information Center on the corner. I wander inside. A tiny woman is standing behind the counter: her name is Morita-san. It's her job to give directions to the local Kabuki theater, help tourists to find lodgings, and tell them which subway will deposit them at the most popular Kyoto shrines. She must have done something terrible in a past Buddhist life because she has the rotten luck to be on duty the day I walk through the door.

I start off easy—directions to a festival and a cheap place to stay for the night. She is so kind and helpful that I find myself standing outside the plate-glass doors early the next morning, waiting for them to open. I describe my documentary. Even with the Tanakas' help, prying open the doors to traditional Japan has been like trying to break into Fort Knox. If I film one more Buddhist temple or manicured rock garden, I am going to have the video equivalent of elevator music.

Then Morita says those fateful words: "Maybe I can help."

I take a deep breath and it all comes pouring out. "Can I stay in a Buddhist monastery? Not as a tourist, as an acolyte. I've been trying to shoot pachinko, but every time I sneak inside a parlor they catch me six seconds later and dump me back out on the sidewalk. Is there a sake-making factory that still uses wooden buckets and paddles to stir the rice? I'd love to go out with the spider crab fishermen—you know, the giant crabs with bodies the size of serving platters. The Naked Festival sounds like fun. Any chance I can join in? What if I wear two loincloths, top and bottom?"

She's writing furiously. When I finish there's a slight pause, like an overly polite host whom you've just informed of your plans to stay another month. Then she smiles and says, "Nobody's ever asked me that before. Let me see . . ."

That night she finds a pachinko parlor whose owner not only lets me film but sits down with me over dinner to explain the entire industry. The next morning I'm once again waiting outside the Information Center, this time with a bag of pastries, a shamefaced smile, and a dozen more requests. I know this is not a part of Morita's job and that she's swamped with work, but she just laughs and shrugs it off. "Your questions are interesting," she says.

Before I leave Kyoto, Morita does something wonderful and terrible and extraordinarily generous. She hands me her e-mail address. I know it's against the rules of the Information Center. I swear I won't take advantage of it, but I do. She is my lifeline, my one chance of success after months and months of failure. If I can't understand Japan through the Tanakas, then maybe I can through my film.

CHAPTER 14

"Karin, come up!"

I haven't heard those words in weeks. I race up the stairs. Yukiko's tiny kitchen is packed with people. Genji is chatting with their son at the dinner table while Yasue, their daughter-in-law, helps Yukiko prepare a meal. Their only grandchild, Sinchan, runs around the kitchen, stopping every loop or two to beg a lift into his grandfather's lap. I head straight for the un-chopped vegetables but get intercepted by Genji, who wants me to speak English with his son.

Ushio is a supremely serious young man with the thin face and stringy body of someone for whom discipline is as impor-tant as oxygen. He followed his father into the prestigious Tokyo University and was immediately snatched up by Nissan, a blue-ribbon corporation. Three years ago he was transferred to their office in Taiwan, where he quickly learned the local lan-guage and got a black belt in one of the country's martial arts.

Genji sits beside him and beams with pride. Ushio dredges up his English word by painful word. Genji won't allow us to speak Japanese. Once Ushio finishes his résumé, he immediately launches into an excruciatingly slow-motion lesson in Taiwanese history. I try to pay attention, but all I can think of are the carrots still sitting on the sideboard. I have this crazy notion that if I don't get up and chop them, they will turn into little flying daggers, all pointed at my heart. Genji decides to have his son demonstrate his martial art on the front driveway and motions me to follow them downstairs. I turn my back on the vegetables and trail off after them.

I spend most of lunch pretending to listen to Ushio when I'm really watching his son. Sinchan is eighteen months old and remarkably well-behaved. He sits quietly on his mother's lap, points to what he wants, and says, "Eat." His mother unfailingly corrects him with "Please . . ." He repeats the word and she lets him have a piece. When everybody's finished, he climbs down and heads for his favorite spot—his grandfather's lap. Genji hoists him up with a laugh and lets the little boy play with his reading glasses.

Yasue and I get up to clear the table. She is beautiful, with short black hair, high cheekbones, and long lashes. She rarely speaks louder than a whisper and never raises her eyes above knee level. She constantly defers to her mother-in-law, knows where all the dishes go, and jumps up to do the chores before she has to be told.

Yasue was handpicked by Yukiko and has turned out to be the perfect daughter-in-law in every way except for one. Genji's parents lived downstairs for fifteen years while Yukiko waited on them day and night. She had every right to assume the same treatment when her son brought home a wife. The Tanakas

182

even built their house in the expectation that Ushio and his family would one day move in. And then disaster struck—Ushio got a job on the other side of Tokyo, too far to commute by train. Now he visits only every other month. Yukiko, after all those years of servitude, was cheated of her reward.

And then I came along—a woman, Yasue's age, and a barbarian to boot. I slid right into that empty space where Yasue should have been. In Japan, it is proverbial that the mother-in-law does not like her new daughter. Even the word—*shutome*—has all sorts of ominous implications. The young woman comes into the house as a stranger. It is her principal duty to learn how her mother-in-law likes to have things done and then to follow her example to the letter. It is assumed from the beginning that she is not good enough. It can take years before she is grudgingly accepted into the family.

I finally realize why Junko would rather stay in her tiny room upstairs than move into the spacious granny suite. It's the first step down the path to a place she doesn't want to be.

Dinner is exhausting. When Ushio finally pulls out of the driveway I wave goodbye with some relief, but the evening isn't quite over yet. Genji pulls me aside as I'm about to say good night. He mentions that he's been put in charge of the Tokyo University quarterly judo alumni meeting—the same association that landed me on his doorstep six long months ago. "I would be pleased," he says delicately, "if you could attend and give a short speech in Japanese."

"Of course." One ten-thousandth of my obligation. I owe him far more than that.

We agree that I should speak for fifteen minutes. I ask him several times about a topic, but he insists that it should be up to me.

I write out four sample speeches, none of which pass muster. "Perhaps," Genji suggests eventually, "you should focus on your judo, both here and in America." I do. He suggests a few more details. I add. And add. I'm now up to thirty polished pages and several tedious evenings hunched over a dictionary.

"It's good," he finally says. "Only . . . it should be in honorific Japanese."

Unfortunately, I only know the plain version of the language. He graciously offers to rewrite it in the proper style. I secretly translate it back into English, only to find that all my jokes have been removed and the speech itself has been flattened like a lobotomy. Never mind. I tape him reading it into my camera, and then I practice every night for two long weeks. I don't care what the alumni think; I'll do anything to make Genji proud of me.

∞

I know my days are numbered when Yukiko's hairdresser won't cut my bangs. I call three times but he's always busy, and finally I get the message and stop trying.

A week later Yukiko tells me that her mother is coming to visit over Christmas. I know they usually put her in the front room with the proper Western bed, but I offer to move out anyway. She instantly agrees.

And just like that, it's over. Nothing left to do but pack my bags and head back to the States. But I've begun a documentary that isn't close to being finished. If I go home now, it will all have been for nothing. I will have failed. It's the one thing I can't face.

I'll stay.

Easier said than done—it's the dead of winter, and I soon won't have a place to live. I call around to half a dozen rental agencies, but I'm told in no uncertain terms that foreigners are required to have a Japanese citizen cosign their lease. I finally check the classifieds in an English-language magazine and find a roommate-wanted add in Osaka City. Shared kitchen, bathroom, living room. In a quiet neighborhood five minutes from the Kyobashi train station. One month's deposit, and my housemate's name is Jerry. It's available by December 20. I take it, sight unseen.

That night I come home from judo to find a note from Yukiko on my kitchen table. I'm to make an immediate copy of the footage I took at the Sanja Festival—six months ago—and send it to the owner of the Asakusa Bar. I'm to include an apologetic letter explaining why it's taken me so long.

There must be some mistake. I made that copy right after the festival and gave it to Yukiko. I go upstairs to talk to her, but she insists she never saw it. Unfortunately, I shipped the original footage home with Mom. I offer to make another copy as soon as I get back to the States.

"*Now*," she says.

The next morning there's another letter on my table with a list of all the people I must apologize to in writing, from Yukiko's friend at the organic restaurant to the woman next door who doesn't spray her hedges. I ask her to help me, but she doesn't have the time. In desperation, I go see Roberto.

He listens in silence, then shakes his head. "I think you need to leave immediately," he says. Yukiko's behavior doesn't make sense, even for Japan.

If only I could tell her how far I've come. That I've learned to put out combustibles on Wednesdays, plastics on Friday, glass and metal once a month. That I now eat sushi instead of Pringles, pickled radishes instead of candy bars. I don't think twice about laying out twenty-eight dishes for three people at the breakfast table. I return my cardboard milk containers, properly folded and tied, to the supermarket. I am more graceful. I slide smoothly around furniture and slip through the crowded subway station without bumping into anyone. I remember when my laundry's almost dry and iron it immediately. I vacuum more. I dry my dishes. I pause when I change into my bathroom slippers, turn around so that they'll be facing the proper direction, back out, and make a small, involuntary bow. I stack those tiny plates in their proper places in the overcrowded cupboard, one by one. I haul my futon outside to air the moment the sun comes out and wake up instinctively if it starts to rain when I've got laundry on the line. I'm still not sure that there is only one Right Way of doing things, but I've learned to take comfort in rolling up the garden hose in precisely the same place, the same diameter, the same direction, every time I water the plants. *Kata*, I've finally learned, is an act of discipline that you practice by doing something the same way day after day, until it becomes completely second nature. It's a sign of respect to those who taught you and to the society you live in. If only Yukiko knew how successful her efforts have been.

I decide to try one last time—not to patch things up but to make a graceful exit and perhaps open the door to reconciliation a few years down the road. I wait until I know she's having lunch and knock gently on the kitchen door. I bow my head and ask what I've done wrong and if there's anything that I can do to make it right. There's a pause as she swallows a small piece of sautéed eggplant and composes herself. I am, she tells me, a completely unmannered lout.

"Could you be more specific?" I ask without a hint of irony.

I don't greet her properly when I come in the door, and I don't wash my bath mat often enough. She once found a stain on the underside of my cutting board, and the maid had to wash it off. I walk in at dinnertime and talk to Genji when she is ready to lay the table.

I can't help myself. "But I asked if it was okay—twice! You didn't say anything."

I should have known by her expression.

"Maybe it's a cultural misunderstanding—"

"Not culture. Manners. You have none."

The list goes on for forty minutes. When it's over, I'm curiously relieved. She said nothing that I would be afraid to tell my mother. I can live with her critique.

I pack my gear and say goodbye to my beloved garden.

∽

I have only one obligation left. I'm meeting Genji in Tokyo tonight to give my speech at his alumni meeting. He's rented a club in a fancy part of town, on the twenty-sixth floor. Hors d'oeuvres will be served and dress is suit and tie.

I show up at the appointed hour. The foyer is dark and elegant, with a breathtaking view of the city lights. A woman stands behind an oversize mahogany-and-satin desk. She seems surprised to see me. I introduce myself as one of the speakers, and a young man steps forward to usher me inside.

Forty men in business suits are standing in small clusters

around room, chatting among themselves. Most are between sixty and eighty-five. I take a deep breath. They won't be an easy audience, but I've practiced this speech inside out and I'm confident that I can hold their attention.

Then a woman walks by in four-inch heels, fishnet stockings, a thong bikini, and a fluffy tail . . . and suddenly I realize I'm in a Playboy Club. More Bunnies drift in and out, offering appetizers and drinks. They fish cigarette lighters from deep between their breasts and lean way over, leaving nothing to the imagination. Several of the men are chain-smoking. The dim lighting does little to hide the furtive caresses and the hungry eyes.

I have two choices. The American in me wants to walk out in disgust; the Japanese is worried about what this will do to my relationship with Genji. I retire to a corner to think about it for a while.

He is my *sempai*. I will stay. A final act of obedience for his help and friendship these many months.

⁀

When it's finally over, Genji and I catch a taxi to the train station. It's well past midnight by the time we walk up the driveway, and he wearily unlocks the front door. There are a thousand things I want to say, but I only manage one.

"Papa-san, I will miss our conversations."

He grins and slaps me on the shoulder and climbs the stairs. I never see him again.

Yukiko shows up in my living room the next morning—the day before my move. "Genji and I are going up to the mountains for three days," she announces. "Do not leave until we come back."

I've already made arrangements to meet Jerry in Osaka, but I'm touched that they want to be around to see me off. I explain that I can't stay, but I would love to take them out for dinner before they leave on their excursion.

"No. You must hand me the key in person."

"I'll set the alarm and put it inside with your spares." It's what I always do when I leave the house and nobody's home.

"In person."

Suddenly, it strikes me. "Do you think I might *steal* from you?"

Her smile is wintry. "Maybe."

I try to swallow past the sudden lump in my throat. No one has ever accused me of . . . that . . . before. She just scored her first direct hit.

"Are you sure you want to say that?" I ask, very carefully.

"Yes."

I'm packed up in an hour. I wash and iron and fold the sheets, towels, dishcloths, and bathroom mat. I clean and scrub and replace the furniture exactly the way it was when I arrived. I count the spoons and forks and align the tiny dishes in the glass cabinet. Then I vacuum up my tears and leave.

I'm not even sure where I'm heading until I look out the window of the train and see the steep, pine-coated mountains of the Kiso Valley. I get off at Tsumago, the ancient postal village where Mom and I spent that lovely summer afternoon a lifetime ago. I remember the ripe tomatoes and crackers and sticking our heads under the waterwheel to cool off. There's the snap of winter in the air now. The last few blades of grass are already covered in silver frost. The afternoon shadows are growing longer, but I have no desire to find an inn, to bow and drink green tea and pretend to make small talk. I turn my feet to the old postal road and set off up the mountain.

It's a hard climb and I'm already bone-weary, my body worn out not from exercise but from the struggle to hold in my emotions. There's an aching spot inside my head that's been there for so long, I can't remember when it started. I don't have enough warm clothing or a flashlight to help me navigate the uneven stones. The last, dim tentacles of blue-gray light slip away beneath the trees. The stars come out bright and hard, and the fallen leaves crackle under my heels.

I feel the bands loosening around my chest and head, like a corset that's been pulled too tight or a *hachimaki* scarf coming off after a long day at a festival. The rage and helplessness are finally trickling away. All this space around me—I feel like I can breathe again.

My pack has molded to my back with the weight of ten thousand steps. I glory in my aching calves. I listen to the tinkling of the half-frozen stream, the rustling leaves as some small animal scurries away. I stumble onto the waterwheel and sit along the bank and dip my fingers into the icy flow.

I'm sure Genji must have regretted it—that moment when he casually raised his hand to host a stranger and unwittingly allowed a large, well-meaning, but untrained mutt into his home.

There were so many things I admired about him, but mostly, I loved his laugh. He'd just throw his head back and dissolve in peals of mirth. It was utterly infectious, completely unself-conscious, and in a delightful way, just the tiniest bit unJapanese. He spent hours helping me unravel the great ball of Japanese culture that on my own I would have plucked and tugged into a Gordian knot.

He bought me children's books so that I could learn to read in Japanese. He gave up his seat to old ladies on the train. He made sure my mother had an umbrella when it rained.

There are a dozen words for "friend" in Japanese, but almost all of them imply some kind of hierarchy: senior school friend, junior coworker friend, and so on. I know how far Genji had to stretch to bridge the gap between us—far beyond our differences in age, social status, and gender: he, an immensely successful man, well connected, socially brilliant, wealthy, and steeped in old-school values; I, career driven, outspoken, foreign, poor, and alone, in so many ways beneath him, according to the hierarchy in which he had been raised. Yet he never hesitated to introduce me to his friends and coworkers. He valued my opinion. He always, *always* treated me with respect.

And that, more than a place to stay, or judo lessons, or even an explanation of the nuances of Japanese culture, was his most precious gift to me.

And Yukiko. She worked her entire life to achieve the ideal of what a Japanese woman should be. She raised two children to take their proper place in society and cared for her husband's parents for years without complaint. She keeps a perfect house, cooks like a Tokyo chef, watches over her family's health and weight. She has every reason to expect a comfortable retirement, children to look after her, and unconditional respect.

Then suddenly, without her approval or consent, I was thrust into her life. Thirty-five and unmarried. A social anomaly, to put it mildly. Heading off to judo with her husband while she stayed home to cook our meals. My very presence was an insult to both her lifestyle and her choices—and to the society in which she lives.

Worst of all, Genji respected my opinion and applauded my achievements. He treated me like an intellectual equal. He complimented me on my language skills and my athletic abilities. He called me up to discuss world affairs while his wife stood by and peeled vegetables. He seemed to value those very things about me that she had been taught to avoid.

Yukiko did her level best to teach me how to be a proper woman and, if I got very lucky someday, a wife. But I was immune to public ridicule and humiliation. Japan is a shame culture, and I am not ashamed of who I am.

CHAPTER 15

My new home in Osaka is tucked into a narrow alley in an older downtown neighborhood. It's a thin, decaying townhouse with neighbors glued onto both sides. Its decor can best be described as Spartan Grunge. There's neither toilet paper nor salt. Several cats howl under the window, and one neighbor comes in after midnight on a noisy motorbike. Two of the four lightbulbs on the bottom floor are burned out, and a third is flickering. I'm halfway through a shower when the hot water runs out. It's a less than perfect environment and I'm absolutely thrilled. My gear—piled into one corner of the bedroom— doesn't require endless apologies. If I forget to hang the tattered bath mat, it will not go down on some permanent cosmic ledger as a black mark of barbarian ill manners. It feels more comfortable than my spacious granny suite ever did.

I have a real bed that doesn't have to be manhandled into the closet at the crack of dawn. I can cross my tiny bedroom in two large steps. In one corner there's a small bookshelf and a grade-school desk. The house has no heating and no insulation, and the walls are so thin that sunlight seeps through the tissue-thin wallpaper. No one ever locks the front door, and when it's time to check the meter, the gas man just lets himself in. There is no microwave, no oven, and no hot running water in the kitchen sink. There's only one electric outlet per room and one low-wattage light. The living room on the second floor opens out onto a balcony that's just large enough to fit a small washer and dryer. The washer freezes up in winter, so it only works on sunny afternoons, once it's had a chance to thaw out. I can touch the neighbor's balcony on either side, and a halfhearted spit will reach the one across the alley. For all its idiosyncrasies, my room comes with one truly priceless luxury: If someone knocks on my door, I can tell them to get lost.

I haul my filthy bedroom carpet upstairs, hang it on the banister, and beat it to within an inch of its tattered threads. I stuff the stained and stinking comforter into the tiny washing machine with a triple dose of detergent. It doesn't come out much cleaner, but at least it smells nice. I run out and buy a small floor heater, and for the first time in weeks, my hands don't ache with cold. I do the dirty dishes in the sink and dis-cover, to my horror, that the plastic toilet seat is covered in an unspeakable crusty coat of mottled brown and gray. I pour half a bottle of disinfectant over it, pick it up with tongs, and drop it under the scalding shower for twenty minutes.

Jerry, my new housemate, is tall and blond, good-looking and gay. He's an excellent dresser and could pass for half his age. He's employed by a private corporation, teaching English part-time to lonely, middle-aged housewives. That earns him enough to live a college-dorm lifestyle and keep him in cigarettes and beer. He's been in Japan for nearly five years and doesn't know if he's ever going back to the States. *Gaijin* men are popular, he tells me, and if you're going to be sexually active, Japan is relatively safe.

He goes to work at dinnertime and either stays out partying or brings someone home at two or three in the morning. He sleeps from mid-morning until late into the afternoon. We so rarely see each other that we communicate mostly via the dry-erase board in the bathroom.

When I finally bump into him in the hallway one morning, I tell him I want to get involved in community activities and ask him if he might introduce me to our neighbors. He laughs at my request. "Last spring I tried to plant that piece of dirt alongside the doorstep," he tells me. "The guy next door dumped a five-pound bag of salt over the soil."

"Why?" Do they not want a foreigner in their little alley, or is it because he's gay?

He shrugs and stumbles off to bed.

Jerry is not alone in his lifestyle. Osaka is awash with foreigners, many of them scraping by part-time in the English-teaching profession. Most seem to skitter across the surface of society, hanging out with fellow foreigners during their free time. Almost all are here on two-year visas, though some extend to three. A few hang on for four, or five, or six more years, until they gradually realize that their skills are no longer particularly marketable back home.

They are exempt from most of Japan's rules and obligations, provided they at least pay lip service to societal conventions. They get paid for little more than speaking a language they grew up with, and they rarely even have to prepare a lesson plan. But they are also looked down upon by the average

195

Japanese. I remember Genji's comment one evening at the dinner table: "The English teachers that you send here, in your country they're not good for anything more than pumping gas." It was unlike him to be so blunt unless he thought he was stating the obvious.

Surprisingly, Jerry agrees. "Most of the teachers who make a life here are misfits, one way or the other. In Japan just being a foreigner already sets you apart, so you can hide whatever else you want behind your gaijin-ness. And you always have a group that you belong to just because of how you look."

But as I get to meet Osaka's English teachers, I start to question his assessment. The gaijin that I meet are all, in their own ways, making herculean efforts to fit in.

Rory has a wicked sense of humor and a gentle streak a mile wide. He's married to a beautiful and brilliant Japanese woman and has an extraordinarily well-behaved three-year-old daughter. Rory was a white-water-rafting guide in New Zealand and spent nearly three hundred days a year away on the river. He decided to teach English in Japan so that he could spend more time with his child. Unfortunately, he never learned to speak much Japanese beyond the basic phrases, and he often doesn't understand what his daughter is saying. He can't answer the phone at home and only associates with English-speaking friends. Most of his daughter's books are in Japanese, so he can't read her a bedtime story. What will she think of him when she grows up and starts bringing home friends? I wonder if he hasn't exchanged the absentee-father's cloak of invisibility for a dunce's cap.

Lou took a job at IBM because they promised to send him to Japan. When the company changed its mind, he quit and came here with the English-teaching program. He has a

Japanese girlfriend, all shiny lipstick and sharp eyeliner and auburn hair. She greets me at the pizza parlor with the phrase, "Roey hath stinky poo." I mentally run this through my Japanese and English vocabulary and come up blank.

"I beg your pardon?"

"Stinky poo! Stinky poo!" she shouts.

"I ate some fish the other day and it didn't agree with me," Lou explains quietly.

I assume her five-year-old's vocabulary is a function of her struggle to speak English, but when I listen to her in Japanese, she talks exactly the same way. And yet she is dressed as though she just stepped out of the pages of a fashion magazine and expertly cadges cigarettes from one of Lou's friends. Her face puckers into a dangerous pout when her food arrives too spicy, and Lou dashes off to get it replaced. Her infant personality is a lifestyle choice, not a form of mental deficiency.

They're planning to get married early next spring.

Mary is twenty-nine and utterly miserable. She works in the public-school system, and her supervisor will not allow her to live on her own. She's with her third host family. The first one kicked her out when she invited her boyfriend over for the night. She snuck him in at midnight in dead silence with all of the lights turned out. The family knew about it before he left the next morning. They said she was a bad influence on their twenty-four-year-old daughter, who got drunk at least three times a week and twice passed out on the front step because she couldn't find the door.

Her second landlord was a seventy-three-year-old retired teacher who only accepted a foreigner into her house under pressure from her ex-supervisor. She had two grown children who never came to visit and three cats that ate off her dinner plate. Mary lived in the granny flat facing the garden in the back. It was three months before she caught a glimpse of an elderly man sitting in an easy chair and realized that her landlady's husband was alive and well. Night after night the cats sat under Mary's window and howled until, in desperation, she got a pot of cold water and poured it on their heads to make them go away. The next day her water heater stopped working. She asked her landlady to fix it, but the weeks ticked by and a repairman never appeared. She tried to do it herself, but the gas had been turned off. Eventually she got tired of cold showers and begged her supervisor to put her somewhere else.

Her third family is nice—they invite her in to eat with them at least once a week and bring her tangerines whenever they go to the farmer's market on Saturday. She tries to smile and make casual conversation, but she just wants to go back to the States.

Sarah is the wife of a high-ranking Osaka businessman. She's been here for twelve years and wholeheartedly embraces everything Japanese. She takes classes in cooking and housekeeping, loves the language, rolls sushi like an expert, and has even tried her hand at the tea ceremony. But she sent her two sons, seven and nine years old, to boarding school in America. She sees them once a year, for two weeks, on her annual pilgrimage back to Louisiana. Already they are forgetting the land they were born in, the culture and their heritage. She's protecting them, she says.

There's an Israeli on the corner just outside the train station. His name changes every time I see him—Thomas, Sven, Michael—but day or night, he's always there. He sells jewelry and handbags from a table on the sidewalk. I catch him during a slow moment and listen to his spiel. "You see this?" he says, grabbing a pair of cheap silver earrings. "I bought them for twelve dollars. You know what I sell them for?" He doesn't wait for me to guess. "Three hundred eight-five dollars. Not bad, huh? I make almost nine grand a month. No office, no politics. In six months I go home with the down payment on a house in Tel Aviv." He rubs his hands together. It's already mid-December and he's blue from standing around outside. He pauses to harass several businessmen, who avert their eyes and quickly disappear around the corner.

He dismisses them with a flick of his wrist. "They never buy when they're in groups like that. You have to look for single men who are in a hurry, usually between six and ten in the evening. They're off to see their girlfriends and they need a gift if they're going to get laid." He picks up a thin silver bracelet: "Eighteen hundred dollars. The Japanese are the most gullible people I ever met. I only have to sell four of these a month and I'm home free."

It takes another twenty minutes before the truth starts to dribble out. "This job is shit," he says bitterly. He works at least twelve hours a day, though more often than not it's closer to sixteen. He's out here seven days a week, and the position doesn't come with vacation, sick days, or benefits. He spent the summer on the sidewalk, frying like an egg in the midday heat. Up to three-quarters of his profits goes to the guy who supplies his merchandise, who in turn pays off the *yakuza* who control this section of the sidewalk. "At least they keep the competition out," he says. "I own this corner from there"—he points to a noodle shop about five stores down "—to there," a bicycle parking lot that laps up against the station door. "Anyone tries to set up on my turf, and some guys show up in ten minutes flat and tell them what to do with themselves."

Unfortunately, the yakuza don't have a similar authority

over the police. "The cops have been here twice this week, and a month ago they actually shut me down just before a holiday weekend! I could have made a ton of money because the shops were all closed for two solid days. I was counting on it."

Not only is he not supposed to be selling from the sidewalk, but he's on a tourist visa, so technically he's not allowed to work at all. If the police decide to prosecute him, he could go to jail, or at least have to pay several thousand dollars in fines and be immediately deported. He's willing to take the chance. "Just six more months," he says. "Three bedrooms, two baths. Great location. If I rent it out and come back here, I can buy a second one in less than a year." He stomps around to warm his feet.

Three days before Christmas, the sidewalk is suddenly swept clean of street sellers. It takes two weeks for the yakuza to make a new deal with the police. I see the table full of cheap trinkets and smile at the seller, but it isn't Michael-Thomas-Sven. It's a skinny young man with thick earplugs and a three-day beard. "Never heard of him," he says.

∞

Through chance meetings in the living room and the occasional potluck party, Jerry introduces me to a side of Japan I would never have known about: its gay community.

"As long as you keep up the pretence of being straight, you can pretty much do what you want on your own time. But you don't tell anyone—not coworkers, not neighbors, not even your own family." His Japanese boyfriend of six months had a good job in a catering business until he posed for a condom ad in an obscure gay magazine. He was fired from his job within a week and disowned by his entire family.

200

"What happens if you're leaving a gay bar and you bump into someone from your office?" I ask.

"You pretend you didn't see them and then act as though it never happened." Of course there will be gossip—whispers in the hallways, strange looks in the men's room—but as long as you say you're straight, they'll go along with the charade.

Until you hit that tricky age of thirty when you're suddenly expected to get married. Some just resign themselves to a heterosexual future, let their parents choose their partner, and live out their lives in misery, punctuated by affairs. Others marry lesbians and live the facade of marital bliss with the private understanding that they will each continue to do as they please.

"It's actually not a bad place to be gay," Jerry says as he puts on a stylish blue shirt that will fill his housewife students with secret fantasies and, hopefully, pick up some guys. "Nobody digging around to find out the truth. Nobody trying to out you. Just keep up the pretense and everyone leaves you alone."

It doesn't sound too bad until I meet a lesbian who's been here for three years and just married a gay Japanese man. She hasn't told her family in the States about her husband because she came out to them ten years ago. No one in Japan knows she's homosexual. Lies within lies. She's going home in seven months. Her life is a hurtling train, just waiting to derail.

CHAPTER 16

I meet Adam Cooley through a most unexpected series of events. It started with a tattered issue of a local English-language magazine I found abandoned on the seat beside me on the train. Inside was a brief article about a Western artist who does street performance. He dresses as a Roman statue, stands on a busy corner, and interacts with anyone who passes by. This seems inconceivably brave to me. I want to meet this guy.

I track him doggedly through several editors at the magazine until they finally give me an e-mail address. He replies almost immediately. No, he doesn't do mime anymore, but yes, he still occasionally puts on a street performance. He'd be happy to get together, and he gives me his home address.

He's tall and fit and soft and huggable. He came to Japan almost seven years ago. He speaks perfect Japanese, though he never cracked a grammar text. "I learned it by listening to my friends," he says. He lives in a tiny room that's filled to bursting with his paintings, books, masks, an entire wall of fish tanks, and a tub of tiny crabs. There's a small tree in the corner, shedding its leaves onto a pile of unfolded laundry.

"I've been looking for a place to release it," he says, following my gaze. "I just found an old cemetery a few miles away. A quiet spot that's full of birds, where no one will prune it to death." He reaches out and gently touches one of its thin branches.

Four months ago he absentmindedly left a carrot on the edge of a bookshelf. In that warm and nurturing environment it quickly took root. It's now got ten inches of filigree leaves, and it's looking healthier than any of my Fujisawa vegetables in their super-rich potting soil. He's watering it until spring, when he can plant it in his miniature veranda garden. I take a peek outside. It's completely overgrown and spilling onto the neighbor's land.

"Do they mind?" I ask, thinking of Jerry's salt patch.

Adam shakes his head. "I planted sweet peas and lots of flowers in the spring and told everyone to help themselves. I like to sit with the window open and hear them snacking on the pods."

He was raised in Rednecksville, America, in a poor household. He never understood why washing dishes was considered woman's work and why boys were always trying to tear the wings off flies. He didn't do the Cub Scouts or sleepovers and never had many friends. "I was terminally shy, bordering on agoraphobic, and I hid myself as much as possible from the world, from strangers, from people I felt threatened by. And from uncomfortable situations." Being gay didn't help.

Then one day he found a place where, for the first time, he felt safe.

"Japan is a country of masks. The Japanese are experts—they learn to wear masks from when they are children. The successful ones know exactly which ones to wear and when. The Japanese respect masks—if you wear them well. They don't try to pry them up to see what's underneath. They're comfortable admiring the beauty of the surface." He pauses and looks up at his wall of masks. They are a pandemonium of color and emotions: pig snouts and blood-red horns and lovely faces and Medusa heads, a laughing clown and a woman crying bright green tears. "They never try to uncover my mask, they never try to expose me. It's not that they're superficial. They're just very patient—they wait until I'm ready to take it off myself."

He smiles sadly. "When I arrived it was like a dream come true—masked boy meets land of masked people."

We talk deep into the night. His mind is full of colors and beauty and the kind of immediacy that you rarely see in anyone over the age of five. His favorite smell? He doesn't hesitate. "Walking by a rice field at night in the countryside two weeks before the harvest and smelling the ripe rice carried on a warm wind." If he could have one selfish wish? "Of course, financial independence, fame, good health, clothes that would make me look thin . . ." He pauses and stares off into the distance, a dreamy expression on his face. "Those would all be good wishes. But if I could fly . . . I think that would take the cake."

He agrees to let me film his street performance. It's not until I hug him goodbye that I realize how much I admire this man who has the wisdom of an old man and the simplicity of a child.

I get back to my room newly inspired to mend fences with my neighbors. Whatever they don't like about foreigners, I'll just prove them wrong. I'll use the Adam Cooley approach: I'll be so nice that they can't help but change their minds.

I set my sights on the old woman who lives directly across the street. Half of her roof is fenced off as a garden with over a hundred potted plants inside, many of them still flowering despite the cold. I often see her up there watering when I do my laundry.

I bake a plate of homemade chocolate-chip cookies, eat half a dozen, then quickly wrap up the rest and knock on her door. Her face puckers up when she sees me, and she almost ducks back inside. "Wait!" I say. I tell her that I'm her new neighbor, and I just want to introduce myself and thank her for the lovely view. I thrust the cookies into her hands and beat a hasty retreat. She steps back inside her house and slowly shuts the door.

After that, whenever I go shopping, I pick up a token—a few apples, a tub of miso paste—and leave it on her doorstep if no one answers my knock. A week later I see her come out to water the plants when I'm on my balcony, scraping ice off the washing machine. She still doesn't smile, but she nods in my direction.

I abandon my laundry and scoot out to the corner store to buy her some tangerines. By the time I get back she's no longer home, so I hang them from her doorknob with a note.

That night I am hauled out of deep sleep by what sounds like a slow-motion jackhammer right beside my head. I unglue my eyes—the clock says 3:00 a.m.—and stagger down the hall. Jerry is in the kitchen, pounding a frozen head of broccoli with an oversize kitchen knife. He's got the blade embedded in the stem and he's slamming it against the counter, trying to break it in half.

"Jerry, it's three in the morning," I say.

"I'm hungry," he replies between whacks.

"We have neighbors." Who are by now all wide awake within a two-block radius.

He shrugs. That's when I realize that maybe he's not hated because he's gay or foreign. It's because he's an unmannered lout.

The next morning my bag of tangerines is hanging from our front doorknob. The old woman never looks my way again.

☙

A week later, Adam calls to tell me that he's ready to perform. We set up near a busy intersection in the heart of hip Osaka. He's brought along two assistants dressed from head to toe in black, with heavy gauze hiding their faces. Adam is in a tight, black, sleeveless top and baggy pants. His skin is covered in white rice powder and his lips are painted fire-engine red. He's barefoot, despite the cold.

He steps onto a thin tatami mat and curls up into a ball. *He is the seed of a young bonsai tree.* Slowly his head comes up. *He sprouts and grows.* His assistants circle around him, gradually adding clumps of fake grass and twigs. A half dozen businessmen pause on their way to lunch to watch. I know the basic story line, but they look rather baffled. That's fine with Adam. He wants to keep them guessing long enough to stick around while he tries to get his point across. He gradually rises to full height, his fingers spread to catch the sunlight. *The young tree grows grand and powerful.* His helpers keep adding branches and bits of greenery. They are helping him to reach his full potential as a mighty tree. They represent society trying to bring out the best in each of us.

And then something starts to go wrong. They tie his arms with rope and try to twist them into painful positions. They deform his natural shape, like Chinese foot-binding or an

Elizabethan corset. They prune and mold him into the kind of person that society thinks he should be. I suddenly understand the carrot in his room—how he celebrated its spontaneous burst of life—and his quest to find a place where his young potted tree could grow into its full potential.

Adam fights at first, his face puckering into an unhappy scowl. The rope digs deeply into his biceps and leaves red welts along his neck. Eventually he gives in, arms sagging, his body drooping to the ground. Like an overpruned bonsai tree, Adam dies.

There's no applause. Two teenage girls chatter into their cell phones. One guy in insect shades and leather pants sits motionless, smoking his umpteenth cigarette. A thick matron gets back on her bicycle and pedals off. It doesn't seem to me like Adam's sacrifice made much of an impression. Then I look again. That was a two-hour performance, and most of them are still here.

"They loved it," I tell him as we're packing up our gear. He nods happily, though I get the feeling that I don't have to lie—that if even one person went home and thought about it for a moment, he would be quite satisfied.

"Adam," I ask suddenly, "do you think most foreigners in Japan are misfits?"

He gives it careful thought, as he does all my questions. "I think a misfit is someone who doesn't belong but still tries to fit in. It's like a square peg in a round hole. If you're a square peg, then you should try to make your own square hole. You should choose what you like most from everything you come into contact with and create a world that fits you best."

As he walks away I realize he's just described himself. Yes, Adam wears a mask. But unlike the rest of ours, his is completely transparent.

207

CHAPTER 17

Gradually Jerry and I reach an uneasy compromise. I take over the top shelf of the refrigerator, where his decaying food won't drip onto my fruit and vegetables. I leave the stove and sink to his dirty dishes and the roaches, and the living room to the stench of his cigarettes. I clean the toilet for both of us but don't set foot inside the filthy shower. Instead, each night I roll up a towel and head off to the public bath.

Many of Osaka's older homes were built before it was considered normal to have a private bath and shower. Everyone just used the corner *sento*—the neighborhood bathhouse—when they got home from work. Despite the advent of indoor plumbing and hot water, the public bath just two blocks from my house is filled to bursting every night.

It looks like a private residence, with a dark blue curtain instead of a front door. For $3.50 you get a tiny locker, an assortment of plastic buckets, and your choice of five different tubs.

The baths are separated by gender, though we can hear the men talking, hawking, spitting, belching, and running the full gamut of animal expressions. The women never make a sound.

The rules are fairly straightforward: Never make eye contact. Never look at anyone's body, no matter how interesting their scars and birthmarks, their tattoos or ingrown nails. Surprisingly, nobody seems the slightest bit embarrassed by their less than perfect figures. The women scoop up their sagging breasts to scrub their ribs. They hardly glance in the wall-to-wall mirrors. They flaunt mastectomies and fallen arches. They seem wonderfully oblivious to the shape of their hips.

I grab a stool and sit under a hip-high showerhead. I scour vigorously—my back, behind my ears, my hair, around each fingernail. A dozen eyes watch surreptitiously to be sure I don't miss the spot between my second and third toe. One must be red and raw and shiny clean before climbing into the *furo*. I scrub, I rub, I rinse. I'm ready.

I put one foot into the medium-hot bath. It's scalding. I know I'm not screaming, but I must have a screaming expression on my face because the woman in the bath across from me smiles sympathetically. Gradually I lower myself in, rubbing each newly submerged area like I just banged it on the coffee table. This is what it must have felt like to be slowly boiled in oil during the Inquisition. I clench my teeth. My hair itches. I try panting, but that agitates the water around my ribs and makes it even more uncomfortable. I hang my head over the edge like a dog out of a car window and stare mournfully at the ground. This will be over soon. I'll pass out and slip under the scalding water and they'll fish me out when I eventually plug up the pipes.

I sit absolutely still, waiting for my body to cool down a

thin, insulating layer of water to keep me from being boiled like a turkey. I watch the clock—the Japanese have rules for everything, and the sign says I'm supposed to stay in for no less than three minutes and no more than five. Has it only been thirty seconds? You're kidding. I can feel my eyeballs pushing out of their sockets.

After four minutes my pulse is up to 135. I clamber out. My limbs are watery. I stagger over to the cold bath and drop in like a stone. Unfortunately, it's the middle of December and the water just came from the place where hell froze over. My lungs convulse and my skin burns like I've tumbled into a patch of stinging nettle. My heart rate drops to 46. I can see mist rising off the water. After three minutes my head throbs with the sound of my own heartbeat and my ears are ringing with the cold. I stagger back to the other bath. This time the hot water hurts even more, and I'm not even in the hottest tub.

But I go back every night, and gradually I am accepted into the evening routine. Women no longer keep a stealthy eye on me to make sure that my underarms are shaved, my hair pinned up, and that I'm properly scoured before lowering myself into the tub. I get better at examining them while pretending to stare at the tiles. One day it dawns on me that I'm not the fattest person in the room. It's been a long time since I've been surrounded by real people who don't look like they just stepped off a fashion runway. I see the occasional sagging buttocks, wilted breasts, thin and twiggy arms. I'm indescribably relieved. For the first time in months, I start to feel a little proud of my body again.

One evening I notice a small tub in the corner that no one seems to use. The sign says DENKI FURO. It looks not unlike any other Japanese hot bath until I examine its surface. It's chattering ominously with little standing waves. *Denki* means "electricity."

I wait until no one is looking. I casually stick one toe into the water. Something shoots up the *inside* of my leg, like a rabies virus working its way into my central nervous system.

This is going to be really unpleasant. Of course, now that I'm in Japan I don't just have discipline, I have face, and that means I can't back out, even if no one is watching. I lower myself into the bath one inch at a time, so carefully that I barely disturb those evil little ripples.

It's one of those times that I'm truly glad I don't have testicles.

And then, an eternity later, it's time to get out. I wait until there's a momentary pause in traffic and no one is in the room. I prepare to leap, screaming, from the tub. I leap. I scream. Nothing happens. My legs are completely and utterly asleep. No pins and needles, just out like a light.

I finally get out by beaching myself on my stomach and using my spindly arms to flop along the ground, like a walrus. I leave a long, slithery trail all the way to the showerheads. The electricity follows me like a bunch of hungry leeches. I prop myself up against a wall and wait for my body to come back to life. Then I put on my clothes and wobble out into the street, looking for all the world like one of those drunken Tokyo businessmen on the train after a sake-night-out with his buddies.

CHAPTER 18

I'm on Teramachi Boulevard in Kyoto—at least I think I am—trying to track down a well-known Japanese paper shop. I've been wandering around the same three blocks for most of an hour, peering at street numbers that seem to bounce around like bingo balls and getting more frustrated with every step.

A group of six businessmen emerge from a nearby subway station and turn in my direction. Four of them are in their late thirties, all wearing carbon-copy suits and identical black shoes. A gray-haired patriarch leads the group, and a youngster—probably along to buy train tickets and keep everyone in cigarettes—brings up the rear. I wait until they're virtually abreast of me and then boldly step out to intercept them.

"Please excuse me for bothering you," I say in my most honorific Japanese. They bunch up like a flock of penguins, smiling nervously. "I'm trying to get to Kamiji Kakimoto," I explain quickly, "and I'm terribly lost." The young fellow's face lights up. He turns and points in the direction they've just come from, his features puckering with concentration as he does the mental gymnastics to get me to the shop. Several others talk among themselves and nod their heads.

Suddenly the patriarch steps forward. Everyone melts out of his way. I know he wasn't listening when I asked my question and that he almost certainly wouldn't know the location of an obscure paper store.

He extends his arm directly over my map. He holds it there a moment, then his finger plummets like a slow-motion bird dropping. It lands somewhere to the east of us by at least ten blocks. The young man glances at the map and pivots like a compass needle until he too is pointing east. His delighted smile is suddenly fixed and constipated. The murmuring among his coworkers gets momentarily louder, then dies away. They all nod in agreement.

I'm hot, I'm tired, I'm wearing a heavy pack, and I'm annoyed that they would knowingly send me off on a wild-goose chase just to please their pompous boss. I nod and smile, say thank you several times, and pretend to study the map while they walk away. I have to wait until they're out of sight so they don't catch me ignoring their advice. Just before they turn the corner, the young man glances back at me. I smile. He ticks his head in bare acknowledgment but doesn't smile back. *He's no different from the rest of them*, I think uncharitably.

Once they're gone I scoop up my pack and head for the nearest train station. I'm fuming silently: Don't they know how it feels to be a stranger in a foreign city, lost and all alone? By time I've covered half a block, I'm feeling profoundly sorry for myself. Suddenly the young man pops back around the corner.

He plasters himself against the wall and frantically scans the street. He must have told them he was going back for cigarettes and secretly retraced his steps. He catches sight of me and his face lights up with obvious relief. He points down the street, the way he did when we first met. I nod. He holds up three fingers. Blocks? I nod. His hand cuts to the left.

I start walking in the right direction. He nods and breaks into an enormous grin. I glance away for just a moment and when I look back at the corner, he's gone.

I get home armed with several new rolls of *washi* paper and immediately set to work making dozens of elaborate cards to thank the people who have agreed to be in my film. With only five months left, I've thrown myself heart and soul into the documentary. Maybe the only way to find what I'm looking for is through the lens of my camera.

But without those six months in Fujisawa, I know I wouldn't stand a chance.

I've learned to control my body language and—most of the time—my mouth. I've even developed a little of the Japanese "belly feel" when confronted with a social dilemma. And I'm just beginning to get a glimpse past the mask Japan wears in public to its more private side. It's almost like an alternate reality—a kind of Japanland—that's right there in front of you, but you can't see it unless you know how to look.

But deep down I know I'll never make it without Morita-san. At least once a week I send her an e-mail at the Kyoto Tourist Information Center. I never know how to begin those messages: "I'm sorry to bother you" or "I promise to make this the last time." I always mean it, and it's never true. She makes call after call, introducing me to Buddhist monks and cattle farmers. She puts herself and her entire organization on the line for my good behavior. She gets me into calligraphy classes and on fire patrols and onto steam trains. But more than anything else, she believes in me.

An e-mail pops up on my screen. She's found me a crab-fishing family in Shimoda. They run a small bed-and-breakfast and would be happy to let me go with them on their next crabbing expedition. I pack my bags.

∞

The Houeis have been hauling crabs up from the depths for at least four generations. Fishing is a part of the family DNA; even those few who don't rise early to brave the icy ocean have become fish-store owners, fish processors, or sushi chefs.

The old man has curly peppered hair. His face is lined and dark from years of too much sun and salty air and diesel fumes. He has thick, bristly eyebrows that are just starting to go gray. He's moody, and he likes to pretend he's hard of hearing so that he doesn't have to participate in the dinner conversation. His sister is calm and quiet and as soothing as a balmy breeze on an airless afternoon. She has no children, and her life revolves around Dom, her beloved yellow Lab. She's taught him how to fetch the paper—"*Shimbun!*"—and to bring her the cordless phone. He never goes after the food set on their knee-high dining room table, no matter how inviting it may seem. His picture is on her nightstand and on the family Web site and on the T-shirts she wears. He sleeps at the bottom of her bed and lays his head in her lap whenever they drive anywhere.

For our first two days a howling gale keeps all of Shimoda's boats tucked safely inside the harbor and their owners at the breakfast table. The meals are huge and satisfying, the kind of

215

belly-fuel that's meant to last through the predawn hours on a rocking boat in the bitter winter wind. Crab legs in a thick brown sauce. Battered fish bones, as crisp and salty as potato chips. Seaweed jam and pickled radishes. Potatoes, boiled greens, and thick fish paste. Fat chunks of sashimi and chewy slabs of home-dried fish. The table downstairs is ringed by a thick comforter and has a heating lamp attached to its underside. We slip our legs beneath the blanket and stay toasty warm despite the freezing air. My room has neither heat nor furnishings. It's a powerful incentive to hang out with everyone downstairs.

The crab season, it turns out, is only three months long, so come spring the Houeis rerig their boat to take tourists deep-sea fishing. They get their customers from among the steady stream of tourists who flock to Shimoda because of the pivotal part it once played in modernizing Japan.

July 8, 1853, was a hot and muggy summer day, just like any other in the timeless Tokugawa era. The fishermen launched their tiny boats, careful not to drift too far from land. The penalty for leaving the country, even by accident, was immediate decapitation. For 250 years Japan had been sealed up like an oyster, determined to defend itself from contamination by the outside world.

Then something appeared on the horizon that would change the course of an entire nation. A puff of black smoke heralded a ship, then two, then four. The temple bells rang and peasants and fishermen fled the "alien ships of fire." That afternoon an American, Commodore Perry, anchored off Shimoda and demanded to speak to the man in charge.

Perry certainly wasn't the first foreigner to set eyes on Japan. Diplomatic missions had been trying to establish communication for decades. Only the Dutch were allowed a tiny trading station near Nagaski, an island barely two hundred yards long and eighty yards wide. It was connected to shore by a single bridge that required special permission to cross. A high wall blocked any view of the mainland. Servants left at sunset, and the gate was locked from dusk to dawn.

But though Japan itself was trying to hold back time, the world around it was changing at a breakneck pace. Steamboats were taking over for the graceful clipper ships that once plied the Asian trading routes. Those early steam engines required huge amounts of coal, and the hunt was on for coaling stations in the Pacific. In 1851 America learned that Japan had abundant natural deposits. Perry, with his square face, double chin, and buttons popping off his chest, arrived shortly thereafter to "request" the opening of trade.

The first exchange of papers happened in complete silence, since speaking to a foreigner was also against the law. The Japanese emissary, Kayama-san, was given gifts of calico, sugar, wine, and books. He wisely drank the wine on his way back to shore. He was later demoted and his remaining booty confiscated and destroyed.

Eventually the Americans were allowed to come on shore. Perry immediately had his men string half a mile of telegraph wire between two buildings. The samurai stood in line for hours to send a message, then raced to the other end, astonished that it had arrived ahead of them. The sailors also built 350 feet of railway track and unloaded a quarter-scale, steam-powered railroad train. The Japanese took turns riding on top of it, their robes flapping in the twenty-mile-an-hour wind.

Although the Japanese were impressed by all the Western gadgetry, the success of Perry's mission was, more than anything, due to lucky timing. He arrived just as Japan was on the brink of famine and social disintegration. The bankrupt shogun no longer had the political authority to control his own citizens, much less defy the Western barbarians.

Within fifteen years, the shogunate was overthrown; feudalism and the entire samurai caste were abolished, and Japan entered the modern age.

The winds of Izu continue unabated, so we spend an afternoon helping a cousin set up his soup stand at a local flower festival. In the evenings we chat, not about the stock market or global economics, but about the old man down the street who pricked his finger on a fish spine and was laid up for a week with the infection. Dom thumps his tail to ask for a piece of fruit and accepts it gently from my hand.

After several days I'm down to my last set of clean clothes, so I do a quick load of laundry in the shower and then scout around for somewhere unobtrusive to hang it up to dry. My room has neither nail nor line. In desperation, I pin a damp pair of socks and some underwear to the inside of my ankle-length skirt and head down to dinner. Once I'm safely tucked under the table-blanket, I discreetly flip the skirt up to let my laundry dry under the heating lamp. When I finally climb the stairs to bed, I hear a burst of laughter from the living room. I look down to see a long white sock trailing behind me like a puffy tail.

After that they take me in like the daughter they never had. Even Dom no longer barks when I come through the door. I secretly hope the weather stays bad.

When it's finally time to go back to Osaka, they won't let me pay for either my room or meals. "You're like family," they say. "Come back as often as you can."

On my way home I spend two days outside of Kofu, filming a local fire festival. As I'm leaving the small pension, it starts to drizzle. The old lady who owns the place calls after me to wait. She ducks back into her kitchen and reemerges with a monstrous purple umbrella. It's made of wood and oiled paper and is sadly scuffed and splintered. She hands it to me. I thank her and hand it back. The umbrella is as heavy as a tire iron. It has a little yellow knob on the top that makes it look like a cross between a giant pimple and a bruise. We stand there and pass it back and forth until I give in, bow profusely, and shuffle off down the road, clutching the center column of my new semi-portable wood-and-paper ceiling.

Two days and several hundred miles later, I can't stand it anymore. The umbrella doesn't fit in my pack or hook over my arm, and since it hasn't rained for a while, it's about as useful as a stick of firewood. I decide to "lose" it. Unfortunately, Japan has only two kinds of public garbage receptacles—one for recycled soda cans and the other for newspapers. I feel funny trying to stuff the umbrella through the little round hole meant for cans and am terrified that someone will catch me frivolously disposing of what is clearly a Valuable Tangible Cultural Asset. So I decide to send it to umbrella heaven—the Lost and Found Department of the Japan railway system—where it can party forever with the hundreds of thousands of other umbrellas that get left on trains every year.

I pick a day when I have to make five connections, two of them on the famous bullet train, which stops at each station for less than a minute.

It takes me one connection to get up my nerve. I'm not

used to publicly littering. Just the thought makes me hunker down and start looking out of the corners of my eyes like a criminal.

Second connection: The train is standing room only. I get up and edge my way to the door. Someone calls out to me. I ignore it. Someone else stops me and gestures over my shoulder. The purple umbrella is making its way toward me, hand over hand. I accept it with profuse apologies, deep appreciation, and even deeper bows, then stand outside the train, waving at a smiling carriage full of good citizens. They wave back.

Third connection: This one is a bullet train, with plush seats and only a scattering of people. I sit down next to an *obasan*—a granny—who compliments me on my umbrella. This is a bad sign. I pray that she either gets off or dozes off. Not a chance—she is alert, awake, and solidly seated. When it comes time for me to go I see her eyeing my stuff and I know it's useless. I reach for my umbrella. She smiles and nods and tells me to take care and good luck.

My next connection is local. I get on. I don't talk to anyone. I don't make eye contact. I quickly stuff the purple umbrella into a rack above me, push it way back, and put something on top of it. When we reach my stop I wait until the last minute, sling on my gear, and scurry out the door. I sprint up the steps and down to the next platform. My train is due in less than three minutes. I half expect the umbrella to magically appear behind me, flying through the air all by itself like Mary Poppins. A minute ticks by. Nothing happens.

I'm free! I feel like doing a little jig. With four less pounds to carry, I may even indulge myself with the luxury of a newspaper at the next station.

I hear a shout, in English. I'm the only Caucasian in the station. I turn; I can't help it. A young man in a schoolboy's uniform is standing on the platform outside my old train, waving my umbrella. I wave back a lot less enthusiastically. Even if I wanted to, I can't go back and get the umbrella or I'll miss my connection. I feel awkward pretending ignorance while this poor fellow is frantically trying to communicate across two crowded platforms, but the problem will resolve itself as soon as my train arrives. Suddenly, he stops signaling and dashes up the stairs. I pray for my train. No good. He's young. He's fast. He's at the top of my platform, taking the steps three at a time. He comes to a panting stop in front of me. He bows. I bow. He offers me my umbrella. I express vast surprise and gushing gratitude. I've already decided to own up to ownership. Someone has clearly seen me with the umbrella and can identify me, and that's how the police in this country solve 95 percent of their crimes.

My train pulls up. He gives me the umbrella. I try to give it back to him as a thank-you gift. He won't accept it. I bow. He bows. I bow. He bows. I miss my train.

Then, as he disappears in desperate bounds up the stairs to his platform, his train pulls away.

When I'm about to get off my last train, I notice that it's raining. I grab my umbrella and tuck it under one arm. What's a couple of pounds anyway?

CHAPTER 19

My Osaka neighborhood is coming into focus in a way
suburban Fujisawa never did. I'm gradually tuning into its
rhythm—or perhaps I've just learned to listen better. The
garbage man comes by twice a week at 6:00 a.m., his loudspeaker broadcasting a peppy, come-get-your-ice-cream tune.
The alley regulars pass a few feet from my window with brief-
cases or bags of groceries, or that one lady with the creaky
stroller and the eternally crying twins. I can hear my left-wall
neighbors answering their cell phones, and I recognize the different rings.

When evening comes, the streets around me fill with
sounds that haven't changed for centuries. The sweet-potato
seller drives by just after dark, his creaky oven whistling like a
lonely owl, calling people to buy his *ishiyaki-imo*—sweet potatoes baked on heated rocks. The Hyoshi-gi volunteer neighborhood fire patrol is a bit less reliable; they often fortify

222

themselves at a local pub before braving the cold. They follow a complicated path through the backstreets and alleyways, calling out "*Hi-no-yoooooooo-jin!*"—"Be careful of fire!"—to remind people to turn their kerosene heaters off at night. I wait to see their flashlights sweep across my bedroom wall before I settle back and close my eyes.

And then there is the noodle man. He comes around at half-past midnight, blaring an ancient noodle-seller's tune through his rusty megaphone. I slip out of bed, throw on a jacket, and prowl the streets until I find out where he's parked tonight. I stand patiently while he cooks the noodles, flipping them expertly in his sieve, then pours them into a bowl of steaming, aromatic broth. He adds a single slice of egg, some pressed fish cakes, and a sprinkling of chives. I dash home, huddle under the blankets, and eat it in the dark. Then I curl up, wrap my arms around my own warm stomach, and drift off into happy dreams.

But Osaka is more than just a spaghetti maze of narrow alleys peppered with corner grocery stores. It's the country's second-largest city, the marketing capital of Japan. Most new merchandise gets tested here—I'm told that Osakans are the world's toughest customers, and if they like a product then it's sure to do well no matter where it sells. There's almost nothing you can't buy along the city's busy streets and endless malls. Osakans aren't the least bit embarrassed by their materialistic reputation. Instead of "Good morning," they often greet each other with "Making any money yet?" Osaka belongs to the businessmen.

Every weekday morning a huge, migrating tide of brief-cased men and women flow out of Osaka's crowded neighborhoods, waterfall down the stairs into the city's subway system, and split seamlessly into long serpent lines waiting to board the trains. I slip in behind them. We all shuffle forward, and when the packed train pulls up, barely squeeze on board. I am instantly locked hip-to-shoulder with a half dozen strangers. I'm still amazed that the Japanese, who so rarely touch each other in public, manage to survive this daily invasion of their personal space.

In such a densely crowded situation, etiquette is everything, and a unique code of behavior has developed to maintain harmony. Nobody ever makes eye contact. Nor do they in any way acknowledge other passengers, not even to say "bless you" when someone sneezes just inches away. They ignore any behavior—like a friendly smile or drunkenness—that could draw them into a conversation. They do nothing to bring attention to themselves. They make space wherever possible, but when contact is unavoidable, they don't take is personally. When they sleep, they do it with decorum—no snoring, drooling, or sliding to the floor.

But mostly, people seem to go into a sort of trance, a Zen and the Art of Commuting by Train. Their faces take on a distant expression, like old folks sitting by themselves at home or nude models posing for a drawing class. They are neither miserable nor rebellious—there's a quiet dignity in their expressions. They've withdrawn into a space inside themselves, a place that's at least a million miles away. Where I waste a lot of energy fighting off the crowds, they hardly seem to notice them at all.

When their stop arrives, some internal clock snaps them back to life. They squeeze out the door like toothpaste and disappear into the gleaming skyscrapers that line Osaka's major boulevards.

When I was still in Fujisawa, I spent long evenings talking to Genji about what went on inside those gleaming skyscrapers. I know about the endless hours, the corporate ranking system, and the way that desks are usually arranged to face each other so that everybody knows what everyone else is doing. But it wasn't until I learned the protocol of business cards that I realized just how dangerously complicated a Japanese businessman's life can be.

The business card offers that single, crucial piece of information: your rank in the social hierarchy. This is a function of the company you work for and your current rung on that corporation's ladder. It determines where you sit at official functions, your place in the elevator, and how you conjugate your verbs when speaking with other businessmen. If you don't have a name card, then in a very fundamental way you don't exist.

Even that first exchange of business cards is fraught with peril. The lower-ranking person must offer first. Being female, foreign, young, and unaffiliated with a major corporation, I'm almost always on the bottom rung. I use both hands when presenting my card—English on one side and Japanese on the other, Japanese-side upward and facing out. I bow long and low. I repeat my name.

I accept the other card with an even lower, longer bow. I study it intently, even if I can't read a single line. I pretend it's abstract art and try to find the hidden picture of a woman in it. I give the ritual greeting, then pull out my custom-made business-card holder and slide it in as carefully as though it were a work of art. I never write on it in public. Defacing someone's business card is an unforgivable sin. This is one of the few lessons that I was lucky enough to learn secondhand.

Not long ago the governor of Nagano met with a top prefectural official for the first time. Upon receiving the governor's business card, the official deliberately folded it in half and stuffed it in his pocket. The event was caught on camera and the footage made the national evening news for three days running. Angry citizens immediately flooded the governor's office with more than eight thousand phone calls, e-mails, and faxes, demanding that the man be fired. The chastened official offered an apology and asked for permission to resign. The governor then announced that he would discuss the situation with the prefecture's Public Corporation Management Chief as well as a host of other bureaucrats. They eventually decided to reject his resignation. A news conference was held and the letter of apology displayed to the public. The folding of the business card was denounced as "thoughtless and unpleasant." The chastised official promised to do his job with supreme dedication, "as though I were newly appointed."

But if I'm going to shoot a documentary, I have to experience at least part of the salaryman's life myself. So I get a good night's sleep, then gather up my cameras and hop on the bullet train. I'm on my way to Shinjuku, a trendy Tokyo district known for its late-night entertainment. Tonight I'm going to film an extraordinary event—the last train leaving Shinjuku station.

❦

Shinjuku is the busiest train station in all Japan; every morning more than a hundred thousand people get disgorged onto its platforms, filter through its underground tunnels like a great termite army, and disappear into the city. Inevitably, some of these millions are still working or drinking or partying at midnight, when they all simultaneously look at their watches and realize that they are about to miss the last train home. For most Tokyo suburb-dwellers, that would put their household slippers and floor-level futon a $200 taxi ride away. What follows is a stampede to the station and a bloody battle to get on the train.

This is good. I could use a little more blood in my film.

Problem is, if I shoot the last train leaving, how am *I* going to get home? I check a map; it's a bit far, but I can walk back to Tokyo Station in a pinch. Or better yet, take a taxi and spend the remainder of the night at the nearby Press Club Library, buried in back issues of the *Atlantic Monthly* and *People* magazines.

I arrive at Shinjuku just before midnight. I run up and down the stairs to every platform until I find one that's jam-packed with people. Standing off to one side is a tall, long-haired Australian who's been in Japan for nine years. He tells me where to wait for the train and offers lurid stories about how terrible it will be. Apparently all the station staff stand outside the carriages and shoulder the seething mass of humanity through the doors. I'm thrilled.

"You know why the trains stop running at 1:00 a.m., don't you?" he asks. I don't. "The taxi lobby is incredibly powerful in Tokyo. The government should run one train per hour through the night, like they do in New York City, but the Taxi Association gives the politicians so much money that they voted to shut the stations down."

A train approaches. People crush forward. The Australian is actively fighting, like a sperm trying to swim upstream, while I am allowing myself to be passively jostled in classic Brownian motion. He gets in and I am shunted aside. Darwinism works.

I hang out through several more trains, waiting for the Big

Moment. I notice that on the next track over, there is still one train bound for Tokyo Station. I even go over to investigate it. I have some good footage. . . . Should I just hop on and not worry about a taxi? No, I have to know what that Last Train is like. It should be spectacular.

More people trickle into the station. I'm watching the clock, urging those desperate hordes to hurry. The last train pulls in. It's virtually empty. Everyone boards in a leisurely fashion. There's plenty of room. The doors close. It pulls away. I'm alone.

Like the great buffalo herds of yesteryear, they never came.

I leave the station. I find a taxi stand just outside the door. There are over a hundred people waiting in line and not a single taxi. The guy at the very front is holding a bunch of flowers. I go to the back. Two drunken businessmen fall in line behind me. It's freezing out, and I've only got a thin jacket in my bulging pack. The moment I stop moving my sweat immediately turns into Tiger Balm. I'm bored and exhausted. I'd give two healthy molars for a trashy paperback.

An hour later—1:30 a.m.—I look to the front of the line and see the same bunch of flowers. Our steady forward motion has been nothing but compression. Everyone is either too drunk or too tired or just plain resigned to the wait. I decide to walk.

Once I've left the taxi stand I pull out my map. My, that's a long way. Looks to be eight or ten miles. I remember that Roberto is usually in a restaurant in nearby Harajuku on Friday nights listening to Brazilian music. Restaurants are warm. He told me to call him if I wanted to come by.

I call. I get his cell-phone message machine. I am in a quandary. Should I walk to the restaurant? It's not on the way to Tokyo Station. And Roberto's a super guy, but he's not exactly . . . reliable. He doesn't reliably have toilet paper in his bathroom, for example. He could be anywhere by now, or the restaurant could be closed and impervious to knocking. I decide to head for Tokyo Station. I'll flag down a taxi when I get tired.

Everyone knows that taxi drivers don't like *gaijins*. I've heard bitter diatribes from the Tokyo party crowd on the subject. Until this moment I've never felt much sympathy. What are these people doing out in the city after one in the morning, anyway? Isn't six hours in an expensive, crowded, smoky bar enough for one night? Secretly, I've even sided with the taxi drivers. Gaijins rarely speak Japanese, usually can't give directions to where they want to go, and have notoriously short tempers. If I were a Japanese taxi driver, I'd probably avoid them too.

But then, I never expected to be out on the streets of Tokyo at two in the morning trying to flag down one of the unfriendly beasts. I hike about a mile down the road until I start seeing empty taxis with their VACANT lights on. I wave. They speed by, their faces as cold and impassive as samurai warriors. I walk to the next stoplight and waylay them there. One pulls up. I tap on his window. No response. His hands have the steering wheel in a death grip. As soon as the light changes, he nearly blows me over as he accelerates away.

Green-yellow-red light. I manage to get the next guy's attention. Infinitely slowly he reaches down to pull the back-door opener. The door opens. Hooray! While I'm scooting around the back to get in, the light changes. The door slams shut and he takes off.

The next wave of traffic has three empty taxis in it. They see me signaling and their VACANT signs blink off like Christmas lights, then blink on again as soon as they're past the intersection. Merry Christmas.

I give up, hike about half a mile back up the road, and find a hotel lobby. Would they, I ask, be willing to call for a taxi? I'd be happy to pay for the favor.

"Absolutely not," the receptionist—another samurai—says. "We offer that service only for our guests."

"If a guest were standing in your lobby then they wouldn't need a taxi home," I point out, but I know it's futile. Back out into the cold.

By now it's three thirty. I'm beyond exhausted. My feet ache from the weight of my pack. *Death to all taxi drivers*, I think. *I'm walking*.

I follow the silent train tracks across the city, skirting the stations. By now Tokyo is virtually deserted but for the homeless, emerging like shadowy wraiths to begin their nightly scavenger hunt for aluminum cans. The restaurants have long since closed, so I keep an eye out for a vending machine. They're on almost every corner and sell everything from cigarettes to cameras, phone cards, and popular CDs. They also occasionally do cold soda, hot coffee, beer, hard liquor, and, depending on the part of town, men's magazines and used women's underwear.

I eventually find one whose blinking sign advertises hot corn soup. As I'm popping the top off the can, I hear a sound behind me. A homeless woman sits cross-legged on a piece of cardboard, sound asleep. She's bent over forward, her head nearly touching the concrete. I sit down beside her and drink my soup, unexpectedly comforted by the way her head bobs in time with her rumbling snores. My body wicks up the cold from the concrete until I'm shivering uncontrollably. I climb stiffly to my feet, feeling a great deal more respect for homeless people and cardboard insulation, and even less for taxi drivers. I leave 120 yen—the price of a can of soup—beside her bags.

An hour later I stumble across a capsule hotel. I know they usually don't take women, but I go inside to ask, just in case. To my surprise the clerk nods his head, accepts my $40, hands me a locker key, and directs me to the third floor. The place has everything a stranded salaryman could need after a hard night's drinking or playing pachinko. A corner of the lobby sells instant noodles, beer, sake, and cigarettes. Clean white shirts and ties are available, as well as an assortment of toiletries. A large television plays baseball games, and the basement offers an entire floor of comic books. When he's finally ready to call it a night, a creaky elevator hauls him up to a cubbyhole bed.

Each floor is actually an endless hallway with cubicles stacked on top of one another like a giant beehive or, perhaps more accurately, a morgue. They are exactly one meter high, a meter wide, and two meters long. A flimsy, roll-down screen offers the pretense of privacy. There's no lock, but then again, you don't really need one. It's not like anyone else is going to fit in there beside you.

There's a built-in light and radio. There's also a television hanging from one corner, but for that you have to buy a special card at eight bucks an hour. I flick off the lights and am asleep before my head touches the pillow.

The first train out of Tokyo Station leaves promptly at six. Two dozen people are already waiting for it in an assortment of wrinkled eveningwear. One woman wears a long, slinky dress and sparkling high heels. Everyone stares vacantly into the distance with guttered eyes and sallow skin.

Four hours later I stagger off in Osaka and hike past the taxi stand. Business is slow. I catch the eye of one driver. I nod. He opens the back door. I march right past. Boy, that felt good.

231

CHAPTER 20

I'm jogging in Osaka Park, in the shadow of its famous castle, when a man on a park bench asks me for a light. I don't have one, but he catches my eye and motions to the seat beside him. He seems harmless and my run is almost over, so I sit.

He's in his mid-forties, obviously a businessman, and a successful one at that. His suit is tailored to perfection and has that subtle, expensive sheen. He must have noticed my appraisal because he starts speaking as though we were old friends.

"It was almost four years ago," he says. "They came into our office and just made an announcement. We were all so ashamed that we couldn't even raise our heads and look each other in the eye." He pauses. "They said it wasn't our fault . . . the recession . . . a bad year in exports. . . . But still . . ."

He's somehow lit a cigarette. I've been staring at the castle rather than looking at his face. I don't have to be a Catholic to recognize an open-air confessional.

"I lost my savings, then the house. After that I sent my wife and kids home to her parents. We all said it was temporary. I went to see them a few times, but it was too painful and embarrassing all around. Now I just don't bother anymore and everyone is relieved. It was the same thing with my friends. It made it worse that I still looked like them—I suppose it was a reminder that it could happen to them as well.

"One day I walked out my door with nothing more than a briefcase and my best clothes, as though I was just going off to work. I never went home again."

He's rubbing a spot on the inside lining of his suit, and I can see that the material has started to fray. "I've learned to sew," he murmurs, almost as an afterthought. He flips his jacket up just long enough for me to see the stitches, tiny and impossibly straight, where he fixed a tear in the lining. "I take it off at night so that I don't wrinkle it in my sleep." He laughs low and without humor. "One night I almost froze to death. It was my first January, and it got so cold. Every third month I save up to have it dry-cleaned, and I have to hide for a night and a day. In between I hang it over a steaming subway grate."

He used English when he first spoke to me, but since then he's switched to Japanese. Sometimes I understand his words, sometimes not, but always from his expression, I know what he's saying.

"Occasionally I buy a cheap ticket and ride back and forth on the train. I can do this because I look just like a businessman. But it has to be during rush hour, when it's the most crowded and uncomfortable. I always stand. Sometimes I catch a young lady's eye." He smiles. "Life isn't so bad."

When he walks among the people at the station, nobody notices him. That minor gesture—or lack thereof—makes him feel a part of things. And he reacts like any good citizen when he sees a dirty man in wrinkled clothes sleeping on the ground. "I will never be like that."

He's smoked his cigarette to the nub. It's an expensive habit—most homeless look for discarded, half-finished fags—but he won't pick them off the street.

"I still drink too much," he says sadly. "A bad habit I brought with me. When I drink I remember the bars we used to go to after work—the camaraderie, the mama-sans, the swirling smoke, and lots of noise and warmth. It was always warm in there. I never noticed it at the time, but looking back . . ."

He can't get another job, despite his clothes. He's not trained for anything else. Stores won't take him because they want young women and he's overqualified. In some ways the suit is as much a deterrent as if he wore old rags. And he has expenses—a haircut once a week. The barber doesn't know his situation, even after all these years. He never asks for a discount and always pays in cash.

The cigarettes are a prop, of course. So am I—a onetime actor on his stage, there for a single scene. The play: that he is a successful businessman taking a lunchtime stroll in the sun. Only he never gets up to go back to work. But the suit—that's more than just a prop. It's his dignity, his face.

He's rubbing the same spot over and over with his thumb. It frays more each time.

"One day," he says, still rubbing, "it will be destroyed. And then everything will be over."

∽

That night I dream about the ghostlike scavengers that flit through the city's gutters and back alleys when everyone else is safely tucked in bed. Osaka, it turns out, isn't just the marketing capital of Japan; it also has the country's largest homeless population. Most of them migrated to the city to work as day laborers during the 1980s construction boom. Once the first recession hit, the housing market tumbled, and the few jobs that were left went to those who were young and fit. The homeless are mostly male and over forty—unemployable in this rigid society. Virtually all have cut off contact with their families because they are ashamed of what they've become. They sleep on sidewalks and under bridges, and in the mornings they carefully fold their futons and brush off their immaculate tatami mats. Most make a living recycling garbage, earning about $10 a day for eight hours of hard labor. I often see them in the shopping malls, pulling carts filled with cardboard boxes, scruffy dogs walking slowly at their heels; or in Osaka Park, where they've stretched blue tarps between the trees, anchored them with car batteries, and swept the dirt around their "houses" meticulously clean. They've been completely marginalized by Japanese society. Like the untouchables in feudal times, they are not counted in the national census. To the average Japanese, they simply don't exist— and they reciprocate in kind. Unfortunately, that makes them almost impossible to meet.

At last, in desperation, I visit Morita-san.

"You want to get to know a homeless trash collector?" She's generally unflappable, but this really sets her back. "I don't know," she says warily, and then immediately comes up with a plan. She calls a local police chief, who tells her about a non-profit organization that makes lunch for the homeless once a week. She wheedles an introduction out of him and the next thing I know, I'm climbing aboard the subway on a rainy Tuesday morning, heading for Kamagasaki Park to feed a thousand men.

The organizers are already hard at work, hauling in buckets of vegetables and quail eggs that were donated by local markets well after their expiration dates. They light up half a dozen scrap-wood fires, lay down huge metal cauldrons, and start pouring in the ingredients. They scrape up every shred of carrot and carefully wash a quail egg that someone found lying on the ground. They know what it feels like to be hungry— they're all homeless themselves.

Tattered men start gathering in the corners of the park. A line, almost three blocks long, forms of its own accord. A few umbrellas pop up here and there, but most of the men just stand patiently and get drenched. When they finally get their mochi ball, they dip it in both sauces, then walk quickly to the side. They find a place among the filthy planks and savor it in tiny, birdlike bites. Food is precious here, not because it's eye candy, but because it fills the stomach. When they're finished they go immediately to the back of the line and wait for lunch.

The meal itself is a generous serving of rice smothered in a vegetable-and-quail-egg stew. I watch the quiet, hopeless faces file by as I hand out bowl after bowl. Most thank me. Some even bow. We run out when there are less than fifty people left in line. They disperse without complaint, despite having waited several hours in the rain. When everyone has finished eating, they stand in yet another line to wash their bowls and chopsticks and carefully stack them back in their original plastic containers. A few stick around to help us tidy up, including a man who introduces himself as Nishida-san.

He's sixty-four years old, born in 1937. He finished two

years of high school before dropping out to work. He got a job in a famous factory, making the cores of dynamite for industrial coal-mine production. He was a union activist—a "rebel"—and at twenty-three helped organize a strike. When it fell through, he knew he was in trouble, so he quit and migrated to Osaka. For two years he worked as a winch operator, moving American scrap along the docks. He got promoted and spent the next fifteen years working with refrigeration lines. "That was my best time—money every day, good friends, plenty of sake, a clean bed, and a dry place to sleep." He shakes his head and smiles at the memory. "Sake and song. Best time of my life."

And then the bubble burst. He was already over forty and didn't stand a chance against the younger, stronger men. Because his work site was controlled by the *yakuza*, he had neither retirement package nor pension. He still can't get unemployment because he doesn't have a home address. Instead he lives on the street and gets up at five to sort through other people's garbage, looking for aluminum cans.

I ask if I can join him. He says yes without hesitation.

On my way home I stop by the Information Center to thank Morita-san and tell her about Nishida and his invitation to go out and gather cans. She offers to find a student interpreter to accompany me—she's worried about my safety on the streets so early in the morning. I'm touched by her concern.

I agree to meet Asao at the subway station and put him up for the night. He turns out to be a thirty-two-year-old student with blackened teeth and what looks like a four-pack-a-day cigarette habit. On our way home we take a shortcut through a covered mall. He stops abruptly outside a liquor store.

"You have alcohol?" he asks.

I think about it. "A little beer, perhaps."

"How many?"

"One."

"Big?"

"Small."

He goes inside. He grabs a bottle of sake. I offer to pay for it. He grabs a second bottle, then a six-pack of beer. "To help me sleep," he says.

I make him comfortable in the living room, ask him not to smoke inside, then sit and keep him company for a while. He opens the windows, turns on the television, and cranks the heat on high.

He's an activist—a self-proclaimed Marxist—though his one real goal in life is to make a lot of money. I ask him what he's active in and he says something about student demonstrations, then quickly changes the subject. He wants to create a 1960s American-style student revolution as long as it doesn't get him into any trouble.

"But now," he says, "I am studying acupuncture at night." He'll have to work for two years once he gets his license, and then he plans to go to Nicaragua and join the Zapatistas. He wants to speak many languages and have an office where his children can run around while he is curing grateful people. He's looking for a wife who is loving and independent and will continue to work after they're married and have kids. That way they'll have at least one income, no matter what happens.

"Who will take care of the children?" I ask.

"She will," he says impatiently. "That's why I need a loving person." He also wants her to be active—he points at my figure—"just like you."

By sad coincidence, he broke up with his current girlfriend less than a week ago.

I can't help myself. "What happened?"

"I could not have sex with her," he says.

I change the subject.

He was living in her house as a "nonpaying guest." Now he has to move into a dorm room with six other people and cough up $230 a month. He's not at all happy about the situation.

I go downstairs and make him dinner, then sit and watch him slurp it down. I've never seen anyone eat so noisily. I couldn't smack my lips like that if my life depended on it. He slurps his beer and pats his stomach, then lights a cigarette. I leave him to watch TV and drink himself to sleep.

∞

We meet Nishida-san in the predawn darkness at the designated subway station. He's already checked his tattered schedule to see which neighborhood is recycling this morning. His bicycle has a small stuffed panda bear tied to the handlebar. A dirty yellow fishing cooler filled with his clothes and daily needs is lashed to the back, and an umbrella and bike pump tied securely to the frame. He also has a locker at the train station, but at $4 a pop he doesn't open it very often. He wears white gloves against the cold and a tattered, cement-grey jacket with fake fur around the hood. He looks like he just showered, except for a rim of pus around his eyes. He's itching to get started.

We struggle to keep up with him as he rides around the neighborhood. He knows exactly when each household puts out its trash and where. He roars past the houses that don't bother to recycle. He pedals furiously, then pulls up without warning to kick a bag of trash. He tells me he can hear if there are aluminum cans inside. Then he leans over and squeezes the bag, feeling for the crinkly softness of aluminum. If there are more than one or two, he gets off his bike, opens a bag, pulls out the cans, carefully reties the bag, puts everything back where he found it, and continues on. I'm surprised to see how few soda cans he finds. The Japanese clearly prefer tea—green or barley—or even a sports drink with the unappetizing name of Pocari Sweat over Coca-Cola, Pepsi, or their ilk.

We circle the same neighborhood again and again, following his complicated mental map of when each household puts out their garbage. He knows a surprising amount about the residents from their trash—which ones have parties, who drinks a lot, what else they throw out and recycle. He also knows who walks the dog before breakfast and which couple just had a fight, and who has children that are smoking or sneaking out at night. He's the first to notice a new car, and he can tell you which train that salaryman is hurrying to catch. Homeless people may be invisible, but they're anything but blind.

But then, neither are we. He stops twice when he thinks we're not looking and grabs a glass of sake out of a vending machine. He tosses it back in two quick gulps. A fifth of his daily income, down the hatch. It's not even breakfast time.

By nine thirty his bicycle is so weighed down that he can no longer ride. Black and yellow bags hang off either side of the cooler and from the handlebars. Finally, he slows down enough to talk.

He has one sister and a brother back in Kyushu. His brother is a carpenter, but he's six years older and probably retired by now. His sister married a salaryman. He hasn't seen them for close to twenty years. Nishida himself never married and has no kids.

"If you found a woman that you loved, would you marry her?" I ask.

He shakes his head. "I don't have the means to support her, and my work is not stable enough." He looks at me. "We are very alike in the marriage market," he says without a hint of malice. "No chance for either of us."

"If you had kids, what advice would you give them about life?"

He answers immediately and with confidence. "Have pride in your work. Be an upright person."

I decide to challenge him. "If you found ten million yen, what would you do with it?"

"I'd take it to the police," he says promptly, "and collect the 20 percent finder's fee."

"Okay, say you won the lottery."

He's momentarily stumped. It's not something he thinks about very often. Perhaps rent a proper apartment for a month or two, he muses, or go to a hot-bath resort for a few days and give his arthritic joints a rest.

He seems quite content with where he is in life. He could probably make a few more yen if he collected cardboard in the afternoons, but he'd rather rest. There is nothing more—except perhaps sake—that he really wants.

We reach the recycle center. He quickly weighs his morning's haul and stares mournfully at the scales.

When Nishida finally gets paid—about $8.50—he insists on taking us to his favorite afternoon hangout. I expect it to be a bar, but to my surprise we pull up at the public library. He heads straight to the magazine rack, grabs a well-thumbed copy of *Science Monthly*, and settles into an easy chair. It's warm, it's quiet, and he has the entire afternoon to enjoy himself.

241

I can't help but think about the tide of desperate salarymen dashing for the train at 7:00 a.m. and staggering home at midnight. Nishida doesn't have nearly their material possessions, but he has another priceless luxury. He has time—to think, to sleep, to read.

∞

I get an e-mail from Asao later that same afternoon. I answer it. Shortly after midnight, the phone rings. He's drunk.

"I have nothing to say to you but I call anyway. I miss you. I want you."

I don't want Asao at all. I want to go to bed. We both got up at four in the morning. He tells me that he misses me, again and again. In between he drinks, loudly.

"I want to see you again, not just for sex but as a friend."

"Gee, thanks." This is my only suitor in most of a year. No wonder Genji went white when I teased him about finding me a husband.

"I want to go out to dinner with you."

I demur, pleading my filming schedule. He complains that I don't have time for him. "You are not interested in an activist like me. . . . "

Bingo.

"I am drunk."

Right again.

I disengage with difficulty. He calls again an hour later, three times at two, then twice at two thirty. I finally tell him I'd rather date Nishida-san, take the phone off the hook, and go to bed.

CHAPTER 21

Morita-san has come through for me again. I'd heard rumors of a village, somewhere on the remote and rugged Ise Peninsula, with an unusual way of celebrating New Year's Eve. Apparently the entire population gathers on the rocky shore and, on the stroke of midnight, slips naked into the ocean. It's a Shinto purification ritual that cleanses both body and spirit for the coming year. Morita-san tracks it down to Ijika, then manages to find a guesthouse that agrees to take me in on the thirty-first of December and even invites me to join them for their New Year's dinner.

On the most ordinary day, Japanese meals are the stuff of legends, but nothing compares to the culinary extravaganza assembled every New Year's Eve. And since Ijika is a fishing village, I'm not surprised that seafood rules the menu, from appetizers to ice cream.

But more than anything, the food is fresh—so fresh that

nothing, it seems, has had more than a passing acquaintance with either the oven or the cooking pot. The rice is covered in a thin layer of raw sea urchin roe, orange and creamy and tasting like something you'd scrape off the bottom of a bucket that's been sitting in the low-tide zone. Oysters with the consistency of boiled tissue paper and a coppery aftertaste, like sucking on a penny. Thin slabs of raw fish layered with lemon, so tender that it melts like butter and has absolutely no smell. Snails whose owners have been evicted, eviscerated, doused in vinegar, and then stuffed back into their shells. Sea slugs, dried and smoked, soaking up a salty seaweed-bonito sauce. Salmon eggs that pop like bubble wrap and smell of stagnant seawater. And raw squid, sliced and left to ferment in their own innards until they taste like the inside of a carburetor and have the consistency of an inner tube. It all goes down the hatch under the eagle eye of the proprietress, who doesn't smile until I've sucked my last crab leg clean of its tender threads of flesh.

I emerge from my guesthouse just in time to see a long line of young men disappear down one of Ijika's steep cement stairs. They are on their annual New Year's trick or treat—going from house to house, where they stand around the entryway and raise their voices in a kind of fraternity chant: *"Yashoi, yashoi, whhoooooooeeeeiiiiiii!"* For this they receive oranges, sake, dried fish, and rice. When their labors are over, they retire to the headman's house and drink themselves silly, apparently in preparation for the icy swim.

I follow for a while, chant a bit, and earn some oranges.

"What time," I ask casually, "do you-all plan to go swimming?"

They tug each other's sleeves and have a quick group think.

"Seven in the morning," one says. "Six," another adds. "Eleven tonight." "Midnight." They smile at me and march off to visit the next house on the list.

At ten thirty I dash down to the ocean, my cameras flapping at my side. Ijika's tiny stretch of beach is completely surrounded by a four-story cement beachhead with a single set of stairs that angles steeply down to the sand. The wind is howling and the waves are tall and sharp as razor blades.

I find a place among the rocks and close my eyes, relishing the icy sting against my face. After two months in Osaka—the smog, the crowds, the blinking neon lights—my body craves the emptiness, the raw and unfettered beauty of nature left to its own devices. I take a deep breath of ocean air. The sea slugs in my stomach catch a whiff of home and abruptly come to life.

Ten forty-five. There is a riot going on inside my intestinal tract. That overly fresh dinner is clawing its way out. The slugs are dragging bags of sea urchin eggs like Santa Claus, and the oysters are slithering around in search of their shells. Even the squid is squirting up the aftertaste of six-week-old fermented ink.

Eleven thirty. I'm completely alone. The village above me is eerily silent—not a soul on the paths, no music, not even the momentary gleam of flashlights. Perhaps the purification rites are no more than a rumor after all.

Midnight. I'm disappointed. I've been working myself up to this for days. Knowing that a spectator with a camera might be frowned upon, I'd planned to take the dip myself, my bathing suit carefully concealed under a modest towel. Just slinking home and climbing into my warm futon seems like a cowardly way to end the night.

But wait a minute: I'm here. The ocean's here. Why not?

I store my gear beside the stairs. Off comes the Woolrich jacket, the down vest, flannel shirt, and long underwear. Since I'm alone, I don't bother with a bathing suit. I pick my way through the jagged boulders to the water's edge. I'm not one for graduated pain, so I dive in and take several quick strokes straight out into the ocean. Instant, icy splinters shoot up into my sinuses and it's suddenly quite difficult to breathe. The waves are steep and unpredictable. It's glorious and terrifying. Ten more feet, I think, and then I'll head back and—

"Yashoi, yashoi, yashoi . . ."

I turn. A long string of lights is making its way down the steep steps of the sea wall. It's the fraternity chanters, sodden with sake and finally ready for their midnight dip.

The beach is only ten feet wide. My clothes and camera are hidden behind some rocks above the high-tide line, right at the foot of the steps. I'm trapped. And mortified. What on earth am I going to do? I make a snap decision to at least level the playing field—I'll wait until they get naked too.

This turns out not to be such a good idea. I'm far more motivated to get out than they are to get in. They take their time, turning the sandy shoreline into an open-air locker room, snapping each other with their towels, passing around bottles of toe-warming sake, and anxiously scanning the black waters for hidden dangers. I, in the meantime, am losing all feeling in my arms and legs. I suddenly remember an article about some trees in Glacier National Park during a recent cold snap. Their cells all froze and eventually exploded.

Finally, I can't stand it anymore. If I get any colder they'll have to help me out of the water. "Good evening, gentlemen," I say in my most honorific Japanese.

246

Everyone freezes—a herd of humans caught in the head-lights. They're searching the black waters for real now.

"Who's there?" a brave soul asks, loudly.

The only thing I can come up with is "Candid Camera." Fortunately, I don't know the Japanese word for *candid* and my dictionary is lying next to my towel. None of those sample dialogues in my assorted grammar books have prepared me for this kind of encounter. More important, I've come to Ijika—to Japan itself—to make a documentary. It's time to choose. My camera or my towel?

"Could you pass me my towel?" I ask with pretend non-chalance. It's my first great failure as a filmmaker.

The Japanese may not be used to dealing with unfamiliar situations, but courtesy is bred into their DNA. At last, here is something they can act upon. Towels instantly snap free of a dozen waists. They hold them out to me like bullfighting capes, eyes modestly averted. Enveloped in a wind-whipped wall of terry cloth, I make my way to my stash of clothes. While I'm dressing, a disembodied hand reaches through the towels, offering me a bottle of sake and a cup.

Once I'm properly attired, they see no reason not to go ahead with their spirit-cleansing swim. Bodies hit the water. I pick up my camera, but given their chivalrous behavior, I just can't bring myself to point it in their direction.

I say my farewells. Unfortunately, Ijika is built on a steep mountainside and my guesthouse is at the very top, 434 steps away. As I climb the steps I feel my body stiffening like a piece of roadkill after the sun goes down.

There is a certain etiquette to the Japanese hot bath. Clothing must be folded and put in a wicker basket in the bathroom foyer. A thorough scrubbing at the midget showerheads.

Hair properly pinned up, fingernails scraped. I manage to kick off my shoes and unshoulder my cameras before toppling, like an oak tree, into the tub. Luckily, it's after midnight and everyone has long since gone to bed.

CHAPTER 22

From Ijika I head down to the southern tip of Kii Peninsula, to join a hard-core group of winter ascetics undergoing *Kangyo*, midwinter purification. One by one, they visit the forty-eight waterfalls along the sacred trail to Kumano and stand for hours under each stinging blast. I only make it to number seventeen. My feet get so numb that I keep stubbing my toes on underwater rocks and not realizing it until I see my own bloody footprints in the snow. Every time I force myself under those icy showers I get an instant, throbbing headache that feels like a needle straight to my brain. I don't learn a thing about enlightenment, except that it's someplace comfortable and warm.

Now I'm back in Osaka, huddled under four thin blankets, staring at the far wall. It's moving back and forth—*breathing*— as the subzero wind whistles down the alleyway, curls around the corner, and runs smack into the front door. I'm clutching a mug of lukewarm tea and dreaming about Indonesia, or

Samoa—somewhere where there's more to buy at the local market than pickled vegetables and ice is something that you put into your drink.

There's one place I really *don't* want to go—a famous winter Kabuki performance in Kuromori, five hundred miles to the north. Morita-san recommended it for my documentary. Unfortunately, Kuromori is near Sakata City, on the back side of Japan, a place so cold that the endangered swans that winter there have been known to kill each other. I'm not sure I can handle another week of that kind of weather.

Ironically, Sakata should have a relatively mild and temperate climate—but for a geological technicality. Every winter, Siberia shrugs off waves of cold, dry air that howl across the Sea of Japan, crash into warm currents flowing northward, absorb huge amounts of moisture, run smack into the Japanese Alps, and drop it all as snow—up to thirty feet of it. No performance could possibly be worth sitting in that kind of cold all day, and the play is seven hours long.

That's it. I'm staying home.

And then Adam tells me a story that changes everything.

"Six years ago I fell in love for the first time in my life." He's digging into a bowl of slippery udon noodles with his chopsticks, but he's got a wistful smile and his mind is far away. "He was a perfect-looking, perfect-acting, intelligent, funny, sexy, charming, interesting, dreamy Japanese guy. Unfortunately, he was already taken—he was dating another foreigner who was on vacation in Australia at the time. He told me he didn't love his boyfriend anymore and things were basically over. He came to my room—back then it wasn't nearly so full of junk. We stayed there for a whole week, ordering food in and sleeping during the day and going out at night for long walks around Hirakata neighborhood. It was this exact week, six years ago. After a few days he confessed that he planned to get back together with his boyfriend at the end of the week and that this was nothing more than a fling. I know it sounds like a silly storybook cliché, but the moment he told me, I felt as if my heart broke. Not sank, but broke—I felt it seize up and break into a thousand pieces. I ended up taking a taxi alone to the hospital, to see if the doctor could try to fix my heart. I rode home later that morning, and I cried and I decided I would take any time I could get with him. It was a wonderful and horrible week—mostly horrible, because we knew that it would end.

"On our last day, a Saturday, I was scheduled to go to the Kabuki theater with another friend. Teary-eyed, I walked the guy back to the station and said goodbye, knowing I would never see him again. He was the only person I'd ever fallen in love with and I was absolutely, 100 percent certain that it would never happen again. He walked through the ticket gates and caught his train. Three minutes later—probably the longest three minutes of my life—my friend, who had no idea that I was gay, showed up and we went off to Kabuki. Of course I put on a mask, as I always do, and smiled my fake smile, but inside my head the last week was playing over and over, burning itself into my brain. Everything was a blur. I just wanted to forget—how could I?—the love of my life.

"We had great seats at the theater, fourth from the front, next to the winged stage—perfect seats. This was my first time watching Super Kabuki, which is basically a modern, jazzed-up version of a traditional play. The story was about Kaguya Hime, the Moon Princess, who doesn't know what love is, so she gets sent to earth and falls in love with a handsome prince. In the end she finds out that she must leave him and go back to the moon

251

and lose all of her memories of him, or stay and have the earth and the person that she loves destroyed. Imagine this story, done in the most elaborate costumes, with people flying out over the audience on wires and the kind of searing colors that you only see when you're delirious. It was like being launched into the sun or being able to visualize a higher dimension." He pauses. "I didn't think about *him* once during the entire four-hour play."

That's it. I'm going.

☙

I head home to pack and discover that Jerry has thrown a belated New Year's Eve party. The living room and kitchen are awash in half-eaten food and spilled glasses of wine. Even my pillowcase smells of stale cigarettes. A scribbled note on the dry-erase board informs me that he won't be back for several days. I gather up my gear, open up the windows to keep the food from rotting, and let myself out the door.

I spend the next sixteen hours in a smoke-soaked bus, then overnight in Sakata City. The gentle drift of dry, white flakes tells me that it's considerably less than freezing out. Two teenage girls wait patiently at a streetlight, their bare white legs protruding from the short skirts of their school uniforms. Several stalwart citizens are braving the slippery sidewalk on bicycles. I'm impressed and a little scared. This place seems completely impervious to the cold.

Kuromori is a hamlet of just four hundred families. Its principal claim to fame is its *natto*—fermented soybean—factory. The village is far too small to have its own theater, so each year, when it comes time for the performance, they rebuild the local Shinto shrine.

By eight in the morning the place is already buzzing with people, most of them well over fifty. The women are bundled up in headscarves, their thick glasses fogging over as they haul lumber to reconstruct the walkway that juts out over the audience. The men are arguing about the order in which the beams should be raised. Several bent figures gamely hack at the snow with shovels, trying to dig down deep enough to find solid ground.

They seem a little overwhelmed. The organizer—the only man in a suit and tie—is completely unconcerned. "They'll figure it out eventually," he says.

"Are you in the play?" I ask.

"Oh, no!" he laughs. "Only locals are allowed to act. I didn't move to Kuromori until I was four. I was born ten miles south of here." He is, however, responsible for choosing the play and signing on enough actors to fill almost thirty roles. That can't be easy, given the temperature and time of year.

He laughs again. "They mostly do it for the sake after the rehearsals."

I suspect it takes more than a bottle of grog to convince a man to memorize several hours' worth of dialogue in a language that he barely understands. But the real challenge has to be finding three teenage boys to play the roles of sensuous young women, complete with heavy makeup, flowery kimonos, and purple paper umbrellas. Only men are allowed to perform in traditional Kabuki, even though it was a woman who started the art form.

Back in 1603, a Shinto priestess by the name of Izumo no Okuni performed a deliberately provocative dance in Kyoto, driving her audience into a wild frenzy. Other entertainers soon followed her lead, adding comic sketches and erotic scenes to the already edgy repertoire. The more enterprising among them took advantage of all those excited customers to practice the world's oldest profession. In 1629 the Tokugawa shogunate reacted by banning all women from the Kabuki stage. The female roles were immediately taken over by young men, who developed them to such a degree of style and perfection that even the geisha started going to the actors for advice on fashion and etiquette. Soon Kabuki troupes were touring the countryside, and homegrown performances sprang up in poor, entertainment-starved rural villages. In a few places, like Kuromori, it took root and flourished.

The play opens in just forty-eight hours. The entire village is turning itself inside out. Two old women sit in the corner, reams of fabric spread around them like giant petticoats. They lean back and stretch out their arms to thread their needles, then gather up an armful of material and begin the first of ten thousand perfect stitches.

Since nobody wants to grow their hair into a samurai ponytail or shave a bald spot in the middle of their head, several boxes of wigs have to be prepared. Two hairdressers are hard at work, scraping mouse droppings out of a dozen scraggly hairpieces and massaging in yet another dose of hair oil. A long line of women are pulling big sheets of Styrofoam out of the storage shed. They are for the audience, who will be sitting on the snow.

I wander over to a wall of photographs. In one shot the entire troop looks like it's performing in front of a snow-covered cemetery. I look again. Those lumps are spectators, curled up like Eskimo dogs in a driving blizzard. The real samurai, it seems, are in the audience.

That evening I go back to my musty hotel room and start reading medieval plays. The floor is tattered with cigarette burns, but I barely notice. Chikamatsu, the Shakespeare of Japan, makes another world comes alive against the backdrop of bare walls and peeling paint.

There's the story of brave Masaoka, the wet nurse who sacrifices her own child to save Tsuruchiyo, the son of her lord and master. The play opens just as Tsuruchiyo's father is forced to retire due to years of dissipation, passing on the title to his young son. This puts the boy in considerable danger, so Masaoka keeps him in the women's quarters on the pretext that he is ill.

Masaoka has carefully trained her own son to taste the child-lord Tsuruchiyo's food in case it has been poisoned. She also cooks for them, tediously preparing the rice with her tea-ceremony utensils, so the boys often don't get enough to eat and are always hungry.

The bad guys have by now eliminated everyone but young Tsuruchiyo. They send an accomplice, the wife of a high-ranking retainer, with a gift of poisoned cakes. Masaoka's son dashes out, as he has been trained to do, and eats one of the cakes. He immediately falls to the floor and writhes about in agony. The evil woman pulls out a knife and stabs him to death to cover up her foul deed. Despite watching her son get murdered in front of her own eyes, Masaoka shows no emotion. Her calmness fools the plotters into believing that she must have exchanged the clothing of the two young boys and that it is really Tsuruchiyo who was killed. They therefore assume that Masaoka is on their side and give her a secret scroll with the names of all of the conspirators.

Once Masaoka is alone, she gives vent to her grief. The evil woman is secretly watching. She dashes out and attacks Masaoka, who stabs her to death without hesitation.

255

At that moment, a giant rat appears and runs off with the scroll. A man eventually reappears with the scroll in his mouth and exits as though walking on clouds.

Okay, so the ending needs a bit of work, but at least it's not as grim as *The Double Suicide at Sonezaki*. Ohatsu is a courtesan of the most famous teahouse in Kyoto. She is secretly in love with Tokubei, a clerk at a nearby soy shop. Tokubei hasn't come by in several weeks, and Ohatsu is heartbroken but trying to put on a brave face.

Tokubei finally appears but has bad news. His uncle is so pleased with his hard work that he has arranged for Tokubei to marry a young heiress. Tokubei wants to refuse the offer, but his greedy stepmother has already accepted the dowry from his fiancée's parents.

Tokubei manages to get the dowry back from his stepmother. On the way home he runs into an old friend who is in dire need of money. Tokubei agrees to a loan on the condition that it will be repaid within three days. His friend takes the money and promptly disappears. Eventually Tokubei's uncle has to pay the dowry back on his behalf, and Tokubei is told to leave Kyoto and never come back.

At this moment Tokubei's shiftless friend shows up. He denies all knowledge of the loan and declares the promissory note he signed a forgery. Tokubei attacks him in frustration and a fight breaks out.

Later, the dishonest friend shows up at Ohatsu's teahouse and tries to buy Ohatsu with the very same money he stole from Tokubei, her lover.

In the dark of night, Ohatsu creeps out of her room, clutching a razor and dressed from head to toe in white. She meets Tokubei outside, and they head off to commit suicide together. After they are gone, Tokubei's uncle learns what really happened. Tokubei and Ohatsu, unaware that they have been exonerated, take their last journey through the forest of Sonezaki, where he stabs her to death and then kills himself.

Though the plots may seem outlandish, these plays were in fact the closest thing the average eighteenth-century citizen had to CNN. Playwrights often took the latest local scandal, changed the names and dates, and had a performance ready within a few days. Like Shakespeare, Chikamatsu wrote about the things that concerned the common people—dressed up with the occasional severed head, lost sword, or wife sold into prostitution, along with lots of sake and *seppuku*. Mostly, his characters were obsessed with the torturous demands of loyalties and obligations versus their emotions and personal desires. The good guys didn't necessarily possess moral virtues, but they had to be loyal to their masters. Heroes rarely made it through the last scene alive, though they were usually vindicated posthumously. Women in particular—or the men who played them—seemed to get the short end of the stick with depressing regularity: the wife who sold herself into a house of prostitution in order to repay her husband's debt or fund his latest vendetta; the girlfriend who agreed to marry some nasty old man so that her lover could retrieve a sword that had been in his family for generations. Their heroism lay in their complete obedience to Confucian values—and their utter submission to the men in their lives.

By 3:00 a.m. I'm thoroughly marinated in feudal values. Of course Masaoka had to sacrifice her son. It was the only thing to do. Tomorrow morning I'll come to my senses, but tonight it seems perfectly clear.

Opening day: The shrine is packed to bursting; it looks like half of Kuromori is busy fitting themselves into costumes and wigs. I wonder if there's anybody left over to man the audience.

The kids are in a back room, putting on their face and body paint. Several mothers are firmly tying bows around their children's waists. Others are slathering a thick coat of pink paint onto thin arms and legs. After that come coal-black lips and dabs around the eyes.

Up against the wall, the old woman who's been sewing for the last two days is finally asleep, her head against her chest and her hands folded serenely in her lap. A needle is still lodged between her second and third finger.

One of the lead actors is smoking a cigarette on the second floor, his head already wrapped in a tight rubber skullcap and his face covered in blue-white paint. This will be his twentieth year on the Kuromori stage. He too started out as a reluctant thirteen-year-old, but he's come a long way since then.

He takes the cigarette out of his mouth. "For one day I get to be like the great Danshiro!" His eyes glow, and for just a moment he's no longer in a tiny, snowbound village but on the elaborate stage of the Kabukiza in downtown Tokyo.

"I'm a merchant by profession. Where else could I ever get to perform these works of art on a real stage in front of a live audience?"

He has a point. In most of Japan's Kabuki theaters, the actors undergo a long and exacting apprenticeship. So long, in fact, that most start their training in early childhood, almost before they learn to walk. Several famous Kabuki families go back seventeen generations. Ancestral styles are handed down from father to son, just like the secrets of sword-making or pottery.

The lead child actor is this man's oldest son. Perhaps he too is starting his own Kabuki family dynasty.

"No, nothing like that." He smiles and his eyes slide away in embarrassment. "I'm just a salesman." But he can't help sneaking a glance at his son, who is getting dressed while studying the last of his lines. His grin turns into a proud parental smile.

I hurry out to get a good spot on the Styrofoam. The audience is filling up. They seem to be mostly older folk and the very young. They take off their shoes, carefully lay out bottles of sake and thermoses of green tea, and settle in for a long, cold day.

I try to remember Adam's admonitions. "Expect exaggerated gestures, flamboyant costumes, glaring makeup, and artificially high-pitched voices. Don't worry if you don't understand a word they say—neither does anybody else in the audience. Learn the plot in advance, but assume they're just going to play their favorite scenes. Wear something warm." He smiles. "And my favorite part—they call it *mie*—is that moment when the actor strikes an exaggerated, expressive pose, crosses his eyes, and holds it for several seconds. I think it's what my mother meant when she used to say, 'If you keep making that strange face, it's going to freeze that way.'"

He looks me in the eye to be sure he has my full attention. "But most important, Kabuki plots move rather slowly, and they don't have to make sense."

The curtain abruptly pulls aside.

A woman rejects her suitor, who flies into a rage and kills her. Young Yasunosuke—our hero—vows revenge. He kills the suitor, then flees town. That's the end of Act 1—three hours long.

My fingertips are glued to my camera. I tear them off, leaving behind several patches of skin. My palms are frostbite white. The play starts up again and I check my notes. It looks like they've skipped Act 2.

Act 3: Our grown-up hero, Yasunosuke, now a drunkard, hears that his friend is in trouble. He rushes off, Kabuki-style, to help, but arrives too late. In a carefully choreographed rage, he kills nineteen bad guys. That ends the show. It's been snowing steadily since noon.

Tomorrow they'll pull down the walkway and stack the numbered posts back in the shed. The sweaty wigs will land willy-nilly in a wooden box along with half a dozen oily hair-brushes. The sheets of Styrofoam will migrate back to the attic and the wooden swords into a barrel barely big enough to hold them all.

For two days each year, Kuromori gathers tight around the shrine like a giant drawstring. It transforms a tiny village into something greater than a cluster of houses and a soybean factory. It's a chance to break free of the daily rules and regulations—to slip on a samurai wig, strap on a glittering sword, and swagger up and down the stage. To become larger than life— like Renzan, the *taiko* master—but without the years of grueling training. To make bold gestures and freeze into dramatic poses. To kill nineteen villains in just under two exquisitely choreographed minutes. To escape the gray and predictable world of the present for a romantic age of swords and honor, sacrifice and grand heroics. That's worth a few evenings of study and a couple of afternoons standing in the cold.

And perhaps one day, a little boy will dream of being a famous Kabuki actor, just like his dad.

CHAPTER 23

There's one traditional Japanese community that
I've been trying to wiggle my way into since the first day I arrived: the geisha. They're so secretive that even Genji couldn't
wheedle me an invitation, even though he once traveled all the
way to Kyoto on my behalf to meet with the owner of a geisha
house. He came back very impressed.

"She asked a lot of questions and knew how to get information without saying very much about herself," he told me
with a rueful shake of his head. "I didn't even realize it was
happening until the meeting was already over!" She was
clearly a strong and confident woman, used to dealing with
high-ranking and successful Japanese businessmen. Gracious
but not easily intimidated. Somebody I'd like very much to
meet.

"What would you say if Junko decided to become a
geisha?" I asked. Classical geisha dance and music are highly

valued in Japanese society, definite assets to any well-bred upper-class girl when it comes time to get married.

"No!" Genji replied, with unexpected force. But when I asked him why, he didn't really have an answer. Most Japanese parents think that becoming a geisha is a great idea—for someone else's child. In part this is because the geisha, by tradition, do not marry. It's a momentous decision for a girl of twenty to enter into a career that will deny her this crucial step into Japanese adulthood—as wife and, one day, mother.

But there's even more to it than that. The geisha personify the type of femininity that is often absent in the role of wife. A wife would never socialize with her husband's colleagues, and if she did she would have no idea what to do or say. The geisha excels at clever repartee. Where a wife is modest, the geisha is risqué. The wife is occupied with home and children; the geisha is independent and answers to no one. The geisha lives, quite literally, outside the rules of modern Japanese society. She neither cooks nor cleans, and she can even raise her children as a single mother without social condemnation.

The geisha community is one of the few places in Japan where women are not the weaker sex. They have clients and sometimes even boyfriends, but deep down, the geisha do not need men. It's Japan's more powerful sisterhood. In other words, the geisha scare men silly. It's precisely what makes them so intriguing.

Her name is Koubai-san. She's sixty-three. She lives about an hour out of Osaka, not far from Kobe City. She has a receding chin and friendly, open face. She looks more like an elderly neighbor than a member of the mysterious Willow World—the geisha profession. I don't think I would have given her a second glance if I saw her in a convenience store.

I stutter through an introduction and bow as low as I can go. I'm terrified that I'll do something wrong, and she'll disappear in a swirl of her kimono and a puff of incense. But Koubai-san is open and down-to-earth. I like her immediately.

"It's a good life," she says. "You have a lot of free time, and you get to meet people from all over Japan. Even if I entertain the prime minister, I speak to him in just the same way I do all my other clients."

But it's only part-time work, and it doesn't come with either guarantees or benefits. If you don't live in Kyoto, where the geisha get generous subsidies from the government, it can be hard to make ends meet.

"Yes, a geisha earns a lot of money, but we also have many expenses." Koubai-san owns seventy kimonos worth up to $15,000 each. "They must be cleaned by *araihai*, a process that is very costly." She cannot keep them all in her tiny apartment, so she has to rent a special fireproof warehouse to store them, as well as a studio to dress in each night.

She sits straight-backed yet completely relaxed. There is an almost monk-like stillness about her; she doesn't wave her hands about, giggle, or play with her hair. I realize how long it's been since I heard a woman discussing her own retirement plans. I feel more comfortable with Koubai-san than almost anyone I've met since coming to Japan.

"I was raised in China by Japanese parents. I came over when I was fourteen," she says. I do the numbers in my head. That must have been just after the war—a time of great hardship and starvation. She glosses over the next few years. "I was married at twenty-four, but my husband died of illness a year later." After that she was too busy working as a geisha to find another man.

"Would you marry now?"

She thinks about that for a moment. "I would have a boyfriend, yes. A husband, no."

She has no children. "I became a geisha because I loved to sing and dance, ever since I was three or four." She knew early on that she would never be beautiful, but that just made her practice harder on her *shamisen*. "Beautiful geisha get clients easily," she says, "but those who are skilled earn their lifelong loyalty.

"The word *geisha*," she continues, "means 'artist.' A true geisha strives to become a living work of art. The way she walks and sits and speaks—she must polish her character until it shines. She creates a dream world, a world of fantasy. She is the embodiment of *iki*." She looks sharply at me to make sure I understand.

Iki. It is neither the bland modesty of a housewife nor the infantile mannerisms of a teenage girl. Iki is sophisticated but not jaded. It is innocent but not naive. It is naturally elegant, never forced or contrived. It has subtle undertones of sensuality but never flaunts itself. True iki is daring and unconventional. And it implies sincerity—not the tumbling emotions of infatuation nor the bitterness of the world-weary. A geisha is extremely protective of her clients and can be trusted never to reveal a confidence.

I nod to a picture on the wall, of a geisha's delicate foot clad in a perfectly white sock and sandal, stepping into the snow—elegant, subtly erotic, yet steeped in steely strength and quiet discipline. Women who are iki have experienced hardships but would never mention them. Iki is powerful and independent, yet gracious and refined. Young girls are hardly ever iki. Few women, even geisha, acquire it before middle age.

No wonder Genji was intimidated.

On the way back to the train station, I ask my student guide if she would ever become a geisha. She vigorously shakes her head. "Only women who have trouble with their family or husbands would choose that kind of occupation," she says.

She's a junior in college. She's studying English but hasn't yet decided on a profession. She wants to get married but has never had a boyfriend. She doesn't understand a lot but always nods her head.

"What do you think of Koubai-san and her profession?"

She shrugs. "They have nothing to do with Japan today. They are," she searches for the word, "irrelevant."

∽

Three weeks later I am invited to an evening with the geisha and their clients in old Kyoto. They even offer to lend me a kimono with all the proper accessories. I can't believe my luck. Kyoto's geisha cater to an extremely selective clientele, those few who wish to spend a few hours inside the mysterious Willow World—and can afford the $5,000 to $10,000 bill.

But if you want to hire a geisha, it's not enough just to show up with cash in hand; you need a personal recommendation from the owner of one of the city's most prestigious tea houses. And after all that expense and effort, you don't—as some foreigners might expect—get sex, or even a fancy meal. The geisha are not waitresses, and they're definitely not prostitutes. They are, quite simply, the world's most exquisite hostesses, and among Japan's corporate executives the most exclusive status symbol.

It takes me almost an hour to find the teahouse; it's the kind of place that makes a conscious effort not to advertise itself.

Inside, traditional sandals are lined up at the bottom of the steps. Alcoves filled with priceless pottery and miniature gardens appear at artistic intervals down the silent, highly polished halls.

A geisha and two *maiko*—her apprentices—are in the back room, waiting for their evening's guests. I introduce myself, then do my best to become invisible. Eventually their clients, four portly businessmen, arrive and are ushered into a traditional tatami room.

The evening passes quickly, with quips and repartee, a maiko dance, and several quavering songs. Sake and laughter flow freely. The older geisha is clearly in control, though you'd never know it from the way she treats the men. She makes them feel like they rule the universe, indulging them like their mothers did when they were five years old, yet never letting things get out of hand. They respond unknowingly to her tone of voice like well-trained border collies. She is gentle and talkative with the shy subordinate, friendly and familiar with his senior, and casually witty with the two who are trying to prove that they can hold their own with her in conversation. The two maiko, who don't have nearly her verbal skills, play the role of young and flirtatious innocents. When the conversation lags, the geisha quickly proposes a party game—picking up slippery stones with chopsticks—then signals to one of the maiko to let the shiest businessman win. It's clear that while the men are flattered by the attention of the sexy young apprentices, it's the geisha that they are trying to impress.

When the evening is finally over, the three women kneel briefly by the door and excuse themselves with expressions of deep regret. They leave their clients in a happy sake haze, quite certain that they can leap tall buildings at a single bound, and considerably lighter in the wallet.

The women glide, whisper silent, down the long and polished hallway, turn two corners, and slip into a room with a bar and a stereo system in one corner. I follow to say thank you and good night, but they motion me inside. One of the maiko pulls out a bottle of Jack Daniels and the geisha lights up a cigarette. They are joined by the teahouse owner and a second geisha who has just finished entertaining two other clients. She peels off her wig in one smooth motion, drops it on the counter, and shakes out her hair with obvious relief. The older geisha chat together and blow smoke at the ceiling. They settle into the Western furniture and laugh and talk about the evening's clientele. Apparently one of the businessmen looked remarkably like his favorite sumo wrestler. They hang out with the kind of ease that comes with years of friendship and a lifestyle that other people neither share nor understand.

∞

I slink along the backstreets of old Kyoto until I find the place I'm looking for: a maiko makeover salon. For an outrageous amount of money they will turn any tourist into a pretender to the Willow World for one brief afternoon.

I slip out of my street clothes and climb into what looks like a dentist's chair. I close my eyes. The woman blots my face with baby oil, then quickly smears a layer of white paint from my hairline to just above my breasts. It feels like one of those clay cleansing masks, but at least the bags under my eyes are spackled over. I crack an eyelid and glance at the mirror. I look completely bloodless, like I've just been sucked dry by a thirsty vampire.

"Don't twitch," she says. She adds a tint of cherry-blossom pink. Much better—I've gone from corpse to porcelain cherub.

She outlines each eye with heavy black mascara, then adds a dab of cherry red to the outside edges. She moves over to my eyebrows, frowns, and bites her lip. I cringe. She smears on some more pancake white and they obligingly disappear. She draws them in again in black and red.

I close my eyes and remind myself how much worse it used to be. In Edo times, the geisha shaved off their eyebrows entirely and drew them back in higher on their heads. They grew their hair as long as possible—a girl was considered particularly beautiful if her locks trailed several feet behind her, like a bridal veil. The geisha whitened their skin with nightingale droppings and a powder called *oshiroi*. This gave them, and any children they might be breast-feeding, lead poisoning.

"Don't smile," the woman says. No amount of toothpaste will make my teeth look anything but yellow next to that artificially white skin. Of course, back then it didn't matter, since coal-black teeth were the height of fashion. The geisha accomplished this by marinating rusty iron in a jar of hot vinegar for several days. They then dipped a brush into the dark brown fluid, rolled it in powdered gallnut, and applied it vigorously to their teeth.

"Don't lick," she says. She's carefully repainting my lips at about half their normal width. I look like I've just eaten a lemon peel.

The hair is next. True maiko have to endure three-hour sessions at the hairdresser and sleep on tiny, bricklike pillows to keep their carefully sculpted coif in place. I've opted for a partial wig. They brush out my hair and dye it black, then rub in a thick white wax and twist and pull and curl it firmly into tubes and waves. They then dab glue all around the edges of my face and slip on what feels like an extra-heavy motorcycle helmet. It's pulling at the skin around my eyes and forehead, making me look like I've had one too many face-lifts. I lean over forward to take the pressure off my neck.

"Sit straight." The wig is built on an aluminum mesh and it's already starting to chafe.

She covers up the glue with another coat of paint, then directs me to a room that's packed wall-to-wall with kimonos. A maiko, I am told, is supposed to be bright and colorful, and to cultivate an air both flirtatious and innocent. I practice my look of virginal sensuality.

"Don't grimace," she says. She puts me in head-to-toe royal purple. I stand, arms outstretched, while she dresses me like a scarecrow. My sleeves fall to my ankles and the belt goes from just below my breasts to just above my hips.

"Breathe out." I do. She pulls it tight.

"More." There isn't any more. She digs two knuckles into my ribs. I grunt and she gets another inch. I feel like a horse that's just been saddled. A few adjustments, and I'm free to go. I look in the mirror. A stranger stares back at me. I've got huge hair festooned with pins and flowers, like a Christmas tree with too many decorations. My body is wrapped up like a mummy ready for burial. I don't feel the slightest bit iki. I feel like a giant Christmas present.

They push me out the door, telling me to enjoy Gion and come back in forty-five minutes. I clump off down the street in my heavy wooden clogs. The obi belt is squeezing my intestines up into my rib cage, and a fake spray of wisteria keeps slapping me across the nose. I have to take tiny steps or risk falling flat on my face. My cheek itches but I can't scratch it without digging a hole in my makeup. The wig is slowly abrading my skull in three different places. I'm dying for a drink of water from a corner Shinto shrine, but I have no idea how to bend over.

I stop for a moment to get my bearings. *Think like a geisha.* I straighten up. The obi loosens slightly and I can breathe again. *Hold your head still.* The glittery stuff in my hair stops jingling like Santa's sled. *Hands up.* I tuck my arms into their sleeves and I'm no longer tripping on the trailing ends. *Glide.* I take a few tiny, shuffling steps and my body stops jerking like a car that's firing on too few cylinders.

Several Japanese are walking in my direction, staring at my costume and chattering among themselves. Their volume suddenly trebles when they recognize my Western nose. I should be embarrassed, but I'm not. The elaborate costume is like a suit of armor—I feel completely impervious to their laughter and prying eyes. It's like putting on a whole new personality.

I make it around the block and back to the studio with sleeves intact and a terrific wig-induced headache. I can't decide which feels better—when they peel off the kimono or the hair. I take one last look at that strange white face and then wash it down the drain. I come out with enormous new respect for the geisha profession and the sacrifices they make. A geisha is never allowed to forget, not for a moment, who she is and what she represents.

∽

A week later, over coffee, I shamefacedly confess my visit to the maiko-salon to Koubai-san. She laughs and laughs, then quizzes me in detail about the colors of my kimono and the kind of pins I wore in my hair. "The kimono," she explains, "is different from Western clothes. Westerners are always trying to stand out—they want to be on the cutting edge of style." A kimono is meant to harmonize with one's environment, depending on the time of day; the woman's occupation, age, and status; and the season and event. "Purple," she shakes her head, "was wrong on almost every count." I hang my head.

"Don't worry," she says, and puts a sympathetic hand on my arm. And then, unexpectedly, she invites me to her home.

Her place is tiny. It's on the third floor of a crowded apartment complex, across from the elevator. The kitchen, living room, and study are all one room, with a small bedroom tucked into the corner. Every nook and cranny is crammed with odds and ends. She has three telephones and a fax machine, but not a single photograph of family or friends. There's a new computer in a tiny alcove under a bunk bed, but she hasn't learned how to use it yet.

"Who sleeps up there?" I ask.

"No one. My mother, when she was alive."

Koubai doesn't cook very often. There doesn't seem much point, and the kitchen is so small. She eats mostly out of the convenience store on the corner.

It seems like a lonely place. But the geisha are such a powerful community—a sisterhood. Every maiko has a geisha "mother" and "older sister" to teach her how to tie her kimono, introduce her to all the teahouse owners, and generally show her the ropes. Those bonds are for life. They even go through a mock wedding ceremony.

"I was never a maiko," Koubai says.

What happened almost fifty years ago, back in 1952? Why did she come home from China, and what sort of world did she find when she arrived? How did she become a geisha, all on her own, when she was still a teenager? I don't dare ask. It would not be iki. That much, at least, I've learned.

271

CHAPTER 24

A sharp, unpleasant clanging slices like a razor blade through the soft and enveloping cloud of sleep. Jerry making popcorn again? I pull the pillow over my head but it continues, metal on metal, jarring me out of friendly dreams and into the real world of dark and bitter cold. I'm in a monastery, and it's four thirty in the morning—time to get up and chant. A dozen slippered feet are already shuffling along the polished wooden floorboards past my sliding paper door.

We nod in discreet greeting and file into a double room hung with dim orange lanterns and dozens of Buddhist ornaments. The monks kneel with the swish of robes and creaking bones, pull tiny sutra books from inside their sleeves, and take a deep breath of the achingly cold air.

The sound that fills the room is deep and resonant, so rich and full that it couldn't possibly be coming from just fifteen sets of lungs. It rises and falls, swirls and eddies, wafts around the room like incense from the central altar.

Koyasan is the monastic headquarters of Shingon Buddhism. Its 120 temples are set in a remote valley, surrounded by eight mountain peaks that symbolize the petals of the lotus flower. It was built by the Buddhist Saint Kobo Daishi, probably the most famous man in Japanese history. He was both a saint and scholar, the inventor of the Japanese kana alphabet, calligrapher, engineer, literary giant, artist, educator, and social worker. And, when he was young, a terrible disappointment to his parents.

Kobo Daishi was born in 774 on the island of Shikoku. Already as a child he showed great promise and was expected to do well in his studies and one day establish the family name at the Emperor's court. But Kobo, from a very early age, had his own agenda. As legend has it, when he was seven he climbed to the top of a mountain near his house. Once he reached the summit he announced, "If there is value to my life then I will be saved," and threw himself off. A celestial being appeared and caught him in her arms. He pledged at that moment to give his life to Buddha and save everyone on earth. Then he went home and wisely decided not to tell his parents what he'd done.

Eventually he graduated and dutifully went on to study at the National University in Nara. Those years, he later wrote, were filled with pain and suffering. He had no desire to become a court official and felt a great emptiness in his life. One day he met a monk who told him that if he chanted a certain mantra one million times, he would acquire such a splendid memory that he would never forget anything again. Kobo packed up his books and left college for a life of ascetic practice. His parents were appalled.

For the next seven years Kobo wandered around Shikoku Island, studying scripture and begging for his meals. His family tried to talk him out of it and finally gave him up for dead. Then, in 804, he was selected to sail to China as a student monk. The ship barely survived a raging storm and eventually limped into a small port a thousand kilometers south of its intended destination. The Chinese governor assumed they were all pirates and refused to allow them to land. The ship's captain, at wit's end, asked Kobo to write a letter on their behalf. Somewhere along his wanderings, Kobo had learned to speak and write Chinese, and had developed a profound knowledge of the country's culture and literature. Kobo's letter was elegant and persuasive, his calligraphy superb. The ship was permitted to sail on.

Six months after leaving Japan, they finally arrived at the capital. It would be another half a year before the Seventh Patriarch of Esoteric Buddhism granted Kobo an audience. When he was finally admitted to the temple, the master said joyfully, "I knew you would come. I have waited a long time." Within three months Kobo had learned all he could and was anointed as a Buddhist master in his own right. He caught the next ship home. He landed on the southern island of Kyushu and languished there for several years, waiting for permission to return to Kyoto. Eventually the old Emperor died, a new one ascended, and Kobo's fortunes abruptly improved. He was given the land around Mt. Koya to build a monastery for his new brand of Buddhism—Shingon. Thirty years later, at the age of sixty-two, he entered eternal mediation. He has promised to return in 5,670 million years. In the meantime, he'll be watching from the heavens.

The monks flip the pages of their sutra texts in the dim candlelight. Their breath condenses in the icy morning air and mingles with the floating incense. Not much has changed since Kobo Daishi walked these halls.

Koyasan is more than just a training center for Shingon Buddhist monks. It's the starting point of Japan's most famous pilgrimage—a seven-hundred-mile trek to eighty-eight sacred Buddhist temples that ring Shikoku Island. It follows in the footsteps of the young Kobo Daishi as he wandered in search of enlightenment. Most pilgrims visit Koyasan just long enough to pay homage to Kobo Daishi's tomb. I've asked to join a temple and learn the basics of Buddhism before attempting the long and arduous journey myself.

Seven hundred miles—it's a moving meditation, a walking Zen. Beauty and austerity in equal measure. They say that if you act with single-minded discipline, then your head and heart will eventually follow your legs.

In two months I'll be going home. I don't feel much closer to finding that elusive sense of inner peace than when I first arrived. This pilgrimage is my last hope. In the next eight weeks it somehow all has to come together, or else I'll climb on board the plane empty-handed.

∞

If discipline is what I'm looking for, Koyasan is a great place to start. Life in the monastery is simple and austere, meant to rid the monks of their desire for worldly pleasures and possessions. All meals are vegetarian—clear miso soup for breakfast and a heaping bowl of rice. A small plate of pickles makes the rounds, but few take more than a single, tiny slice. The monks pick out every grain of rice and then pour green tea into the empty bowls. They use the pickles as scrub brushes, drink the liquid, and eat the brushes. They tidy up their places and chant a thankful sutra, then disperse to their daily assigned chores. Several young acolytes gather up the bowls and rush them to the kitchen to be washed.

I offer to help with the daily chores and am immediately assigned to the cleaning crew. We wipe down every inch of the burnished hallways while the water gradually freezes in our buckets and our hands stiffen with cold. When we're finished, the acolytes scurry off to a nonstop schedule of assemblies and sutra lessons that won't finish until well after dark. The head priest invites me to join him, with a smile and a wave of his hand.

His name is Koichi-san. His father was once in charge of this temple, and it has since passed into his hands. Koyasan has always been his home—the simple robes and slippers, the maple trees that blush bright red beside the entrance gate. He has two sons, one of whom will inherit the position in his turn. Koichi-san laughs often and easily—usually at himself. He sits and talks to me with perfect equanimity while one of the acolytes shaves his head. His young apprentices jump to do his do his every bidding, but I never see him angry or hear him raise his voice. He reminds me in many ways of Genji, though Koichi-san lives by a simpler set of rules.

There is a buoyancy about him, a contentment that doesn't just show up from time to time but seems to permeate his life like ginger in a piece of gingerbread. He takes things seriously, but somehow doesn't seem to be affected by them.

"How," I ask him one morning after a particularly ugly awakening, "can you accept that clanging bell with such equanimity?"

"When you realize that the world is an illusion, then sleep no longer has a hold on you," he says.

"But if the world is just an illusion, then why not stay in bed?"

He laughs. "Because there are things that must get done." And with that he puts on his scarf and steps out into the cold.

That night I watch him rake the sand garden. His movements are slow and deliberate, and the arcs that emerge from his ministrations are perfect and evenly spaced. He works with complete attention to his task, his entire body following each stroke. He does it with such satisfaction that it seems more like a privilege than a chore. I don't think the secret is in the sutras that he chants or in the hand gestures that he has learned, or even in the delicate and complicated mandalas that adorn his temple walls. I think the key to Shingon Buddhism is somewhere inside of Kouchi-san.

And yet . . . Koichi-san's attitude doesn't jibe with the central precept of Buddhism: that all life is suffering.

He chuckles. "Suffering is caused by our desire to hang on to things, by clinging to worldly attachments. Like youth or money or"—he runs one hand ruefully over his scalp—"hair. Especially in winter."

"So be flexible?"

"And have a sense of humor. That always helps."

"Koichi-san," I take a breath, "do you know the meaning of life?"

He doesn't hesitate. "The first and most important task in life," he tells me gravely, "is to keep the temple clean."

As the days go by, I get to know the acolytes. I like these young men for their shy smiles and the way they look out for each other if one of them is late. I like the way they scrub the floor with their entire beings. They are every parent's dream—well brought up, polite, obedient—but they seem somehow too serious for their youthful faces. Even the youngest, nine years old, doesn't show a hint of rebellion at the rigid and grueling lifestyle. The spirit of the stubborn young Kobo Daishi, who followed his own path no matter what the cost, seems almost to have disappeared under the weight of rules and etiquette.

Then late one night, as I'm lying on my futon, I hear a scurrying sound. It's the quick shuffle of monastic feet. I throw on a robe and follow. I chase a dim flash of saffron through endless corridors, up stairs, and around corners, to the very back of the monastery. There's an unearthly neon glow coming from one wall. I watch a monk feed coins into a soda machine and retrieve a diet cola. Kobo Daishi can rest easy after all.

A week later I take a wrong turn from the kitchen and walk right past the acolyte's quarters. They are anything but austere—in fact, they look like miniature versions of a college dorm. One entire wall is dedicated to CDs and a bulky stereo. The bunk beds obviously don't get straightened very often. A set of hand weights litters the floor, and there's a *television* in one corner. A fourteen-year-old monk is playing a sumo video game. All those hours of monkish concentration are finally paying off—he blows through level after level. His roommate prods him to finish so that they can watch their favorite baseball team.

At last it's time to leave this exquisite place, peopled with orange-robed monks and set amid the pine trees and cedars of the sacred mountain. It's a perfect sanctuary, where nature, spirituality, and compassion are woven together in a warm and soothing mantle that wraps around the soul. I'll be sad to go.

As I'm putting on my shoes, Koichi's mother comes out to

bid me farewell. She gives me a bright red apple that's been sitting on the altar for several days. It smells strongly of the temple's incense. At this time of year fresh fruit is an unheard-of luxury. I store it carefully in my backpack, between several soft layers of clothes. Whenever I want to remember Mt. Koya, I will take it out and breathe in the smell of incense and peaceful contemplation.

∞

Shikoku Island is a rustic appendage stuck onto the belly of Japan. I stand on the deck of a ferry cutting through the icy blue waters and watch its towering peaks gradually draw nearer. A thin belt of coastline clings to the mountains, punctuated by the occasional fishing port. I imagine endless stretches of empty beach, the white sand squeaking beneath my bare feet . . . twilit bamboo forests, mossy and striated, their tops knocking hollowly in the wind like ghostly bones . . . tiny, forgotten temples surrounded by enormous cedar trees . . . I can't wait to get started.

I disembark at the bustling port of Muya and hike along the busy road to temple number one. It's lined wall-to-wall with pilgrim-supply shops. I pick one and duck inside.

I don't have to be a Buddhist to walk the pilgrimage, but I do need to look the part. I must wear white—the color of death—from head to toe because on this journey I will be re-born. This dress also doubles as a burial shroud, should I expire along the way and impolitely leave my body in the hands of some village official. There were several versions of pilgrim-suit conveniently on sale, all in the you-have-to be-kidding price range. The deluxe models can be stamped by the temples along the route, for an additional fee of $250.

"Is it washable?" I ask, fingering the flimsy cotton cloth and hurried stitching with some concern.

"Oh, yes!" The clerk informs me enthusiastically, then adds in a low voice, "Though the temple ink has a tendency to bleed."

"So I keep it clean by . . . ?"

"Not getting it dirty."

Not my strong suit. I buy the plain white version. If it falls apart, I can always wear my judo *gi*.

I hang a small brass bell from my backpack, where it rings piercingly with every step I take. It's meant to scare away demons, though it also attracts stray dogs. Most important, I must carry a wooden staff that represents Kobo Daishi. The phrase "We two—traveling together" is written down one side. When no one's looking I drill a small hole in the top so that I can use it as a camera monopod.

A half dozen semi-optional accessories complete the pilgrim's plumage: A small wooden box that holds a fistful of paper strips with the pilgrim's name and address, which you give out whenever you meet another pilgrim or receive a gift from a shopkeeper. (This also helps identify your body if you expire along the trail.) An official pilgrim pouch to hold candles, incense, and money, and a narrow purple scarf that seems purely cosmetic. Finally, a rosary, a straw hat, and a pair of rice-straw sandals that disintegrate after the first ten miles.

I opt for the hat and sandalwood rosary, which will keep me dry and smelling good, and forgo the treacherous box and other trimmings. My bill comes out to $185. This pilgrimage is clearly not for the faint of wallet.

But at least I now look the part. In Japan, that's even more important than knowing where you're going.

Which I don't. I get lost three times on my way to the first temple. I'm using an old walking pilgrim's text from a friend who jogged the entire route. She got it from her neighbor, who got it from the parents of some friends. It's in Japanese, of course, and apparently there's been a good deal of construction since it was written. I finally arrive at temple number one well after lunch and run smack into a radio crew. They've come out to do a story on this year's crop of bright-eyed pilgrims. Unfortunately, they're about two months early. Most pilgrims—the smarter ones, at least, and those without looming visa deadlines—show up after the first spring thaw. The radio announcer—a tall woman, as skinny as Yukiko—pounces on me. "Are you a pilgrim?" she asks breathlessly. In my white outfit and ringing bell, I can't very well say no. She's obviously desperate for fodder for her show.

"Can I interview you in Japanese?" she asks. No way. I'm already late, and I have to get to temple number five before dark or I'll be spending my first night under a bridge. She offers to have her crew drive ahead of us and show me the way to the next temple. "Okay," I say.

They go live in less than six minutes. I rush through the proper ritual: Rinse out my hands and mouth, ring bell, put slip of paper into box at main hall, light candle and incense sticks. We dash off down the road, her recorders flapping around her waist and the van following us like a reluctant puppy.

She's given me a small headphone to plug into my ear. It's supposed to be connected to her producer, but I can't hear anything but vague crackling. *Three-two-one-LIVE.*

"Why are you doing this pilgrimage?" she asks me abruptly and pushes the microphone under my nose. I was hoping for something a little easier, like my name and nationality. I panic and revert to Miss America. "Peace and friendship," I say.

281

My stick-thin interviewer glows. I try to gesture that I can't hear what the studio guy is saying, but she cuts me off with wave of her hand. There's a burst of static in my ear, and the microphone is once again against my face. "*Hai hai,*" I say. *Yes yes.* It's what the female sidekicks always repeat excitedly on the evening news when their male anchors pause to take a breath. For the next eight minutes, every time I hear static or see the microphone, I say "*Hai hai!*" with a smile in my voice. I feel like Pavlov's dog, but it seems to work.

At last she wraps things up, waves down the van, and gratefully hauls herself inside after all that unexpected exercise. "Wait!" I say as she's about to close the door. "How do I get to temple number two?"

She consults briefly with the driver, then wiggles three long thin fingers down the road. "This way. You'll run right into it." They roar off to their next assignment.

Three miles later/I double-check my map. I'm going in precisely the wrong direction. It's not until long after dark, when I stagger into temple five, that I realize in the rush to do the interview, I left my all-important staff back at number one.

∽

My days are made up of endless numbers: the kilometers I've gone and how many I still have to do; a running inventory of the blisters on each foot and whether I have enough moleskin left to cover them; how much the temple cost last night and whether I have time to stop at a noodle place for lunch. I wonder if the entrance to Nirvana has a combination lock and you can open it once you figure out the right digits in the proper order.

The path runs mostly through urban Japan, along asphalt roads with few shoulders and fewer sidewalks. The landscape is flat and dreary—fields covered in row upon row of those ugly plastic tubes without a hint of living vegetation. Exhaust fumes hang in the air at every intersection. The thin icing of snow is as gray as the ominous clouds that pile up on the horizon most afternoons.

There are few other walking pilgrims this early in the season, so when we do run across each other we almost always share a few miles on the trail.

Kayoko and her new husband are walking for the second time. They met at temple forty-three two years ago and decided to retrace their steps for their honeymoon. They don't act like newlyweds. The tension in the air is palpable.

"It was better last time," she tells me quietly when he's gotten bored and walked ahead. "He didn't expect me to wash his socks and underwear."

They're only at temple nine.

I set off with two young men to cross the high pass between temples eleven and twelve. It's sixteen kilometers over three mountains, and I'm happy for the company in the snow. They are clearly purists, from the tips of their carefully polished Kobo Daishi staffs to the heels of their straw-wrapped hiking boots. They pass the time poking fun at the elderly bus pilgrims who get ferried from temple to temple in the increasingly popular, all-inclusive, package pilgrim tour. They do the entire trek in just eleven days. I slog up the steep and slippery trail and try not to think about that warm and cozy bus filled with the laughter of old women. My sneakers are slowly getting soaked.

"What's in there?" one of them asks abruptly and pokes a finger at my backpack. It's at least three times the size of theirs.

"Cameras," I say. An impure motive. His face turns sour. They forge up the trail without another word and leave me with nothing more than the outline of their footsteps and the occasional echo of their bells.

That very night I run into my first bus tour—the "instant pilgrims" that the young men snickered at. I watch them get off the bus, turning to smile and bow to their young tour guide before walking quickly across the street and through the temple gate. There are over forty of them, mostly older and female. They are dressed in identical pilgrim outfits, all the way down to their undershirts and socks. They mill about in the courtyard for a few moments, admiring the curling temple roof and the statue in the pond. A few dig out candles and pass the flame around to light smoldering incense sticks. When the tour guide rings the bell up front, they move obediently into position, put their hands together, bow, and start to sing. The sutras swell and fill the courtyard—not the resonating boom of Koya's monks but the clear, sweet sound of women's voices. *Namu-daishi-henjo-kongo* . . . Their eyes are closed and their arthritic fingers are wrapped tightly around each other. The voices die away with the final ringing of the bell, and they move off to repeat the sutra at the Daishi hall.

That night the temple bath is full of laughter and sagging breasts. All pilgrims are fed in the common room at six thirty sharp. They slide around to include me at a table.

They are mostly widows and widowers, though a few have left husbands at home to water the plants and keep the sofa warm. They're happy to be together and enjoying themselves enormously. They hit eleven temples in twelve hours and sang the sutras almost thirty times. They are dreamy-eyed with exhaustion and the intensity of their spiritual experience. And yet only half say they are devout Buddhists.

They happily repeat their stories in response to my eager questions. They encourage the shier women and make sure no one is left out. Two short days ago they met as strangers. Now they are a community.

One woman in her mid-forties is a teacher. She's had hundreds of students but no children of her own. "I just feel emptiness," she says. She has come looking for something to fill the space. The lady across from me had a digestive illness and survived it by praying to Saint Kobo. She has come to give thanks. Her husband doesn't believe she was sick in the first place, so he stayed at home. Now she's thinking of divorcing him. She'll see what Kobo says over the next few days.

One of the only two men on the bus has come on the pilgrimage to apologize to his wife for not paying enough attention to the family all these years.

"I'm sure she'd like to hear that in person," I say softly.

He hangs his head. "She died of cancer last August," he mumbles. "This is the only way I have left."

They point out a woman at another other table who is carrying a small vial of her husband's ashes. When she gets home she'll sprinkle them in the garden, where he loved to plant his daffodils each fall. Her neighbor—that young lady—is carrying her grandfather's record book from the time he did the pilgrimage over twenty years ago.

They know almost everything about each other after just forty-eight hours. They sit on the bus together, eat identical meals, bathe communally, sleep in one big room, wear the same kind of clothes, snap photos of each other. And yet they don't seem any more bothered by the lockstep life than the monks at Mt. Koya minded the bell at four thirty in the morning.

☙

In two weeks I visit all twenty-three temples in Tokushima, the prefecture devoted to a pilgrim's spiritual awakening. The next stage—Kochi—is dedicated to discipline. The temples spread out and the path zigzags over steep headlands and beside long stretches of deserted black-sand beaches. It's often below zero and always raining. I try hard to think about enlightenment, but mostly I end up worrying about the traffic, money, mileage, and whether I have dry socks for tonight.

The eighty-eight temples along the pilgrimage are meant to represent the panoply of Buddhist vices. As you visit each temple in turn, you snuff out that particular desire. I should be feeling lighter, more buoyant, from shedding all those sins. Instead it all just seems to blur together.

☙

One afternoon I find myself in a tiny village nestled into a cleft along the coast. The air smells of shellfish and seaweed, and rowboats are squeaking up and down against their moorings, just like a pod of dolphins. Seagulls hover overhead, and I can hear the Muzak from a ferryboat tied up to dock. Fish are coming to the oiled surface in the twilight, making rainbow ripples that gradually dissipate.

I find a tiny bed-and-breakfast right on the waterfront. The stairs are steep, and the largest slippers in the hall are three sizes too small. There's no hot water for a shower, so I scoop it out

286

of the bathtub. The walls are peeling long strips of paint, like a paper eucalyptus tree shedding its bark. The terrace lights are greasy bulbs, the walls are caked with years of grime, and my futon rattles with dried bugs. The grandmother who runs the place speaks a dialect that you have to be at least seventy and brought up in the backwater of Shikoku to understand. She is deaf as a Buddha statue and almost blind without her glasses.

"I'm seventy-seven," she tells me proudly. Her husband was a fisherman, dead these last ten years. He'd lost his middle finger in an accident while working on his boat engine. Stripped the flesh right off the bone. He asked the doctors to clean the bones and wire them back onto his hand, but they obviously had no sense of humor and only grudgingly gave it back to him at all. He kept it in a jar in the kitchen, insisting that it accompany him into the next life. Eventually she made him put it in a closet because it was bad for business.

She has two children, both gone to the city, first to Okayama and then to Osaka and Tokyo. They rarely come home. She fingers the dusty plastic flowers crammed into every nook and cranny. They remind her of her family when the children were young. She used to buy fresh flowers in the market whenever she went shopping. She wanted her children to love nature, hoping they would choose to stay on the island as she got old.

"Are you married?" she asks me suddenly.

"No," I say, then remember what country I'm in. "Not yet."

"How many years have you been in Japan? Three? Four?"

I forgive her the peeling paint that rained down on my head while I was bathing.

"You are strong like a man!" I forgive her my dinner, which was 98 percent rice with only the thinnest layer of egg.

"You weight about forty-five kilos?" Her eyesight must be worse than I thought. I forgive her the lumpy futon and the toilet that won't flush.

A half dozen bits of Styrofoam have found their way into my miso soup, along with a several unidentified pieces of greenish plastic. I don't care. I tell her she looks fifty. She gives me some more pickled cabbage.

"How old are you?" she asks me. "Twenty-five?" I forgive her absolutely everything and leave her a huge tip. She chases me upstairs, trying to give it back.

Once I'm in my room I shake the insect carcasses out of my bedding, try in vain to find an unstained corner of the pillow, and lie down to sleep. Somewhere in the deepest, darkest well of dreamtime I feel a prick on my inner thigh, as though I just rolled over onto a cactus spine. I reach down to sweep it away. A second prick, this time like a thumbtack pushed in flush to its head. I sit bolt upright but the third jab comes almost instantly—this time a one-inch, red-hot nail. I throw off the covers. Even in the darkness I can see an enormous centipede, as thick as my finger and long as a ballpoint pen. Its fangs are firmly anchored in my thigh and it's corkscrewing itself into writhing knots as it tries to bore in deeper. I backhand it—twice—before it skitters across the covers and flows smoothly away under the folds.

I pad downstairs. Grandmother is asleep beside her blaring television set. I call out to her, gradually raising my voice as my leg begins to throb and then go numb. She finally wakes up. I realize, belatedly, that I don't know the Japanese word for "centipede." I draw one on the back of my hand. "*Ah*," she says, "*mukade*," and hands me a can of insecticide. I mention, casually, that it bit me. Three times. She rummages around some more and comes up with a small round bottle. Antivenin? No, just iodine. That's reassuring. I spread the stuff on the stings, two inches below my panty line along my inner thigh. I pad back up to my room, wondering briefly which direction the centipede was coming from when it decided to dig in.

I shake out the bedding and spray the beast. It takes half an hour to die, twisting itself into half a dozen sailor's knots while gradually working its way closer to my futon, where I flip it back against the wall with the corner of a magazine I'm reading. Those flexing, half-inch spiky jaws trigger an unwanted memory—a nature documentary I once saw of just such a creature attacking a newly molted tarantula. The centipede falls upon the hapless spider. It frantically pumps venom through hollow, needle-sharp fangs—venom that will eventually turn the spider's flesh and bones into a predigested soup. I imagine three large liquid ulcers forming inside my leg as the fat and muscle gradually dissolve. I stand up and stomp the centipede.

I shake out the bedding again, this time acutely aware of the meaning of those dried-out insect wings and heads. I watch TV for an hour until the pain in my leg begins to subside. Faced with another four hours of darkness, I take the coward's way out. I go to sleep.

I don't always find accommodations, and the temples are often more than a day's walk apart. On drier nights I sleep in graveyards and bathe at the spigot they use to clean the headstones. Occasionally I end up in a cave. I wake stiff and bleary-eyed, and wonder how Kobo Daishi could have managed this for seven long years. And then one day I look in my well-thumbed guidebook and find scribbled directions to Hashimoto's bus. Hashimoto walked the pilgrimage himself and, disturbed by the lack of pilgrim accommodation, parked a bus at the back of his property and outfitted it with everything a traveler might need for the night: a television, coffee, tea, and sugar, a hot-water maker, and, best of all, a small heater and lots of blankets. It starts to rain. I listen to it drumming on the metal roof and drift off into a deep, contented sleep.

The weather warms for several days, and I strip off layers of clothing until my pack is bulging and my arms are bare. I should be flying through the countryside but instead I seem to be slowing down. I wake up exhausted in the morning and can barely move by noon. The weeks of relentless forward motion are finally taking their toll. I pack up my heavy winter jacket—I don't need it anymore—and send it back to Osaka.

Two days later it starts to snow.

∽

I stumble into Zentsuji temple just in time for their yearly Naked Festival. Four hundred loin-clad men are supposed to gather at the base of a pagoda and fight for a small stick that the senior Shinto priest throws down to them. The lucky guy who catches it scoots off the field in triumph and celebrates for the next twelve months.

I talk my way up to the second floor of the pagoda. I'm seven hours early, so I stake out a great position directly below where the head priest is supposed to stand. Unfortunately, it's also well below freezing and the wind is tearing at my meager clothes. I spend the afternoon hunkered down and shivering while a flu virus slowly incubates inside my mucous membranes.

Five o'clock. The police are starting to gather. They line up thirty deep beside the pagoda and ring the fence that keeps the spectators in check. I hear a distant chant of *"Yashoi! Yashoi!"* and

Sleep shuts down my brain before I come up with a solution.

I wake up to a metal cart covered with a dozen tiny dishes. Each has two perfect pieces of sushi and artfully arranged garnishes of pickled ginger and horseradish paste. There's no one else in the room. It tastes divine, and I eat until I'm too exhausted to chew.

Every time I wake up there's a new set of plates on the metal cart beside my bed. I suspect the nurses, though I hardly ever see them. I don't know whom to thank. They leave more food for me each day than a healthy sumo wrestler could eat in an entire week. I write "thank you" in soy sauce on an empty plate, and the next time I wake up it's been replaced by a smiley face.

I get up from time to time and stagger around the room. I still can't lift my backpack—it's only thirty-five pounds but it might as well be a grand piano. I haven't even tried to do a pushup. As soon as I can carry my own gear, I can check out of the hospital and recover in a cheap bed-and-breakfast.

Two days slip by, then three, then four. It feels like a dream—the nurses' gentle offerings, the doctor who comes in from time to time to keep me company and talk about his pilgrimage. I would be so happy to settle back and let the days blend into nights and back into days, but I know that sooner or later the bill will come due. I finally tell the doctor that I have to leave tomorrow.

"You're not ready," he says flatly.

I nod and look away. "I can't afford it," I admit miserably. The shame rises red and hot in my face and I have to force out the words.

"You are walking with Kobo Daishi," he says quietly. "Have some faith in him."

295

I nod. I wish I had learned more of Kouchi's equanimity at Mt. Koya's monastery. Even that lovely apple is long gone. "I still have to go," I say. Kobo could be stubborn too, when he wanted something.

That night I wake up from a sound sleep to find that my backpack has disappeared. After so many months it's become almost like an extra limb. It's my home, my security, my worldly possessions. I feel naked without it, no matter what I'm wearing.

So this is how they're going to keep me here. I toss and turn, and don't drift off into restless sleep until dawn.

When I wake up a few hours later, the pack is back, though it's not the scuffed and ratty version I've come to know so well. It's as clean and crisp as the day I brought it home from the store. A small tear in the left shoulder strap has been sewn up with matching thread and the finest stitches. A long-ago bloodstain has disappeared from the lower left-hand pocket. I pull open the drawstring and look inside. Every single piece of clothing—from socks to shirts to underwear—has been washed and dried and ironed. My spare batteries are right where I left them, only now they're wrapped in red ribbon to keep them together. A bread roll—stale when I bought it a week ago—has been replaced with a small pack of homemade cookies. Everything is exactly where it's supposed to be, although it has all clearly been removed, examined, cleaned, and replaced. How did they do it? Did they draw a diagram when they took everything out? I sit down on the ground with the pack between my knees and swallow hard to hold back the tears.

When I finally emerge—fully clothed and trying not to stagger under the weight of the pack—the doctor is waiting by the reception with several of the nurses. I thank them all, then thank them again, for the food and the care and the friendship. I don't have the words in any language to tell them how much it meant. They smile and bow their heads. And then I ask the question I've been dreading since they brought me in. "What do I owe you?"

The nurses look to the doctor, who steps forward. "*O-setai*," he says with a smile. It's a gift you give a pilgrim because it increases your own good karma for the next life. No pilgrim is allowed to refuse o-setai.

But this isn't o-setai. Nor are the dozen carefully wrapped rolls of homemade sushi that the nurses press on me when I finally walk out the door. It is the purest form of generosity— the kind you offer to a stranger who you know you'll never see again. It's that core of kindness that is so fundamentally Japanese.

I wobble a little as I step outside, but it's not because I'm ill. It's because I'm crying uncontrollably.

I only get a hundred meters before I duck around a corner and slither down a wall. The doctor was right—I'm not ready. I buy a week's supply of instant noodles, take a taxi to a local inn, and sleep for four days and nights. Then I strip my pack down to fifteen pounds, throw away my walking vows, and reacquaint myself with public transportation.

CHAPTER 25

They say that Kagawa is the prefecture for entering Nirvana. The weather warms miraculously, and the days float by on the scent of plum blossoms and gentle rain. A woman working in her garden hears my bell and looks up with a smile. "Oh!" she calls out gaily. "The sound of spring!" I spend hours in the temples, enjoying the gardens, the ringing bells, and the incense that by now has permeated my hair, my clothes, my skin. I watch flocks of *bus-henro* shuffle by. We smile and nod to each other, and sometimes I join them when they sing. I am standing at a bus stop when a driver rolls down his window and shouts, "*Gambatte, O-henro-san!*" *Go for it, honorable pilgrim!* For the first time something is more important than the shape of my nose or the color of my skin. Finally, without even knowing it, I've found a way to fit in.

These days are picked in gold out of the struggle of the last twelve months. Everything is surrounded by a warm and soothing glow, like sunlight through a *shoji* screen. I get up when I'm finished sleeping, walk until I'm pleasantly tired, then take a bus or a train. When a gauntly ascetic pilgrim sees me climb aboard a bus and makes a dismissive gesture in my direction, I laugh and wave back to him.

I wander along the beach for a while, then push my staff into the sand and sit beside it. "We two, traveling together" it reads down one side. They say Kobo Daishi walks with me, but I find myself thinking more and more about all the people I've come to know since I first arrived. They are also here beside me, waiting patiently for me to notice them. It's the first time I've sat still long enough to listen to what they've been trying to tell me all these months.

Roberto, who has learned to blend in despite his round eyes and barrel chest. He can grind a sword to perfection using nothing more than water and stone and herculean patience. He has the discipline of a samurai and a burning passion for the blade. He shows his courage by conforming to society, not revolting against it. He has traveled halfway around the world to fulfill his life's desire—given up his family, country, and language—and accepted with equanimity the slurs and slanders of a system that cannot reconcile itself to the landscape of his face.

Adam, so shy he hid from his own boyhood, yet brave enough to travel to distant shores and try to capture foreign hearts and minds with a daring street performance. Who understands masks and body armor better than the Japanese and yet offers up his soul to anyone who asks. He is an outsider who, unlike Roberto, has no desire to fit into society. He too lives his life by the twin values of passion and integrity. They are so different—and so much the same.

And Yukiko. She had the courage to take a stranger into her home and the patience to give me a hundred times more chances than I deserved. She has built her life upon a Gibralter-like scaffolding of dedication, hierarchy, and obedience. She's here with me as well, and she's no longer mad.

She's in good company: Koubai-san, my favorite geisha; the homeless Nishida-san; Kaneko-san and his archery team; the monks at Mt. Koya, who have found peace in a world of change and uncertainty; Yuka, with her callused hands and beloved smile; the Yamabushi, who shared their sweat and fears and dreams with me; and Morita-san, who had no earthly reason to help me—but did. The countless people I met along the way— the shopkeepers and fishermen, the nurses and strangers on the train—who extended a hand in friendship or offered to help. Even the salarymen; they may wear ties instead of topknots and cell phones in place of swords, but they still share the ancient values of their samurai ancestors. I was wrong about them: their conformity to the system is not a sign of weakness, but rather a great inner strength.

And the answer? In the end, I found it in the place I least expected . . . .

WA

I've walked twelve miles today. It was mostly road—busy and congested—and my feet hurt from the heavy pack and the asphalt. I arrive at the last temple just as the sun is going down. I light incense, chant a halfhearted sutra, and check in for the night. And then I ask, reluctantly, if there are any judo clubs nearby.

I'm hoping they'll say no. I'm nursing two blisters and a bruised toenail. The day-old sushi I had for lunch was more than a day old. I want to soak in the hot tub, do my laundry, and curl up for the night.

"Yes!" the priest tells me with enthusiasm. Yominuri dojo is just around the corner. He gives me rapid directions, then draws a map. When he finds out I have a black belt, he offers to drive me and mentions that the sensei once taught his son. I'm committed. I limp upstairs and dig out my uniform.

The place is tiny, no larger than a two-car garage. Nine students file out onto the plywood floor. When it comes time to do the opening ritual, the sensei passes over me and points to a lower rank. He must not like foreigners, or women—or both. I'll probably be ignored for most of the night. I'm secretly relieved.

We pair up and start practicing our favorite throws. My partner is a stick-thin teenager, just entering that awkward age when he's hyper-aware of my gender and doesn't know where to put his hands. I smile and crack a joke or two, but he still looks like he has indigestion. I loosen up my body and make myself light as a feather when it's his turn to throw. If he's even halfway accurate, I topple over like I just got hit by a lightning bolt.

The sensei watches from the sidelines, both hands wrapped around a hand-carved wooden cane. He's ancient—stooped and gray-haired. His wispy beard has no more than half a dozen hairs. He shuffles with each step and barely manages to climb up onto the mat. He's not wearing glasses, and he's squinting so hard his eyes are almost closed.

My partner makes a halfhearted attempt to sweep my leg. I'm about to suggest a better starting point when I feel the tap of a cane on the back of my calf. The sensei is standing beside me. My partner evaporates. The old man gets a grip of my judo collar and nods his head for me to do my best technique.

I concentrate on picking him up smoothly and laying him down on the mat as gently as I can. He looks almost translucent, like a delicate piece of porcelain. I'm afraid I might break him into several pieces.

I never see it coming, but it feels like a ten-ton truck at forty miles an hour. I hit the ground so hard that for a moment I can barely breathe. I'm not even sure what countermove he used.

I struggle to my feet. He grabs my *gi* without a word. I try again—faster this time—with a little less concern about his physical well-being. I hit the ground before I'm halfway through my first step.

I get up again, trying not to let my frustration show. I don't understand why he's treating me this way. These practice rounds are meant to teach students confidence in their techniques. If someone always counters you then eventually you expect to fail.

I try again—a different throw this time, to catch him off guard. He blocks me easily. I can't believe his speed, his accuracy, and his strength.

The other students have stopped even the pretense of working out and are watching us in silence. They have that attentive, predatory look of a wolf pack waiting to see death.

The clock above the door creeps past seven thirty, then eight. I try a dozen different strategies, from speed to fake-outs to combinations. Every time I hit the ground my resentment grows. He never corrects me or shows me what I'm doing wrong. He hasn't said a single word to me since I walked in the door, except for that annoying, high-pitched giggle he lets out every time I fall. This is absolutely pointless. He's not a teacher—he's just an ugly sadist who gets his kicks out of torturing anyone foolish enough to come into his world.

A year ago I would have told him exactly what I thought of him and stormed out the door, but I'm not that person anymore. For better or worse, I've acquired pride, or face, or discipline. I'm going to stick it out.

Nine o'clock. When I fall, I concentrate on getting up. When I stand, I think about my next throw. When it fails, I think about how to hit the ground to minimize the pain.

And then, almost at random, I set my forward foot two inches further left. I pull and lock and drop and turn, just like all my other attempts. He bends forward as easily as a young willow branch. I twist and he lands full-length on the ground.

The room is absolutely silent. I know that one day I will relive this moment. I will feel jubilation, pride, satisfaction. I will commit every motion to eternal memory, to savor when I am ninety-two years old and in a rocking chair. But right now I just feel empty. I stand and wait for whatever is coming next.

He climbs slowly to his feet. My body hurts so much that I can barely hold myself upright. Tomorrow I will not be able to pick up my pack or even bend my wrists.

He raises his right hand as though to grab my collar for another throw. For the first time I notice that his fingers are permanently twisted and his knuckles grossly swollen. It must be agony for him to grip the coarse cloth of a judo gi.

Instead he reaches out and taps me sharply on the chest. "*Commit*," he says in Japanese.

His finger moves upwards until it touches the middle of my forehead. "*Believe*."

And then he giggles, calls for his cane, and shuffles off.

ACKNOWLEDGMENTS

An expedition is an iceberg. The people in the field do only a fraction of the work that makes this kind of journey a success. The real credit belongs to the unsung heroes who toil tirelessly behind the scenes. Those who drop everything to ship out equipment in response to frantic e-mail requests. Long-suffering friends who breathe a sigh of relief when I finally wave goodbye and are still steadfastly—and inexplicably—at the airport a year later to sweep me off the plane. Generous strangers who miraculously appear when my courage falters and give me faith when I have lost my own. They are the ones who made the trip—and this book—possible. They are the ones who make my life worthwhile.

These are my heroes.

Jodie Rhodes—my agent, my friend. She will fight like a tiger for the people she believes in and she never, ever gives up. There is no one I'd rather have on my side.

Chris Potash, a truly brilliant editor with an extraordinary sense of character and storyline. He is unfailingly polite, as gentle as a summer rain, and a magician with words. One of the best things that came of this book was the chance to work with him.

Dominic Fucci, who generously (and foolishly) answered·a technical question I posted on the Internet. What Dom didn't know about post-production and media management wasn't worth knowing, and he was unstinting with his advice and time. Over the next year I sent him nearly seven hundred desperate e-mails, and he never once failed to respond. Along the way I made a documentary and, better yet, a life-long friend.

Cathy and Dave Staples at Images Group, Inc., who believed in me long before there was any reason to think I deserved it. Their confidence has given me the strength to weather the tough times, and their good advice has helped me to stay the course.

There are few companies in the world with the talent and vision of Woolrich, Inc. They put together an extraordinary line of clothing which performed magnificently through a year of relentless wear and tear. I rode in them, hiked in them, swam in them, and slept in them. The only thing that kept me warmer than their fleece jackets was remembering the people who made them. Roz Brayton, President and CEO at Woolrich, who lives by the twin values of caring and integrity. He has been there for me from the very first day. Lederle Eberhardt, Vice President of Merchandising and Design, whose impeccable taste in clothing managed to be both comfortable and to impress the style-conscious Japanese. Tim Joseph, the Director of Marketing and Media, whose enthusiasm is utterly contagious. Every time I talk to him I'm so buzzed that I'm ready to head out the door again. Jerry Rinder, the Vice President of Sales, and his team for their steadfast support and encouragement.

Then there are those people who you meet on the road. They have no reason to help a stranger but they do anyway, sometimes going to unbelievable lengths for someone they may never see again. I can't begin to describe them all, but there are two to whom I owe a special debt. It is my deepest and most humble wish that I may meet my host family again someday, and perhaps be friends. And Setsuko Morita. "Just doing your job" doesn't begin to cover it. Without you, none of this would have been possible. Thank you.